SPECIAL EDUCATION SERIES
Peter Knoblock, *Editor*

CONTESTED WORDS, CONTESTED SCIENCE

Unraveling the Facilitated Communication Controversy

EDITED BY
Douglas Biklen
AND
Donald N. Cardinal

Teachers College, Columbia University
New York and London

Published by Teachers College Press, 1234 Amsterdam Avenue, New York, NY 10027

Library of Congress Cataloging-in-Publication Data

Contested words, contested science : unraveling the facilitated
   communication controversy / edited by Douglas Biklen and Donald N.
   Cardinal.
       p.   cm. — (Special education series)
    Includes bibliographical references (p.   ) and index.
    ISBN 0-8077-3602-3 (cloth : alk. paper). — ISBN 0-8077-3601-5
(pbk. : alk. paper)
       1. Communicative disorders—Patients—Rehabilitation.
2. Communication devices for the disabled.   3. Handicapped—Means of
communication.   I. Biklen, Douglas.   II. Cardinal, Donald N.
III. Series: Special education series (New York, N.Y.)
RC423.C66   1997
616.85′503—dc21   96-52240

ISBN 0-8077-3601-5 (paper)
ISBN 0-8077-3602-3 (cloth)

Printed on acid-free paper
Manufactured in the United States of America

04 03 02 01 00 99 98 97   8 7 6 5 4 3 2 1

CONTENTS

Acknowledgments

We want to thank the many people who have helped us in the formulation and preparation of this book. In addition to expressing gratitude to each of the contributors, we owe special thanks to Rosemary Crossley, who introduced us to the method of facilitated communication. Further, we wish to thank the staff and associates of the Facilitated Communication Institute. Special thanks to Carol Berrigan, Bob Bogdan, Marilyn Chadwick, Sue Lehr, Diane Murphy, Annegret Schubert, and Robin Smith for reading and discussing with us various drafts of chapters. Thanks also to other colleagues who have read and commented on particular chapter drafts, especially to Dawn Hunter and Judy Montgomery. Thanks to TaShera Jenkins, Sherry Lord, and Barb Pauley for preparation of tables and figures. Special thanks to Steve Drake for his comments as well as for his extensive bibliographic work in the library and on the Internet and to Bob Rubin for his consultation on statistics.

We wish to acknowledge the financial support provided by the Nancy Lurie Marks Family Foundation to the Facilitated Communication Institute at Syracuse University.

Our extended families lived through and commented on nearly every step of the process of creating this book. We lovingly thank them all, especially Sari, Noah, and Molly Biklen and Kathy, Megan, and Nicholas Cardinal.

Finally, we would like to thank the many friends who have been our teachers and who use facilitated communication as their primary method of "voice."

Introduction

This book examines a method of communication used by many people with autism, Down syndrome, pervasive developmental disorders, and other developmental disorders. The method has engendered extreme controversy, with some researchers claiming the method has allowed some individuals to demonstrate unexpected literacy and others suggesting it is a hoax, whereby users of the method are influenced to write the thoughts of their facilitators. In the chapters that follow, we and other researchers address the controversy over authorship. In several cases, the authors explain why they selected particular frameworks and approaches (e.g., quantitative as well as qualitative; storytelling, word completion, or word reporting), the changes they made along the way, the results they obtained, and other observations. Together and even individually, these studies challenge prevailing dogma about autism and other developmental disabilities, ultimately calling into question current conceptions of mental retardation.

In every instance, the people involved in the studies were presumed mentally retarded prior to being introduced to facilitated communication. In most of the studies, detailed diagnostic data and/or relevant information about communication abilities prior to introduction of facilitation are provided.

We have selected these particular studies with an eye toward diversity of design and method in order to exemplify the different perspectives and kinds of findings that can be drawn from disparate research approaches, ranging from controlled quantitative designs (i.e., quasi-experimental) to more open and reflexive quantitative approaches as well as to more interpretive qualitative research. Further, these studies illustrate how scholarly and public controversy influences and even shapes research agendas, research strategies, and interpretations of research. From these studies, we will examine the range of subtle factors (e.g., motor disturbances, sensory sensitivities) associated with certain disabilities that may explain test and other communication performance.

Chapter 1 frames the discussion by exploring how individuals can be alternately defined as competent and incompetent. Similarly, through accounts of early and recent studies of facilitated communication, we begin to uncover the contextual conditions that interact with people's performance in authorship tests. It seems that recent experiences with facilitated communication parallel certain historical events and the social understanding of intelligence testing.

In Chapter 2, Cardinal, Hanson, and Wakeham provide the largest-scale study (to date) of facilitation, involving more trials than all the trials in all other studies, published prior to mid-1995, combined. In this study, "Who's Doing the Typing? An Experimental Study," the authors examine the ups and downs of individual performances. The study involves 43 individuals, ranging in age from 11 to 22 years, attending public schools. This study asks the most basic question regarding the validation of facilitated communication: Given "ideal" conditions, can a person using facilitated communication who has previously demonstrated that she cannot pass a message to a blind facilitator without facilitation do so under certain other conditions? This study supports the notion that a facilitator–user pair can generate output that is completely originated by the facilitated communication user.

In Chapter 3, Biklen, Saha, and Kliewer report on a study entitled "How Teachers Confirm Authorship of Facilitated Communication: A Portfolio Approach." Despite the controversy over facilitation, thousands of teachers, parents, and researchers continue to use the method nationally and internationally. We might ask why. What do practitioners point to as evidence that convinces them that the words typed are those of the people with disabilities, not of the facilitators? This chapter looks at that question though the experiences of 7 facilitators and 17 students, examining in detail the kinds of evidence they amass, often informally through daily use. The chapter, set in the tradition of qualitative, ethnographic research, suggests a portfolio analysis approach to confirming authorship. This chapter, as do all of the chapters, examines the ways of understanding that underlie the method of inquiry used in the research and the kinds of understandings that can be derived from it. Related to this, the authors examine the dilemmas encountered in doing the research, for example, problems of separating the perspectives of those observed from the researchers' own perspectives and debates about how to present the data and how much data to include. In this account the authors also describe motor disorders that may influence individuals' communication difficulties.

In Chapter 4, "Factors Affecting Performance in Facilitated Communication," Baldac and Parsons report on a six-person experiment involving a variety of message-passing tasks. Parsons is a leading Australian scholar in the field of communication sciences and has observed the emergence of facilitated communication in that country over the past two decades. Crossley was one of the facilitators in the study and comments from her perspective as a participant as well as analyst of facilitated communication research in the Postscript. Crossley rediscovered the use of facilitated communication training in Australia in 1977. As noted in Chapter 1, she has written about this period in the book *Annie's Coming Out* (Crossley & McDonald, 1984), filmed as *A Test of Love* (Brealey, 1984); she is also the author of the standard account of the method, *Facilitated Communication Training* (Crossley, 1994). In her postscript to this book, Crossley discusses the communication theory underlying message transmission through facilitated communication. She illustrates her remarks with examples from Australian validation tests conducted between 1979 and 1994, ending with the current study by Baldac and Parsons, which includes people who have Down syndrome or diagnoses of autism or intellectual impairment.

In Chapter 5, "A Controlled Study of Facilitated Communication Using Computer Games," Olney reports the results of a study in which 9 experienced facilitated communication users between the ages of 16 and 42 and their regular facilitators engaged in computer game play over a series of 7 to 10 sessions. A "closed condition" (i.e., blind)—in which the facilitated speakers, but not the facilitators, could see the computer screen—was introduced after the facilitators and facilitated communication speakers learned the requirements of the games. Although the introduction of the closed condition was initially problematic for all participants, a number of them demonstrated authorship by providing accurate responses to game items in the absence of facilitator knowledge. The study provides insights into the complexities of testing facilitated communication. One of the most interesting aspects of this study is the author's collection of typed commentary, by the people with disabilities, concerning how they experienced the closed condition. In her own reflections on the study, Olney identifies implications of this study for future investigations.

Chapter 6, "Sorting It Out Under Fire: Our Journey," is a test designed by the person being tested. Unlike any of the other studies, it has been carried out by a person who uses facilitated communication. Marcus, a young man with autism, heard about the Wheeler, Jacobson, Paglieri, and Schwartz (1993) study that had been carried out at a large state institution in upstate New York. The test had been described on the Public Broadcasting System's *Frontline* exposé of facilitated communication (Palfreman, 1993). Hearing of the controversy, he asked a friend, Shevin, who is a linguist and a consultant to the Facilitated Communication Institute, to assist him with trying to pass the test himself. His goal was to prove he could pass it and then to help other people with developmental disabilities pass the same test. In fact, he wanted to design a study for other people who use facilitated communication. Together Marcus and Shevin set about replicating the well-known O. D. Heck study (Wheeler, Jacobson, Paglieri, & Schwartz, 1993). This chapter is their narrative of the experience.

Chapter 7 takes an altogether different approach. It is a report of two case studies, the first of which concerns a boy who was thought to be severely retarded prior to being introduced to facilitated communication. The authors, Weiss and Wagner, recount their efforts to have the student listen to stories and then to report on them to his facilitator, who had been kept blind to the stories' content. In a second case, the researchers describe a student's progress from being unable to communicate through typing or writing to typing independently. When the authors first heard about and observed facilitated communication, they thought it made no sense and were convinced it was a hoax. Then over a period of weeks, after observing individuals using it, they began to be challenged by their own research. In this chapter, they describe the process they went through and the questions they now believe must be asked by disability researchers.

Chapter 8 examines the perspectives of facilitated communication users toward independent typing. Located in the tradition of qualitative research, this study examines the experiences of eight school-age students who have learned to communicate with facilitation. Three of the students have achieved the ability to type some sentence-level communication without physical support; the other five are at varying levels of support. They talk about the various meanings independence has for them. These accounts are then analyzed in the context of classroom observations in which the researcher looks at how, when, and what they type.

Chapter 9, "Suggested Procedures for Confirming Authorship," examines the factors in study procedures that appear to influence the likelihood of facilitated communication users' success or failure on authorship tests. The authors present a rating system for evaluating research studies and then demonstrate the rating system by applying it to six of the recent, major studies of authorship. The chapter concludes with advice to researchers who may be planning to evaluate facilitated communication.

In Chapter 10, "Reframing the Issue: Presuming Competence," we examine the politics of disability research and the meaning of mental retardation. The controversy over facilitation has been fueled by other questions concerning the nature and meaning of disability, prevailing assumptions about competence and incompetence and its measurement, conflicting notions about science and research, and the context of popular culture. We address these issues through an examination of one of the most controversial aspects of facilitated communication—allegations of abuse made via facilitation. At the same time, this chapter includes an analysis of contextual issues related to the discourse about facilitated communication, drawing parallels between this discourse and other historical and contemporary debates in the fields of education and social science.

In Chapter 11, we conclude with an accounting, based on our reading of the research, of what *should not* and what *can* be said about facilitated communication.

CHAPTER 1

Framing the Issue: Author or Not, Competent or Not?

Douglas Biklen
Donald N. Cardinal

Diane More was born in the 1950s in the south of England. She was in some ways precocious. She spoke early and memorized several stories by heart. But between the ages of 3 and 4, Diane seemed to withdraw into herself. Her mother recalls, "She stopped chattering, lost interest in books, never smiled, dangled a string of beads, and had tantrums." At the local children's clinic, she was assessed as psychotic. Her parents enrolled her at a nearby kindergarten, then in an infant school, and finally at a special school, but she was rejected by each in turn for her disruptive behavior. In the early 1960s, Diane was classified as autistic. Her parents placed her at Camphill, a special village for people with developmental disabilities, but again she was dismissed, this time after six years, having made little progress.

At that point, her parents could find no school to accept the 15-year-old. Her behavior was difficult. Her mother took meticulous care to see she was well groomed, but she "behaved like a mischievous toddler, spilling, throwing, causing chaos in the house. Her speech consisted of angry sounding repetitive demands." Diane wouldn't or couldn't do any house chores, her mother recalls, so her activities were limited to going for rides in the car and long walks in the park.

Taking advantage of her own background as a primary school teacher and for lack of any alternative, Diane's mother decided to try to teach her reading and writing. According to all the prior school reports, she could do neither. For approximately 45 minutes each day, Diane's mother forced her to sit at a kitchen table, keeping Diane contained by wedging her between herself and a wall. Initially, she held Diane's hand firmly and had her point to whole words in beginning reading books. Then she placed a felt-tipped pen in her hand and asked her to write, using block letters. She was quite sure at this stage that Diane was a passive instrument, little more than an extension of her own arm. It was her mother doing the writing, not Diane. As they produced the letters, her mother sounded them out phonetically. After several weeks, to her surprise, her mother thought she "felt her hand move slightly under mine." But she found that hard to believe. The next day, January 13, 1969, she was more certain that Diane's hand was initiating the movement. As Diane's mother relaxed her grip on her daughter's hand, Diane indeed took over the writing, but instead of producing block letters, she wrote in cursive! It was then that Diane's mother realized that Diane might have more abilities than anyone had previously recognized. She declared, "Diane, I do believe you *know* how to write."

While at Camphill, as is the policy in that community, Diane had been instructed with material suited to her chronological age, *not* to her presumed intellectual abilities. Perhaps this education had allowed her to develop the literacy skills her mother now observed.

At first, Diane's mother dictated words, finding that Diane's spelling was usually correct, although some words were creatively spelled, for example "beest" instead of "beast" and "stu" instead of "stew." Next, she asked her questions and Diane wrote answers.

During this period, Diane's parents placed her in a mental hospital. But on home visits and even at the hospital, Diane continued to write with her mother's facilitating touch on her arm. Diane did her writing in the park, in the car, even while lying in bed. The world she unveiled was of her unremitting struggle with anxiety, of behavior she often could not control, and of her desperate wish to enter the typical world. Her writing included idiosyncrasies: She often wrote "what it is" at the beginning of sentences in which she explained something she had said or was thinking or feeling; she reversed pronouns, nearly always using "we" instead of "I"; and she sometimes used words in unconventional ways. The following sequence occurred one Saturday, a warm August 1, 1970, when Diane was home for the weekend:

DIANE: What nice shoes. When we only in my right mind we very very nice to Mummy. When is my only one to not be an abominable unfit one to be a new one to my only nice kind Mummy.

MOTHER: I haven't found you abominable.

DIANE: What it is we surely more like a real person now.

MOTHER: Diane, I like your dress. [She was wearing a smarter-than-usual hospital dress.]

DIANE: We soon must take more interest in my looking nice. [*At this point Diane spoke, saying something about dustmen.*]

MOTHER: What was that you just said about "nasty dustment"?

DIANE: Some of my clothes into the dustbin should go only they arent mine. [Diane lived in an institution where clothes did not belong to any one patient but were passed around among the patients after each laundering]. [*As she wrote, Diane spoke again, this time so her mother could note it: "Nasty, nasty dustmen despair."*] What it is we an only rubbishy person to be disposed of.

MOTHER: You are very precious to your family. You are *not* rubbishy at all.

DIANE: We are not like a more real one to be an only helpful one to Mummy in the house its not my fault to be a kind of freak to only write my feelings to Mummy. . . . What it is we such a very unwhole person still.

In all, Diane has written hundreds of pages about how she experiences life. Hers are among a very few lengthy accounts of autism written by a person whose speech is limited to echoes and stereotyped phrases (see also Sellin, 1995). At the time it was written, it may have been the most elaborate such account by anyone so disabled by autism.

Like other autobiographical accounts of autism (e.g., Barron & Barron, 1992; Grandin & Scariano, 1986; Sellin, 1995), Diane's writing confirmed certain theories about autism and contradicted others. She wrote about extreme anxiety, a condition often associated with autism, yet at the same time, in contrast to all prevailing theories of autism, Diane was aware of other people's feelings—she cared what her mother felt—and she had an active imagination.

CONTROVERSY OVER AUTHORSHIP

Interestingly, despite her parents' efforts to get leaders in the fields of autism and developmental disabilities to recognize the importance of Diane's writing, she was ignored. She lived in relative obscurity, moving from one residential setting to another. She continued to write, but now less frequently, as her mother was the only person with whom she did write.

It would take 20 years before the professional community would systematically examine the method of communication that Diane used—actually, scholars would focus on a variation of the method, one involving typing, called facilitated communication. The debate would occur not around Diane's communication at all, but rather primarily in Australia and the United States, where large numbers of professionals, parents, and people with autism, Down syndrome, cerebral palsy, mental retardation,

and other developmental disabilities began to use the method. This examination would lead to a furor over whose words were being typed, those of
the individual with the communication disability or of the person providing physical and emotional support. The controversy would be replete with
charges by some that it was a hoax and with claims by others that its
results warranted a rethinking of basic concepts about disabilities such as
mental retardation (Biklen & Duchan, 1994; Green & Shane, 1994).

This book explores and presents research on facilitation, focusing
mainly on the issue of authorship but also addressing far broader questions. We and the other authors consider the implications of the scientific
and public policy discourse on facilitated communication to gather understandings of ability and disability.

The method of facilitation has been described as an alternative to communicating by speech that may be useful to individuals who cannot speak
or whose speech is highly disordered (i.e., limited). Examples include speech
that is characterized by echolalia—words and phrases that the person has
heard in the immediate situation or previously (e.g., an advertising jingle)
and that the person then repeats, often seemingly out of context—or speech
that is limited to labeling objects or by one- and two-word utterances, not
sentences, *and* where these individuals cannot point reliably (Biklen, 1993;
Crossley, 1988). Diane's speech seems generally to be a form of delayed
echolalia, that is, repetitions of words and phrases she has heard others say
in other situations plus parts of thoughts that become understandable only
when she elaborates on them in writing. For example, one day she repeated
the phrase "Every day's so easy to do, I'm just a fool" several times and
then "Nighttime isn't clear to me." In writing, she explained that she was
"feeling worried about the night and dying during the night." Later, when
her mother complimented her on her speaking ability, Diane wrote, "with
the best will in the world we not adequate enough."

Facilitated communication typically involves hand, wrist, or arm support, as the person attempts to communicate by pointing or, in Diane's case,
writing. Crossley (1994) has referred to it as a training method, noting that
the ultimate goal for most users of the method could be independent point-
ing/typing or writing (Crossley & Remington-Gurney, 1992).

The rationale for the method has to do with the difficulties these individuals evidence with reliable pointing. Crossley has described the following hand functions as typically problematic in such individuals:

Finger isolation
Tremor
Radial ulnar instability—the wrist bends and the person veers to the left
    or right, depending on whether left or right handed, when pointing

> *Perseveration*—repeating the same action multiple times
> *Initiation difficulty*
> *Proximal instability*—difficulty separating movement of limbs from the trunk
> *Proprioceptive awareness*—awareness of location of body parts in space

Another explanation (obviously related to Crossley's list of hand functions) is that these individuals may experience developmental dyspraxia (Biklen, 1993)—difficulty in initiating and carrying out voluntary actions that cannot be explained by an obvious physical disability such as cerebral palsy—as well as other sensory difficulties that may or may not relate to developmental dyspraxia. D. Williams (1994a), who has autism and who can speak and type in conventional ways, would have us broaden the analysis away from "a mere 'movement' problem" to conceive of autism as a disorder "affecting all systems of functioning" ranging from awareness of proprioception to "analysis and retrieval skills relating to information on all levels (sensory, emotional, mental, proprioceptive, social-interactive) and the integration of those systems" (p. 196). She believes that she experiences some of the same difficulties reported by people who use facilitation. She defines her dilemma as one of systems-management (i.e., integration) and systems-forfeiting. In order to get one thing to work, it is often necessary to abandon or neglect another. For example, the person may have to switch off emotional signals in order to accept factual information, or switch off auditory input to take in visual stimuli. Research and theorizing on dyspraxia and systems or resource management are discussed more thoroughly in Chapter 3.

At one level, this book concerns the prevailing controversy over facilitation, that is, whether the words attributed to Diane and others using this method of communication are their own or instead those of their facilitators (e.g., Diane's mother). Then, too, the book concerns science, ideology, and inquiry or, simply, how researchers investigate something new and controversial. And finally, the book concerns the larger society's understanding of ability and disability.

COMPETENT, INCOMPETENT, COMPETENT AGAIN

The failure of experts to celebrate and announce Diane More's writing may have been due to her many signs of incompetence: her score in the severely retarded range on a standardized intelligence test, her unusual behaviors, her tantrums, and the fact that she did not write with anyone other than her mother. This was a person who seemed more unable than able. Besides, it may have been hard for experts to believe in her ability to write and think complex thoughts if that belief required them to question prevailing ideas about autism: People who appeared as she did were presumed retarded; how could these be her words?

In 1974, teacher/writer Rosalind Oppenheim wrote a book in which she challenged that idea. Her notion was that the context, the scaffolding of good learning environments—she operated a school for students with autism—made all the difference. She exemplified this thesis through her account of two teenage boys with autism, one 16 and the other 17. Both were alternately thought to be capable of academic instruction, then incompetent of any educability at all, and finally, able again. Oppenheim explained the case of 16-year-old Bill first.

One educational account of his abilities found that he was "capable of learning only simple tasks," that despite efforts to instruct him, "he is performing at the same level at year-end as he was at the beginning" (p. 65). That evaluation classified his intellect in the "profoundly retarded" range; he was presumed unable to benefit from schooling or, in the parlance of the day, ineducable. The irony of this assessment was that only three years earlier, another teacher had described him as "a model student," provided he was given challenging work and told that he was "*required* to do it" (pp. 63–64). It was found that although he had difficulty speaking sensibly, even in reading aloud—he seemed unable to get the right words out— he could demonstrate his understanding of written passages by responding to multiple-choice questions. Even though the questions might be sentences of 6 and 10 words each, his responses were "almost invariably correct" (p. 64). At times he would make errors, but this seemed to result from his difficulty in using his eyes efficiently, of looking at the questions before attempting to answer. Bill could also generate his own thoughts and write them out. Yet, to accomplish the latter, "to do it at all," his teacher wrote, "he needs the touch of the teacher's finger on his hand, very lightly—not guiding, but merely touching. . . . Nevertheless, his choice of words and the composition of his sentences reveal the existence of a considerable reservoir of inner language" (p. 64).

The third report of Bill also finds him competent in reading, writing, and doing mathematics, but "only in brief flashes" and only when his teachers were particularly persistent. This latter account was from Oppenheim's own school. Getting Bill to show his thinking competence was a struggle. Yet the gains were demonstrable, in terms not only of the content but also of execution: "In writing, Bill has gained more control . . . at both desk and chalkboard, he can often write now for brief periods without requiring the touch of the teacher's finger on his hand, and he shows real pleasure in his success" (p. 66).

Oppenheim's description of Don is no less dramatic and also no less turbulent. He, too, was viewed as competent, then retarded, then competent again. His mother was the first to recognize his reading, writing, and calculation skills. When he was 6½ years old, his school confirmed her assessment, reporting that he was capable of abstract reasoning at the high school level or above. He was "able to solve problems in probability in a second year high school algebra book" (p. 70). Yet, at the end of the school year in which he was 16, at a different school from the one that had assessed him competent, he was found to "display little ability to conceptualize or use reasoning ability" (p. 72). His conceptual deficits were deemed so pronounced that it was impossible to distinguish them from possible perceptual deficits. He was judged retarded. Just one year later, now in attendance at Oppenheim's school, Don did a turnaround, or perhaps we should say his teachers created the conditions for a reversal of fortune. Now 17, his year-end report bore no resemblance to the account from his previous school: "His written answers to the exercises which accompany his reading material are original and show good insight and wit" (p. 72). The report explained that there was a "discrepancy" between the high quality content of his writing and the poor quality of his "letter formations in the actual writing itself" (p. 72). He accomplished the latter through what Oppenheim referred to as "the touch system" in which he insisted on being touched in order to write (p. 72).

Unfortunately, neither Bill nor Don could act reliably. While each had the physical ability to ambulate, to pick things up, even to point, they both had difficulty doing tasks on command. Bill was described as "sure footed and fleet" when raiding the refrigerator, yet "it was hard for him to execute bodily movements on command" (pp. 65–66). And Don "demonstrates some good gross motor abilities, but they are not always at his command" (p. 73). Often, when given crafts-type, manipulative activities, Don left the work undone on his desk. We will discuss the topic of movement or motor disturbances more elaborately in Chapter 3.

The lesson of Bill's and Don's erratic performances for educators is one of orientation. Should the educator base his actions on the numerous instances of observed incompetence on the part of the student with a developmental disability? Or should the educator act on the basis of glimpses of competence or even on hoped-for competence? Oppenheim's advice is simple and unequivocal: Do not let problems of general functioning, disordered speech, or even absence of speech ever serve as "an index of the likelihood" that a person might be "able to absorb and benefit from teaching at higher cognitive levels," including reading, writing, and mathematics (p. 90). Donnellan (1984) has referred to this kind of decision as the principle of least dangerous assumption: "In the absence of conclusive data, educational decisions should be based on assumptions which, if incorrect, will have the least dangerous effect on the student" (p. 142).

As we will come to see in this book, the ups and downs of facilitated communication, like the turbulent adjustments in assessments of Bill's and Don's competence, have much to do with educational philosophy and practice and the social meaning of disability (Biklen & Duchan, 1994; D. L. Ferguson & Horner, 1994; Goode, 1994; Halle, 1994; Hitzing, 1994; Horner, 1994; Kaiser, 1994; D. Williams, 1994a). Nevertheless, some will argue that it has mainly to do with individuals' capabilities or potential (Green & Shane, 1994; Levine, Shane, & Wharton, 1994b; Whitehurst & Crone, 1994).

EARLY ACCOUNTS OF FACILITATED COMMUNICATION

In the mid-1970s, Australian educator Rosemary Crossley rediscovered the method of communication that Oppenheim (1974), Diane More's mother, and others had happened upon. It involves providing physical and emotional support to a person with developmental disabilities (e.g., autism, cerebral palsy, Down syndrome) and limited or no speech: enabling the person to point reliably—either at pictures, at whole words, or at letters to form words—and thus to communicate. Crossley's first use of the method was with Anne McDonald (Crossley & McDonald, 1984), a girl with cerebral palsy who resided in an institution for children with multiple handicaps, all of whom were presumed severely retarded.

St. Nicholas, the institution in which Crossley found Anne, was in every sense what sociologist Erving Goffman (1961) meant by a "total institution." It was prisonlike, cold, stark, "actually built of different materials from the ordinary house," with "doorframes . . . bathrooms, . . . cupboards . . . all of steel," "an entirely abnormal environment" that "produces abnormal behavior" (Crossley & McDonald, 1984, p. 8). It was a setting in which children never learned what it was like to go shopping, where they could not participate in food preparation, where there was no opportunity for a child to select what she might eat or even drink. For those who could not feed themselves, meals were pureed "to make feeding quicker" (p. 10). Their heads were tilted back so that they could be fed like birds. There was no time to swallow; choking was easy. Drinks did not even come with meals; they were "given at 6 a.m., 10 a.m., 2 p.m. and 6 p.m." (pp. 9, 10). St. Nicholas was a custodial institution, not a center for education.

When Crossley began to teach Anne a method of communication, first by having her thrust out or withhold her tongue to indicate yes or no (Anne gave this up a few years later), then by supporting her arm as she pointed to letters, Crossley could not know Anne's thinking abilities: "I took Annie home for a weekend in the middle of April 1977. She was an unknown quantity, a sixteen-year-old girl with a comprehension perhaps equivalent to that of a normal six-year-old, although I could not be certain of that" (Crossley & McDonald, 1984, p. 40). Crossley had the same difficulty in assessing Anne that Oppenheim experienced with Bill and Don. It was hard to know how to assess someone of limited expression.

Crossley described facilitated communication with Anne as a process of helping Anne control the spasms that "impaired Anne's control of her movements" (p. 53). With her arm resting on a table, she pushed down so hard that she could not move it to point. If it was up in the air and she tried to move, "it would shut up like a rabbit trap" (p. 53). Crossley's remedy was to provide enough support for Anne to control the extension of her arm, but not so much that Anne would seize up in a reflex. She supported Anne's upper arm on her outstretched hand, "acting as a responsive item of furniture," supporting but not moving Anne's arm (p. 53). Anne pointed by moving her arm from the elbow and by moving her hands and fingers. "These movements," Crossley explained, "would be very difficult to influence by manipulating the upper arm" (p. 53).

Crossley's protestation of "difficult to influence" is strikingly similar to the report that Oppenheim shared for Bill, in which it was noted that his writing involved touch but not guiding. In fact, Crossley's method evoked a storm of controversy over the very point she had raised: Was her facilitation controlling or influencing Anne's typing? Thus, when Anne typed that she wanted to leave the institution and go to live with Rosemary Crossley and her husband, the institutional authorities challenged the method of communication, arguing that Anne was retarded and incapable of the literacy claimed for her.

In the first documented authorship test of facilitation, Anne proved her competence to the satisfaction of the court, typing words mentioned to her but not to Crossley (her facilitator in the court): "She spelt, finally, 'string' and 'quit'" (pp. 241–242). In Crossley's absence, the court master had given Anne two words he wished her to type, "string," and "quince." The presumption was that Anne had prevailed even as she was interrogated; she had typed QUIT to say "stop the testing." Prior to this courtroom test, Anne had taken a Peabody Picture Vocabulary Test in which she selected from a set of four pictures the one that illustrated the meaning of the word said by the examiner. Before the watchful eye of a court-appointed psychologist, she pointed without physical support. "The psychologist reported that even on a partial test Annie had achieved a score in the average range, answering sixty-eight questions correctly out of seventy-five attempted" (p. 238).

Anne had won, but the dispute over facilitated communication was just beginning. There had been 11 others at St. Nicholas with whom Crossley had begun communication training. A government Committee of Inquiry (1980) prepared a report that all but labeled facilitated communication and Crossley a fraud: "Not one of the 11 children shows any evidence of a level of intellectual functioning beyond that expected of children of two and a half to three years of age" (p. 247). All were said to be functioning in the "severe or profound mental retardation" range (p. 247). None were found able to use the alphabet for communication. None showed "evidence of even the most elementary level of literacy or numeracy" (p. 247). The report labeled Crossley's training of the children inappropriate and harmful and urged that she be barred from any further contact with them.

The report was angrily denounced by various disability groups and led to submission of a *Supplementary Report* to the Committee of Inquiry (Cummins & Bancroft, 1981), charging the committee with "an imbalance between the Committee's findings in certain areas and the weight of evidence provided to it" and with placing unfair, "unilateral onus of proof upon the claimants (p. 59)." The *Supplementary Report* elaborated:

> There is no reason why the onus of persuasion should have been cast on those contending that the children are intelligent. If anything, as the liberty of the subject was involved, we contend that the onus should have been on those asserting the contrary. At the least, unless the lack of intelligence was unequivocally demonstrated, the Committee should not have concluded that the children are not intelligent, even if they were not satisfied that they are intelligent. (p. 59)

Anne McDonald had already left St. Nicholas to live with Rosemary Crossley. The Committee of Inquiry report was disastrous for the 11 children, but the *Supplementary Report* effectively rebutted it. It was finally discredited when papers obtained under FOI showed the Committee had concealed positive test results. Within a few years, the St. Nicholas institution itself was closed and all of the residents moved into community living arrangements. In 1994, Anne McDonald earned a bachelor's degree from Deakin University. She also traveled and lectured in the United States, had her autobiography (Crossley & McDonald, 1984) made into a feature film, *A Test of Love* (Brealey, 1984), and is continuing her studies by pursuing an arts and humanities master's degree at Melbourne University. Without any physical support, she can now use a Macaw—a communication aid in which utterances can be stored as digitized speech, thus allowing the communication user to initiate speech output by hitting one of several large, preprogrammed keys—but she still requires facilitation for use of a letterboard.

IS FACILITATION REAL?

The controversy over the method revolves around one central question: Are the people with disabilities authors of the facilitated communication? Yet while this is a crucial question that will surely influence the future use of facilitation, the details of such studies are potentially as valuable for what they reveal about how the method works and what aid it affords, if any, in particular circumstances.

The first formal, published investigation of this question produced results that left many observers of the method in a quandary. It seemed to provide evidence to the supporters of the method as well as to critics. This study (Intellectual Disability Review Panel [IDRP], 1989) was initiated in Australia by the Victorian Community Services Ministry in response to concerns raised by critics (Interdisciplinary Working Party, 1988). The Victorian study involved two different procedures: one in which three individuals, considered to have severe communication impairments and mental retardation, were given gifts—with their facilitators being kept unaware of their nature; and one in which three similarly disabled individuals were given two sets of questions—one the same and one different from those given to their facilitators. The facilitators in the second part of the study wore earphones that transmitted the same or different information. The results of these two experiments were mixed: "the validity of the communication while using the 'assisted communication technique' was demonstrated in four of the six clients who participated in the two studies" (IDRP, 1989, p. iv).

The individuals who were given gifts were all able to validate their ability to communicate through facilitation, but all three exhibited severe word-finding difficulties. For example, one participant was able to describe an article of clothing he was given, but only after 45 minutes of conversation and questioning. He described the color of the clothing, but again only after numerous false tries. In addition, he conveyed other information about events that had occurred during the outing when he was given the gift by the IDRP staff (see Postscript for a detailed description of the events). Another participant reported correctly that he had been given a book but could not give the title; it was *The Man from Snowy River.*

Three other individuals participated in a more controlled experiment in which they were asked different questions from those given their facilitators, with the facilitators wearing headphones to prevent them from hearing questions posed to the subjects. The one individual who correctly answered two of the questions given to him, which were different from those given the facilitator, also showed that he could give correct responses to the questions that had been conveyed to the facilitator, thus demonstrating facilitator influence.

Although the report stated that some people had succeeded in proving their communicative competence with facilitation, critics were not satisfied (Cummins & Prior, 1992). Interestingly, one of these critics was the same person who had been principal author of the *Supplementary Report* (Cummins & Bancroft, 1981) so critical of a government Committee of Inquiry that found facilitated communication baseless. The new charges against the method were as harsh as those of the Committee of Inquiry. Its authors wanted more investigations and no presumption of competence in the interim. Indeed, Cummins and Prior (1992) argued that the research on language learning among children with autism had long since found little to celebrate: "The disappointing fact is that such trained language fails to generalize outside the training conditions and that these children do not spontaneously produce new word combinations and use language creatively in the way that other children do" (p. 232). As for the purported successes of facilitated communication, Cummins and Prior (1992) discounted them as mere artifacts of cuing. "All of these peculiarities," they wagered, have "very little to do with emotional support . . . and very much to do with physical control by the assistant" (i.e., facilitator), whether overt or covert (p. 233). They related this kind of cuing to the "Clever Hans" effect, referring to the nineteenth-century horse who counted on cues from his master (Sebeok & Rosenthal, 1981).

Sharp on the heels of this criticism came a spate of controlled studies, appearing in peer-reviewed journals in the United States, all claiming no evidence that facilitated communication fostered communication by people with disabilities and instead claiming that it only produced either nonsense communication (i.e., gibberish, unrelated words) or words influenced or cued by the facilitators. The first and perhaps most often cited of these studies was carried out at a New York State mental retardation institution, the O. D. Heck Developmental Center (Wheeler, Jacobson, Paglieri, & Schwartz, 1992, 1993). In that study, twelve individuals classified as autistic were shown colored pictures of familiar objects and asked to name them: in the condition of the facilitator not being shown the item, in the condition of the subject being unfacilitated, and in the condition of the facilitator being shown the same or different items but not being aware of what the subject (and vice versa) was being shown. *None* of the individuals gave correct responses when shown items different from those shown to the facilitators, except that in two instances, individuals named categories for the items they were asked to identify but not the precise items; these responses were "vehicle" instead of "van" and "food" instead of "bread." Five of the twelve were uninfluenced when facilitators were shown different items; of these five, three individuals gave five correct responses when neither they nor their facilitators knew they had been shown the same item cards. The latter data are not provided in Wheeler and colleagues' article in *Mental Retardation* (1993) but are reported in their preliminary account of the same study (1992). Of 120 total responses, 80 were words, but not words related to the stimulus cards. Individuals did as poorly in the distractor condition as in the same-stimulus condition. Interestingly, overall performance in the same-stimulus condition (where the facilitator's card was the same as that shown to the person) was poor (14 out of 60 trials); overall performance in the different-stimulus condition (where individuals typed the name of the facilitator's card but not of their own) was 12 of 60. All responses in the unfacilitated condition were said to be nonsense responses.

Eight subjects were judged to be profoundly retarded and four to be severely retarded, all were teenagers or older (i.e., 16 to 27), and all had been using facilitation for five months or more and were supported by familiar facilitators. The pictures they were asked to identify were ones they had seen previously and were of common objects: broom, scissors, pan, brush, television, pencil, desk, belt, watch, pillow, books, car, fork, bread, crayons, puzzle, toothbrush, foot, shirt, coat, van, pants, eyeglasses, comb, light switch, keys, socks, bowling ball and pin, shoes, and telephone. Each person had 15 chances to produce correct responses when the facilitator was unaware of what had been asked, or 180 for all twelve participants. Out of 180 tries, there was no success, save the two instances of same-category responses.

Despite the overall poor performance by participants, this study left several troubling questions about how the respondents had performed. Why, for example, did clients do as poorly in the same-pictures condition as the different-pictures condition? Also, in the first report of the study (Wheeler et al., 1992), subjects were said to point without looking at where they were pointing. If that is an accurate report, it suggests that the approach taken actually contradicted Crossley's prescription for facilitated communication, which specifies that individuals should be required to look at the target (Biklen, 1990, 1993; Crossley, 1994).

Several subsequent studies did little more to boost confidence about the method and much to undermine it. One such study (Klewe, 1993) was nearly a replica of the O. D. Heck study, for it involved seventeen institutionalized adults considered severely and profoundly retarded: Eleven could not speak, six could speak but uttered words "of doubtful relevance" (p. 560), and none had any history of formal instruction in reading or spelling. Working with experienced, familiar facilitators, they were asked to view same and different pictures from their facilitators or pictures when their facilitators saw none. The researchers concluded that facilitated communication offered them no benefit: "None of the patients were able to communicate independently using spelling boards. It also is clear that any appearance of communication during the experiments came from the facilitators rather than from the patients" (p. 565). Four participants did not complete the Klewe study; their facilitators indicated that the participants wished to drop out and that they regretted having previously agreed to participate.

An even simpler version of these naming-task studies was carried out using pictures of geometric shapes (Regal, Rooney, & Wandas, 1994). That is, the people using facilitation were not asked to read anything; they merely needed to point to shapes and numbers. Here's how it worked: Nineteen adults, nine males and ten females, ranging in age from 23 to 50, with a mean age of 31, participated. All were classified as profoundly or severely mentally retarded, five of whom had the diagnosis of autism and four of whom were classified as having cerebral palsy. They were assisted by five familiar facilitators. The participants were to examine and report on one of a hundred 5-by-7-inch cards, each of which had three variables: a shape (square, circle, triangle, star, or cross), the number of that shape on the card (1 through 4), and the single color for the shape on the card (red, blue, yellow, green, or orange). Participants could indicate their response on a letterboard or by pointing to the answer on a facilitator's response sheet. The cards were shown to the participants away from the facilitators, for up to three minutes. Then, with the facilitator providing support, the person was asked to answer. If the person failed to respond, the facilitator was instructed to move to the next question. Each participant examined five pictures and thus had 15 questions to answer. The responses of all were judged to be no better than chance.

Even more than the previously mentioned studies, this one was designed to be simple, brief, and easily scored. Yet the results were dismal. They bore no resemblance to the participants' announced prior abilities with facilitation: "Some of what they were reported to communicate (with facilitation in non test conditions) was revealing, sensitive, and at times highly personal" (Regal et al., 1994, p. 354). Hence the experimenters were surprised: "The absence of any support for FC under the simple conditions of the experiment was striking" (p. 354).

Seeming to admonish those who had made any claims of literacy via facilitation, Regal and colleagues (1994) championed their kind of experiment. Responsible people, they argued, could not ignore "the convergent nature of the results from controlled research" (p. 354). While they recognized that other research issues might arise, they announced that any communication by facilitation must be "treated as speculative at best" and warned that the research issues were best resolved through "experimentally sound methodologies" (p. 354). It would be perilously easy, they cautioned, for "all who toil in the field of human services," in hope of improving lives, to get caught up in "the allure of a simple quick fix," particularly when the problems they face seem "intractable and desperate" (p. 354). Particularly because of this "allure," Regal and colleagues exhorted their readers to pursue and honor the results of controlled research, "to ferret out information whose reliability leads to true understanding" (p. 354). Any lesser standard, they argued, would "ignore the emotional impact these claims can have on both clients and their families—especially if the claims should prove to be false" (p. 354).

Such total failure is perhaps more understandable in two other studies (Eberlin, McConnachie, Ibel, & Volpe, 1993; M. D. Smith, Haas, & Bekher, 1994), for these introduced hurdles for participants that were not present in the Wheeler and colleagues (1993), Klewe (1993), and Regal and colleagues (1994) studies. The subjects all had their first encounter with facilitation as part of the study, working with facilitators who also had no previous experience with the method. In other words, these were as much tests of the training process introduced as part of the studies as they were of the abilities of the people involved.

Eberlin and colleagues (1993) attempted to introduce facilitation to twenty-one school-age students who attended a special school, also in New York State. The students ranged in age from 11 to 20; were all thought to be mentally retarded, ranging from mildly to profoundly; and were all classified as autistic, with the exception of one who had a related diagnosis of pervasive developmental disorder. Of the twenty-one, only two had any previous history of reading, writing, or typing ability. The procedure involved training facilitators for four hours; building rapport between facilitators and students over a two-week period in which no facilitation was tried; baseline testing without any facilitation; initial exposure to facilitation; pretest with facilitation; 40 sessions of training in facilitation over several months; posttest warm-up with facilitation; and posttest with facilitation.

The types of questions used in the pretest and posttest included such items as the following: Where do you live? Who do you live with? What is your mother's name? What is your father's name? What is your favorite song? What is your favorite game? Other questions included: What is your diagnosis? How do you feel about being called autistic? How do you feel about your parents? How do you feel about school? Why don't you speak? In other words, some questions called for specific naming and others for explanations and statements. The facilitators were blinded to the questions; they wore headphones transmitting white noise.

The students actually did less well in the pretest with facilitation than in the baseline test without it. And "after 20 hours of FC training no student demonstrated emerging literacy skills or communicative competence that exceeded their already established communicative abilities" (Eberlin et al., 1993, p. 526). The researchers expressed strong pessimism about the method, declaring that "there has not been one scientifically valid confirmatory finding supporting the claims that FC produces independent client-generated communication" (p. 528).

The more recent study by M. D. Smith and colleagues (1994) provided facilitators and the study subjects with even less preparation. The subjects were ten individuals with autism, six male and four female, all classified as mentally retarded (one as moderately, five as severely, and four as profoundly), ranging in age from 14 to 51, with a mean age of 31. Three subjects spoke in unclear sentences, four used fewer than 10 words, two used limited manual signs and pictures, and one used only sounds and gestures. The facilitators had no prior knowledge of the method other than what they had been able to garner from attendance at workshops. The subjects were trained to use the method in two sessions and then participated in six experimental sessions, three with one facilitator and three with another. Actually, each participant received facilitation in only one session per facilitator; in the other sessions they were asked to point without support or with physical touch but no resistance. They were asked to identify pictures of action scenes or objects, to identify objects, or to convey information related to something explained to them orally, about all of which the facilitator was either aware or unaware. The result was similar to that of Eberlin and colleagues (1993) and Wheeler and colleagues (1992): "In no instance did a subject type a correct communication when the facilitator had been exposed to a different stimulus than the subject" (M. D. Smith et al., 1994, p. 363). Further, without facilitation there was no communication. And, when shown different stimuli, "under full support there were 50 instances in which typed output matched the stimulus to which the facilitator had been exposed and of which the subject had no knowledge" (p. 364). The authors concluded from these results that the method "is actually a form of facilitator control rather than facilitated communication" (p. 366). They advised cessation of use of the method for "clinical and educational" purposes and limiting it to experimental use.

A somewhat similar study was carried out in Australia with basically the same results, although there was an interesting twist to the participants' typing (Moore, Donovan, & Hudson, 1993). Unlike the Smith and colleagues (1994) study, all of the five participants in this study had been using facilitated communication for more than 17 months and were able to work with familiar facilitators. They ranged in age from 24 to 41 and in measured intellectual ability from moderately to profoundly retarded. In the first part of the study, with the facilitator absent, the participant was shown one of twelve concrete objects (e.g., ball, balloon, tape, flashlight). Then the facilitator returned and the person was asked to identify the item. In the second part of the study, the participant was spoken to about his perceived favorite television program or some other event in which the person was presumed to have some interest. Then with the facilitator present, the person was supposed to report on what had been discussed. Each participant was shown between three and five objects and heard comments about between three and five topics. A total of 18 objects where shown and 17 topics discussed. None of the responses were judged correct. However, in the process of the study, some of the facilitated typing revealed protests, including: STOP; COMMUNICATE HOW I FEEL IT IS HAPPENING I HAVE GOT A PROBLEM; and DO YOU MAKE UP YOUR OWN MIND IN EVERY CASE ABOUT MY COMMUNICATION IT IS NOT VERY EASY TO DO THIS I CAN'T REMEMBER ANY LITTLE THING ABOUT (Moore, Donovan, & Hudson, p. 546). The researchers found this language noticeably more sophisticated than "the required task of naming the object that had been discussed when the facilitator was out of the room, a task that could not be successfully 'facilitated' when the facilitator returned" (p. 546). Given the participants' apparent difficulty with the simple object-naming task, the researchers concluded that "these particular observed communications are originating from the facilitators" (p. 547). It simply did not seem conceivable that people who could not pass a test as basic as naming a ball or balloon could turn around and type out sentences protesting the testing. And so this test, like all of the others, with the exception of the IDRP (1989) study, was judged by its authors to have failed to produce results of any communicative competence by people using facilitation.

In addition to the findings of a failure to communicate in these post-1990 studies (e.g., Klewe, 1993; Smith & Belcher, 1993; Smith et al., 1994; Regal et al., 1994; Wheeler et al., 1993), they also revealed extensive cuing. In many instances, the words typed were ones *only the facilitators could have known.* While the possibility of cuing/influence had been raised by Biklen (1990) several years earlier—"it is possible in any instance of facilitation involving forearm, wrist, or hand for the person's communication to be influenced by a facilitator" (p. 311)—the controlled studies yielded specific evidence of it. And, disturbingly, facilitators seemed not to be aware of when they might be providing cues (Wheeler et al., 1993). Thus, even if subsequent studies might still demonstrate authentic communication with facilitation, one had to be concerned that people using the method as their means of communication might not always be in control of the words produced.

PASSING TESTS

In the midst of the failure-to-replicate studies came several in which people *did* succeed in passing some tests. The evidence of communication being controlled by the person with the disability was far from earth-shattering, but these studies did furnish some modest evidence that facilitation might enhance communicative ability.

The first of these studies involved only two participants, Ben and Eve, both classified as autistic (Vazquez, 1994). The study employed three different activities: picture identification, a video task in which participants were to describe a short video scene, and object identification. In each instance, the facilitators were kept from observing the content viewed by the person with the communication impairment. In addition, "efforts were taken to preserve external validity by avoiding the use of techniques not part of normal facilitation, for example, headphones, screens obscuring stimuli between subject and facilitator, or unfamiliar facilitators" (p. 369).

In the picture identification, Ben got none of the blind trials correct but all of the nonblind trials correct. Eva got the nonblind trials correct but only two out of ten of the blind trials correct. Their incorrect responses to the blind trials were words, but not the correct ones, for example "jumprope" for "ear" (p. 374). On the video task, Eva could not identify either of the two scenes she observed. Ben was successful in one of three that he observed, describing and responding to questions about a video on canoeing. When they produced wrong information, it was nevertheless coherent: Ben described a video about a rocket as something involving doctors and patients; Eva indicated that a video on whales was about a girl in a jungle. Ben did not participate in the third task, object naming, but Eva starred in this.

Eva was informed that they were going to play a game in which the experimenter would hold up an object from behind a screen as the facilitator looked away. Eva was to name the 20 common household objects (e.g., sock, book, fork, glove, sponge, dollar). The experimenter looked away as Eva typed so as not to provide visual cues. Eva got nine of ten nonblind items correct and nine of ten blind items correct as well. Actually, her incorrect responses were partially correct, for they seemed indicative of word retrieval difficulties; she typed CUP for bowl and COART (coat) for glove (p. 372).

There were two other studies (Ogletree, Hamtil, Solberg, & Scoby-Schmelzle, 1993; Simon, Toll, & Whitehair, 1994) in which some participants were asked to convey information about activities in which they had engaged. These were variations on the Moore, Donovan, Hudson, Dykstra, and Lawrence (1993) study, which asked participants to describe prior activities, and also resembled the naturally occurring message passing reported by Crossley and McDonald (1984).

The study by Ogletree and colleagues (1993) involved one child, age 4½, who was diagnosed as having pervasive developmental disorder/autism. He was given two kinds of tasks, naming objects shown to him from behind a screen and describing activities in which he had engaged. He was not successful in naming the objects. Yet he was able to name the activities to a high degree: "agreement between interpretations and actual events for free-play contexts ranged from 40% (2 of 5 responses) to 83.3% (5 of 6 responses). Agreement across free-play contexts for all four sessions was 70.6 % (12 of 17 responses)" (p. 5). Without facilitation, this child was judged to have the expressive ability of a 6-month-old child; he did not speak. With facilitation, which he had been using for eight months, his written utterances included single words, but also reached three to five words, and often included spelling errors.

In the study by Simon and colleagues (1994), seven students, ages 13 to 16, who had been reported to converse at conversational level with facilitation but to have no "discernible English" without it, were asked to report on activities, such as vacuuming a living area, visiting a vending machine in a leisure area, painting wood in a project center, reading a book in the library, and playing ball in the gymnasium. The incidence of message passing in this study was not as high as in that of Ogletree and colleagues (1993), but some of the participants did demonstrate communicative competence using facilitation: "Our results showed a large degree of facilitator guiding and a small amount of 'validated' communication" (Simon, Whitehair, & Toll, 1995, p. 338). The basic approach was for participants and "an escort" (a familiar staff person from the student's class, not the facilitator) to engage in an agenda as described on a card that had been placed in a manilla envelope. The facilitator then arrived and was given an envelope with a description of the activity, a description of a different activity (misguided condition), or a blank card. The envelopes reviewed with the participants during the study included photographs of the target location and the activity, the name of the activity and the location written in large print on separate cards, and the agenda written on a single card. Input about the activity was provided by the escorts through sign, verbal statement, and writing.

Four of the seven students in the Simon and colleagues (1994) study did convey information unknown to their facilitators. For example, a student typed ATE when he was given a sandwich. Another typed MRSKRBOOK after visiting the library. And one typed, WEATVENDINGMACHINESLLETME-POUTDOLLAR-INLOTOFORIDLFLDL and FORITOS after experiencing an activity during which he went to the vending machine, put a dollar in the machine, and purchased Fritos. With the facilitator naive about the activity, the students were successful 7.26% of the time. When the facilitator was informed correctly of the activity, the students were successful half of the time. And with the facilitator misguided, success dropped to 3.57% of the time. And in the misguided condition, students were influenced 56.25% of the time. Subsequent to publication of this research, Simon and colleagues (1995) wondered if the facilitator for participant 7, the one who discussed the Fritos, had possibly "been responding to olfactory cues from the Fritos that Student 7 had just eaten" (p. 338).

The researchers noted that not only could students be influenced, they could also be inhibited by the facilitators from giving responses that would have been correct. Their recommendation was to emphasize independent typing as a goal and to explore the feasibility of asking individuals to type independently first and then provide progressively more support as necessary, rather than providing the same amount of support in each session while working on fading support. In this study, all participants were supported at the hand/palm or wrist; one received support of the sleeve cuff.

A study in Australia incorporated a similar strategy of asking individuals to report on events in which they had participated or on other personal information, but unlike all of the above studies, it was carried out over many months in multiple sessions, using teaching and conversation sessions as opportunities for validating communicative competence while using facilitation (Steering Committee, 1993). Four preschoolers participated. Twenty adults participated: eleven with autism, two with cerebral palsy, one with Down syndrome, and six with no specific diagnosis other than mental retardation. Without facilitation, all tested in the profoundly retarded range.

Analysis of "transcriptions indicated that thirteen (65%) of adult clients were able to communicate information using visual language which was accurate and not previously known to the facilitator" (p. 10). Other measures of validation were also present:

> Five clients appeared to have a significant idiosyncratic style and nine adults and three children (50% of clients) were able to respond correctly to questions in multiple choice situations where the facilitator did not know the correct response. Thus, twenty-one (87.5%) of the client sample of 24 had their communication validated using content and structural analysis. (p. 10)

When given an oro-motor assessment for dyspraxia, in which participants were asked to imitate tongue and lip postures, twenty-one participants failed. They evidenced extreme dyspraxia in even this simplest action associated with speech. Only one participant was able to communicate more than "basic need" information by speaking. Thirteen participants were judged to be "noncommunicative with speech or augmentative systems" (p. 20).

This study, conducted over an entire year, recorded evidence of correct answers that were spontaneously given, elicited through preplanned situations, and evidenced in multiple-choice selections for which the facilitator did not know the answers (e.g., family information). In the spontaneous as well as the preplanned situations, the individuals could give incorrect information and correct information simultaneously. For example, a facilitator asked, "What did you have for lunch?" The participant responded, typing, ROAST BEEF SANDWICH. Later, when informed that the answer was incorrect, the facilitator asked what he really had for lunch. This elicited both incorrect and correct information including: PIZZA HUT A SUPREME SMALL PIZZA SOAMRGHTLAGERBEERCLANBANGINGER BREADMAN (p. 122). The correct information (underlined) was embedded within incorrect information from the same category (i.e., food, food establishment). A 5-year-old participant correctly answered 16 of 18 multiple-choice questions about various family information. The preplanned activities were similar to those described in Simon and colleagues (1994) and in Ogletree and colleagues (1993). The following is an example:

FACILITATOR: Tell me what you did today.
CARE WORKER: Did you play *cricket* or go shopping?
CLIENT 2: CRICKET
FACILITATOR: I wonder where you went for cricket.
CARE WORKER: Did you play cricket at *Brazzles* or Bundamba?
CLIENT 2: BRAZZLES
FACILITATOR: Did you *watch* cricket or play cricket?
CLIENT 2: I DID NOT WATCH

The last response had been unanticipated but was nevertheless accurate. The participant had neither played nor watched but instead had walked away from the group (p. 130).

Interestingly, message passing, even if it involved a favorite activity, was not always simple, as evidenced when participants exhibited word-retrieval difficulties, as in the following example:

JANE (facilitator): Tell me what you showed Judith last week.
CLIENT: ON MONDAY I INSISTED JUDITH LET ME SHOW HER MY EASY
JANE: Start again.
CLIENT: TO SHOW HER HOW I MAKE SOUNDS IN MY LIVING ROOM

JANE: mm.
CLIENT: I SANG IN THE LIVING ROOM IN MY FINGERS EVER SO
    EASY. DO IT TONIGHT IN THE LIVING
JANE: Keep talking like this until you remember the word.
CLIENT: THE SOUND FROM MY FINGERS. TABLE BLACK BUTTONS ON
    IT (P) TIRED
JANE: Keep trying you're getting there.
CLIENT: STUMPS. PLAY MACHINE CALLED A REAL NICE YOU TELL

Jane had no prior knowledge of the fact that this person had played a piano and a pump organ for Judith. The client never did retrieve the words "piano" and "pump organ," though she described the activity: SOUND FROM MY FINGERS. TABLE BLACK BUTTONS. PLAY MACHINE (p. 31).

The Steering Committee study helps explain the results of all the others. With the exception of two studies (Eberlin et al., 1993; Moore, Donovan, & Hudson, 1993) that employed new facilitators as well as people with communication impairments who were relatively untrained in facilitated communication, this one and the others evaluated people with experience with the method. Yet the Steering Committee study yields a far higher degree of success than all of the other post-1990 studies and is in many respects very different from the others in its conditions. Unlike most of the others, it involved collecting evidence over long time periods; utilized naturally occurring, if sometimes orchestrated, events; used multiple modalities of assessment (e.g., multiple choice, message passing); provided participants ongoing feedback as to whether they had given correct or incorrect answers; and allowed multiple opportunities for individuals to pass their tests. In this sense, each assessment of participants became a practice session for the next. Also, the Steering Committee assessment involved scaffolding of answers, whereby individuals were asked follow-up questions and given lots of time in which to answer. The studies conducted by Vazquez (1994), Simon and colleagues (1994), and Ogletree and colleagues (1993) incorporated some of these qualities; for example, Vazquez used multiple modalities, including the natural condition of a game situation, and Simon et al. and Ogletree et al. used naturally occurring events as their substance. But these experiments as well as the others cited above gave no more than one or two opportunities to be tested; they were one- or two-place-in-time tests.

The condition of scaffolding—whereby participants were queried repeatedly, albeit in a friendly and supportive way—was also characteristic of the message-passing part of the IDRP (1989) study in which three of three individuals passed the tests by conveying information about gifts they had received. The implicit presumption of researchers who designed these studies was that participants could answer the questions asked if given time, multiple opportunities to answer, and the chance to give wrong answers along with correct ones—all under natural (i.e., relaxed and normally occurring) conditions.

THE METHOD WAS BECOMING WHAT THE TESTS SAID IT WAS

The effect of the research debate over the method was to frame all discussions of facilitated communication in terms of "validity" or "invalidity," thus tying its meaning to the tests. The tests ceased to be representations of the method; rather, the test situation (e.g., identifying pictures, passing messages) was presumed to be synonymous with facilitated communication.

A similarity between facilitated communication testing and intelligence testing is unmistakable. Intelligence testing reified the idea that people possess amounts of intelligence, that these amounts can be measured, and that these amounts can be articulated as scores (intelligence quotients). The fact that the very idea of intelligence, let alone particular notions about what it is or how it might be measured, is a social construction is soon forgotten. In the wake of extensive testing, IQ has become an almost tangible thing. Hanson (1993) has described the process by which this can occur, where the idea of intelligence as a single thing reflects the fact that intelligence test results are nearly always reported in terms of the intelligence quotient, or IQ, even though the test is actually comprised of different parts measuring different skills. The idea that intelligence can be quantified and that some people have higher amounts than others also seems to emanate from the intelligence quotient or quantification of test results. Thus, the notion that individual intelligence is something that people "have" or "do not have," and that it is basically "fixed for life," in other words a personal attribute, "stems from the belief that intelligence tests measure not what one already knows but one's *ability* to learn" (p. 255, emphasis in original). Thus, while factors such as opportunity and even desire to learn may vary throughout one's life, depending upon circumstance, ability to learn (intelligence) is presumed "hard wired in the person. Hence each individual's intelligence is considered to be fixed by heredity" (p. 256). Such ideas are not naturally self-evident, though many people believe they are, for such notions about intelligence have "achieved the status of bedrock assumption" (p. 256), treated as "a simple fact of nature" (p. 256).

Facilitation is, of course, newer and not yet as monolithically defined. Yet ideas about testing the method have led to assumptions that people are either "communicating" or "not communicating" and "influenced" or "not influenced," implying that influence in communication is abnormal, bad, a type of contamination. Failure to pass a test is taken as evidence that the method does not work and that the people using it are truly retarded (Klewe, 1993; Smith et al., 1994), unfortunate pawns of a fraud (Green & Shane, 1994), prisoners of their facilitators (Palfreman, 1994), or vehicles for other people's words (Smith et al., 1994).

Alternatively, however, we might ask what factors in the experience of people with communication impairments the researchers have considered. Most obvious among these, have they examined the individuals' lack of experience with test-taking and considered how to overcome this? Have they considered problems of failed confidence and ways to boost confidence? Have they considered the role of practice with test-taking? Have they considered multiple strategies by which individuals might confirm authorship? Have they investigated those instances in which people *have* demonstrated success with confirming authorship to discover the conditions that might have aided their success?

The possibility that individuals could perform well at home or in class but miserably in a standardized test situation is not novel. If it were, we would not have a term such as "test anxiety." Elizabeth Moon (1992) describes the phenomenon in her article "Test Child/Real Child." She pictures the child in a formal clinic evaluation who cannot jump over an eraser on the floor, barely totters up steps, cannot stand on one foot, and fails to perform a simple task with blocks but who at home hops between laundry baskets gleefully, climbs steps with ease, sometimes skipping a tread, hops the length of a hallway on a single leg, and constructs complicated mosaic-tile puzzles. The difference, she argues, may have to do with whether a child is tense, frightened, or merely uncooperative. "An evaluation which doesn't find the 'real child'" Moon argues, can never form the basis for a useful diagnosis or treatment. In some sense, Moon explains, the "real child" is both children—the stiff, seemingly incompetent one in the evaluation and the skipping, agile one at home, "but the one we want to encourage is the lively, competent, adventurous one at home" (p. 18). It does no good to label the child as having problems in attention or in pursuing goals, Moon argues, if the real problem is "which goals he chose to pursue" or his level of comfort (p. 18). And it certainly does no good to focus on evidence of incompetence or, more accurately, failure to demonstrate competence, when there is other evidence that contradicts this conclusion.

In each of the facilitated communication investigations, the test taker, like the clinic child, is portrayed in a position of ambiguity. That is, the test will presumably determine whether the person can communicate or not. The test giver, on the other hand, holds a position of legitimacy, not only to judge the test taker but also to determine the standards by which the test taker will be judged.

Not surprisingly, testers typically project their own unambiguous, legitimate status onto their tests, treating them as essentially objective, valid, scientific, and fair. At least this was the case in the early accounts of facilitated communication testing, in which authors of the tests systematically discounted arguments that might question their test designs (see, for example, Eberlin et al., 1993; Wheeler et al., 1993). The test is treated as unproblematic.

The purpose of tests is ostensibly to ask questions and seek answers. The kinds of questions they ask, however, are limited by the framework of tests. While test givers may make pretenses that the test situation approximates reality, clearly tests impose conditions that are not emblematic of most communication situations. This is especially so in those test situations that introduce false information (e.g., the misguiding described by Simon and colleagues [1994]; the different pictures shown to facilitators and participants by Wheeler and colleagues [1993]) to the two people involved in communication. Also, test apparatus, amount of time for testing/answering, collection of test data, scripted questions and statements, and other aspects of testing make most test situations unlike typical communication events.

The questions asked tend to focus on aspects of larger, real-world events and attempt to reduce complexity to manageable factors, hence the term "controlled conditions." In the case of facilitated communication, tests typically have asked "Are people who use facilitated communication able to convey their own thoughts?" "Is the communication that can be verified as their own reflective of unexpected or previously unseen literacy abilities?" and "Is there facilitator influence/cuing involved in facilitation to the point that the typing reflects content from the facilitator and not from the person with the communication impairment?" Related to these questions, the test results imply answers concerning the intellectual abilities of those tested.

The question "Are people able to convey their own thoughts" is not answered when someone fails to convey an expected answer to a question or any answer at all, for example, to "Where do you live?" (Eberlin et al., 1993) or "What is this a picture of?" (Wheeler et al., 1993). The only thing revealed is that the person did not answer these questions, gave incorrect answers, or gave some other response. It does not explain how a person might respond to a different question or, perhaps more importantly, how the person might respond under different circumstances. Similarly, failure to respond in sentence-level communication does not prove that the person lacks literacy skills. It is conceivable that under different circumstances or with different content, the person would respond differently. Particular tests may fail to explain other observable events as well, for example, that a given person types content that has a distinctive quality to it. For instance, when Diane More uses the phrase "what it is" and nearly always refers to herself as "we," she distinguishes her facilitated communication from her mother's own communicative style. Failure to pass a test or, in Diane's case, conveying information that seems jumbled or simply incorrect does not negate the facts that she has written correct information unknown to her mother/facilitator or that her communication has a distinctive style.

Thus the issue with regard to testing is not whether to test, but rather what kinds of tests are used, the meaning of particular test results, alternative test strategies, and the implications of testing for understanding facilitated communication. While one of the editors has observed that testing was not a part of early facilitated communication training in the Australian model (Biklen, 1990, 1993), this aspect of the method has been altered by the Queensland group (Steering Committee, 1993), which introduced controlled testing and a variety of other validation strategies into early assessment and training activities. As revealed in Chapter 4, controlled testing has become part of DEAL Communication Centre facilitated communication training as well. Yet, neither the Queensland nor DEAL programs view such assessments as pass-or-fail tests; rather, such experiments provide information about facilitated communication training, about facilitator skill, about skills and abilities/disabilities of facilitated communication users, and about issues in test design and implementation.

If researchers or others treat given test results as actually capable of determining who can communicate and who cannot, then they render the test more than a mere representation of facilitation. Rather the test produces what facilitation is, in a way analogous to Hanson's (1994) description of how intelligence testing produces social understandings of intelligence.

What we observe happening with testing of facilitated communication is that the purpose of testing—to find out something specific about the person, to prove the person's competence—somehow gets transformed; instead of helping the person examined, it can become a serious impediment to the test takers if, for whatever reason, failure on the test becomes fodder for an argument that none can pass (American Psychological Association, 1994), that the method is unreliable (American Speech-Language Hearing Association, 1994), that the method is dangerous (Green & Shane, 1994), and that science has spoken (Jacobson et al., 1994). Failure to question the test protocol has as its natural complement questioning of the person.

Analogies to this situation and the resultant interpretations can be found in the use of intelligence testing of African American, Hispanic, and poor students and subsequent disproportionate assignment of them away from gifted classes and into special education classes for mildly retarded students (Heller, Holtzman, & Messick, 1982; *Hobson v. Hansen*, 1967; Oakes, 1985) or in early-twentieth-century army "intelligence" testing (Gould, 1981).

In the latter example, immigrants entering the army, mostly "Latins and Slavs had arrived recently and spoke English either poorly or not at all; the main wave of Teutonic immigration had passed long before" (Gould, 1981, p. 220). Unfamiliarity with the English language was supposedly dealt with through the use of pictorial tests, though it was still found that English-speakers averaged 101.6 and "nonspeakers averaged only 77.8" (p. 220). Robert Yerkes, one of the leading testers, explained away such differences, preferring to cling to his nativist beliefs. What makes this history particularly relevant to today's debates over facilitated communication is that Gould found great anomalies not only in the differences between whites and nonwhites and between longtime residents and recent immigrants but between test conditions, that is, between individually given and group tests and between the Alpha test for English-speakers and the Beta test for recent immigrants who were non-English-speakers. He concluded that the "Draconian conditions of testing made . . . a thorough mockery of the claim that recruits could have been in a frame of mind to record anything about their innate abilities. In short, most of the men must have ended up either utterly confused or scared shitless" (p. 205). He described the procedure for those taking the Beta test—in which it was presumed that the test takers knew no English—as one in which a test giver pointed to a man at a blackboard who apparently demonstrated what it looked like to write on a test form. The tester then announced to the men with their test papers "Ask no questions. Wait till I say 'Go ahead!'" (p. 205). Gould contrasted this to the Alpha test for English-speakers in which they were told more or less exactly what to expect and what to do. They, too, were told to pay attention and to ask no questions, but unlike the miming instructions given the non-English-speakers, the English-speakers were treated nearly as the testers' peers: "The purpose of this examination is to see how well you can remember, think, and carry out what you are told to do. We are not looking for crazy people. The aim is to help find out what you are best fitted to do in the Army" (p. 206). The results of the test, they were told, would help determine their assignments in the army. Parts of the test would be easy and parts hard. But the tester reassured them, saying, "You are not expected to make a perfect grade, but do the very best you can" (p. 206). Less prepared culturally and in language familiarity, the Beta test subjects were further disadvantaged by a hostile procedure.

After experimenting with the test on his own Harvard University students—as Gould points out, they were hardly comparable to recent immigrants in their understanding of the culture and its language—Gould concluded that the test never gave the recruits a chance. Apart from the fact that many of the test takers could not understand the instructions, and in some instances could not hear the instructions, or that they might have experienced test anxiety, exacerbated by instructors who periodically exhorted individual recruits to hurry their responses, "add to this the blatant cultural biases of . . . (elements of the test), and the more subtle biases directed against those who could not write numbers or . . . (write) . . . at all, and what do you have but a shambles" (p. 212).

Of course, this procedure was hardly any less precise or scientific than other strategies of the time. One of the most famous accounts of feeblemindedness was Goddard's report of the Kallikak family (Goddard, 1912), founded largely on the work of field workers through observation and interviews of neighbors and others, some of it conducted after the person in question had long since died. The field workers assigned levels of intelligence, even if they lacked direct evidence. Goddard found himself having to defend his research practices in which he identified the mother of the Kallikaks as feebleminded, yet did not know her first name (J. D. Smith, 1985). He felt confident in his abilities and those of his field workers to know mental retardation on sight. After all, his field workers were "carefully trained" and had "spent weeks and months in the institution, talking with and observing all grades of defectives" (Goddard, cited in J. D. Smith, p. 71). It was well known, Goddard explained, that institutional superintendents could easily diagnose patients simply by looking at them, determining not only "whether he is a fit subject for their institution or is normal and does not belong there, but . . . also . . . his grade" (Goddard, cited in J. D. Smith, p. 71).

We are reminded that those taking validation tests on facilitated communication have also often been judged on the basis of their appearance. Indeed it is the fact of people's appearing to be retarded in speech and adaptive behaviors that makes the prospect of their being the authors of coherent, complex communication via facilitation so hard for many observers to consider, much less accept.

Another parallel between the testing movement and the current pressures to validate authorship of facilitated communication deserves our attention. With both kinds of testing, the testees were potentially at risk. The testing movement of the early twentieth century could lead a testee to conscription, rejection from military service, and even to deportation— Goddard was apparently proud that deportation increased by between 300 and 500 percent in the years 1913 and 1914, at the same time mental testing was implemented (J. D. Smith, 1985). Similarly, failure on authorship tests of facilitated communication could leave testees classified as severely or profoundly retarded and could signal removal of their facilitation, rendering them speechless. Who but they are to say what amount of terror, confusion, and defeat they may feel upon entering, enduring, or exiting the test?

NEXT ACCOUNTS

At the heart of the controversy over facilitated communication is a debate over how mental retardation is defined and assessed, fundamental assumptions of particular research orientations and practices, the ways in which people with severe disabilities learn, and the impediments of social attitudes to recognition of intellectual abilities in people who have significant expressive difficulties. In discussing the public policy and public debate about facilitated communication that has created a tense, contentious environment within which to do research on the topic, we have begun to explore social stereotypes, infringement of civil rights, marginalization, even nihilism endured by people using facilitated communication. In the succeeding chapters, we explore distinctly different research strategies oriented toward understanding authorship of facilitated communication and understanding the method's complexities, noting the differential effects of particular research conditions and scrutinizing the nature of discourse over facilitated communication.

CHAPTER 2

Who's Doing the Typing?: An Experimental Study

Donald N. Cardinal
Darlene Hanson
John Wakeham

In this chapter, we explore the possibility that the reason so many users of facilitated communication have failed to validate their authorship in past quantitative studies may not be because they lacked literacy or because the facilitator controlled their communication but, rather, because the procedures by which their competency was judged may not be a valid measure of the facilitation method. We arrived at this hypothesis after observing over 100 students using facilitated communication in public schools for several hundred hours. When traditional test-taking conditions existed, facilitated communication production was much less complex, even to the point of nonexistence at times, when compared to what was observed in other educational, nontesting environments. When those conditions were strategically controlled, it appeared that facilitated communication was easily apparent and more complex. The question, then, was how one arranges for a set of conditions that would satisfy the scientific controls of a valid experiment while still providing for a conducive environment. After a year of meeting with social researchers, practitioners, and students, and after several pilot studies, a "naturally controlled environment" that included the procedure of extensive "practice" was developed and became the experimental design used in this study.

The research group also felt that past studies had been too complex, making it impossible to determine which conditions may have aided or hindered an individual's ability to communicate. This diffusion of protocol conditions made it impossible to determine whether the study subjects had failed the test due to their inability to use facilitation or whether the testing procedure was invalid for the measurement of facilitation. After all, a procedure or a test is only valid if it can demonstrate that it is able to measure what it purports to measure. If, for example, a test is said to measure a person's ability to read but everyone who takes that test is judged by that test to be illiterate, then the test has failed to be validated. It may be valid, but it is not proven as such and thus should not be considered as a valid measure of reading. This is no different from measures of authorship that consistently fail to measure facilitated communication. There is no more reason to conclude that the facilitated communication is invalid than there is to conclude that the test is invalid, since no one has been able to pass that test. Therefore, scientifically speaking, when authorship studies conclude that no one was able to pass a test under controlled conditions, it is no more accurate to conclude that the subjects failed to validate their communication ability than it would be to conclude that the test itself may not be valid. Consider the following possibilities when trying to measure the existence of a phenomenon. If, under controlled conditions, the phenomenon is not measured at all, then two equally reasonable conclusions compete where the evidence leans no more in one direction than the other. Either the phenomenon does not really exist or the measure of that phenomenon is not valid or not reliable. Setting the question of reliability aside, the conclusion that the measurement is not valid should have equal weight to the conclusion that the phenomenon is not real. For these reasons, this study tests the most basic research question of authorship in facilitated communication: Can facilitated communication users transmit rudimentary information to a facilitator when that information is not known to the facilitator? This investigation, then, is as much a test of the protocol as it is of authorship.

METHOD

Great effort was taken to control for obvious, and not so obvious, threats to internal and external validity. Below is a thorough account of each of these controls as they relate to this study.

Participants

Participants of this study include the subjects (we call them students in this study), recorders, facilitators, and the research observers. Each participant group is discussed in detail.

Students (FC users). To qualify for this study, a participant had to possess the following characteristics or conditions: (1) been facilitated for at least six months; (2) be able to spell out at least a single-word response using FC; (3) possess a communication evaluation documenting a logical array of communication strategies that had been attempted with the student prior to FC and an anecdotal history of events, and confirmation of those events, where the student communicated information via FC that was not known to the facilitator (Cardinal & Hanson, 1994a); (4) demonstrate a willingness to participate in the research study as expressed through the student's best communication method (often FC) with their communication specialist; (5) receive informed consent from all four sources: family/guardian, the school district superintendent, the district's director of special education, and the school principal; and (6) have a mean unfacilitated (baseline-1) score of not more than one in five words correct.

Although a student needed only a single-word facilitated communication ability to qualify for the study, according to their most recent communication evaluations, 86% of the students demonstrated language skills that allowed them to respond to open-ended questions through written language when facilitated. Over 80% of the students were using FC as their primary form of communication in core curriculum classes. It is important to note that none of the students in this study demonstrated the ability to generate written language prior to the use of FC. At most, prior to using FC, the students had educational objectives that indicated they were learning to "read" community sign vocabulary or to write their names.

Forty-six students qualified to be in the study. This represented all eligible students at 10 participating schools, located in four school districts. Participants ranged in age from 11 to 22 years, with a mean age of 15.6 years. There were 63% male (27 students) and 37% female (16 students) participants. The participants' diagnoses were autism (17 students), mental retardation with known etiology such as Down syndrome (16 students), mental retardation with unknown etiology (6 students), cerebral palsy and mental retardation (2 students), and other developmental disabilities (2 students). Each student carried the label of "severely handicapped" according to California State Education Code Title V definition and was reported to have severe communication disorders (Section 3030j, Title V). Three students did not complete the study for varying personal reasons—consequently 43 students remained at the conclusion of the study. Each of the 3 students not completing the study, or their parents/guardians, reported that the students had symptoms of "stress" during the study period, such as sleeplessness, atypical aggression, extreme fatigue, and so on.

Recorders. The 27 recorders for this study were either teachers (6), program specialists (2), communication specialists (2), or teacher assistants (17). Each recorder had previously participated in similar educational activities with the student. Recorder responsibilities for this study included presenting the words to the student, requesting the facilitator to enter the room, recording the letters that were typed by the student using facilitated communication (the letters were actually said aloud by the facilitator as the student touched them; it was this oral response the recorder wrote down), and then filing the responses in a secure location.

Facilitators. The 31 facilitators were either teachers (15), program specialists (3), communication specialists (2), or teacher assistants (11). Each facilitated an average of 1.39 students—18 facilitated a single student, 9 facilitated 2 students, and 4 facilitated 3 students. Each facilitator was one of the student's typical facilitators in school. Each facilitator had been trained in theory and strategy before she began facilitating a student. This included ongoing hands-on training and supervision provided to each facilitator by a facilitator trainer, either a speech and language specialist assigned to each site or the program psychologist who was also an FC trainer. Each trainer received his training through one or more workshops by personnel from the Facilitated Communication Institute at Syracuse University. Hands-on training involved showing the trainee how to support the student(s) he would be working with and describing the language or communicative needs and skills of the student. During training, the facilitator trainers observed the use of the strategy for each student and trainee and provided ongoing feedback to both the trainee and the student. All facilitators participating in this study were deemed "experienced facilitators" by the facilitator trainers prior to the beginning of this study—training was not part of this study but occurred prior to it.

Research Observers. The authors, a program specialist, a communication specialist, and a university professor served as observers. The observers monitored each experimental dyad (recorder and facilitator) continuously until the protocol was followed exactly and then at least once per week (i.e., 33% of sessions) after that until the end of the data-gathering period—this included both baseline conditions. The observers monitored for protocol inaccuracies and/or contaminants (e.g., any verbalization from the recorder during a trial; any verbalization from the participant while the facilitator was in the room other than a simple greeting; unsanctioned movement by the recorder, such as looking at the participant or facilitator during the typing stage of the trial; inconsistency between what the FC user typed and what the recorder noted). If found, they were corrected and that trial and any previous trials subject to the protocol inaccuracy were not counted in the study results. This occurred only four times throughout the entire study and resulted in eliminating approximately 75 trials (compared to over 3,800 total trials). In all but one case the inaccuracy involved collecting data after the ninetieth trial was completed for a specific student, which resulted in 70 eliminated trials. The other inaccuracy was a failure to use the proper randomness technique for word selection, which occurred for one student during the third session (day) of trials, resulting in all five trials for that session being eliminated—proper randomness techniques had been used during the first two sessions.

Settings

There were ten sites used in this study. Each site was a classroom on one of five general education school campuses—there were two classes per campus. The five campuses were located across four school districts. Each classroom was one that was very familiar to the students and was viewed as their resource room or homeroom. Each student was included in general education classes from two to four periods a day.

A specific portion of each of the classroom sites was identified as the testing area. In each case, the testing area was one that could be "closed" to the remainder of the classroom. This testing area was one that typically was used by the classroom teacher as an instructional area; thus it was an optimal environment to be "controlled" but yet was "natural," in that the study environment consisted of the complex social, cultural, and physical conditions affecting the nature of the individual being tested. This tended to be the environment in which the FC user had historically and most successfully learned.

Equipment/Materials

Keyboards used in this study were laminated photocopies of keyboards (alpha and QWERTY in uppercase letters), which are the "devices" used in everyday communication by all students in this study. Most students periodically used electronic devices for their facilitated communication output during times of computer use, typing at home, or when communicating with specific facilitators who prefer an electronic device. Again, for this study, all facilitation dyads used the laminated keyboards.

The test material was a word set of 100 words consisting primarily of nouns, with some verbs, containing no more than six letters (see Figure 2.1). The words were selected because they were considered to be familiar to

FIGURE 2.1 Presentation of Word Set

Apple	Cat	Food	Paint	Sock
Arm	Chair	Fork	Pants	Spoon
Baby	Coat	Frog	Paper	Stop
Ball	Comb	Girl	Pear	Store
Bear	Come	Green	Pen	Stove
Bed	Cup	Hair	Pencil	Street
Bell	Dog	Hand	Penny	Table
Big	Doll	Help	Phone	Taco
Bike	Down	House	Pizza	Talk
Bird	Drink	Jump	Play	Tape
Black	Drum	Key	Put	Towel
Blue	Duck	Leg	Read	Toy
Book	Ear	Man	Red	Train
Boy	Eat	Milk	Run	Tree
Bread	Egg	Money	Shirt	Truck
Brown	Eye	Mouth	Shoe	Walk
Brush	Farm	Nail	Sing	Wallet
Bus	Fire	Nickel	Sit	Water
Cake	Fish	Nose	Sleep	Woman
Car	Flag	Orange	Soap	Work

the students in that they were part of the age-appropriate, community-based, functional curriculum presented in an included school program. Additionally, one purpose of this study was to create a rudimentary protocol that was not contaminated by student characteristics such as age or grade level. The selected words minimized this problem by including words that were encountered by even the youngest study participant. In the curriculum, some of the words had been presented in written form as sight-word vocabulary, in picture line drawing form as communication vocabulary, or in other places in their everyday school curriculum—along with hundreds of other words. The words compiled specifically for this study had not previously been introduced to the students as a word set. Facilitators did have open access to the word list.

Procedures

The test condition was designed specifically for this study, so the participants had no previous experience with this exact procedure. However, since the procedure was developed to be "natural," it was similar to procedures used in typical instruction.

Test Conditions. The following test condition was used:

1. The recorder showed the student a single word on a flashcard, then orally presented the word. The meaning of the word was said orally by the recorder (e.g., "chair—this is a chair—the word is chair" as the recorder would point to the chair or "nickel—like a coin or money—nickel"). See Figure 2.2 for the room layout. The flashcard was then placed face down away from the facilitation dyad.
2. The recorder asked the facilitator to come into the room.
3. Upon entering the room, the facilitator asked the student to type the word that had been introduced by offering physical support for facilitation and saying "type the word."
4. The *facilitator* said the letters aloud as the supported student typed them on the keyboard, and the *recorder* wrote those letters on the data sheet exactly as said until either the student voluntarily stopped typing, typed a period indicating completion, or typed eight letters—two more than the longest word in the set. Letters corrected on the keyboard by touching the "Delete" key did not count in the eight letters.
5. The facilitator left the room and the recorder introduced a second word as per number 1 above and the process was repeated until the five trials were completed for that session.
6. Sessions containing five trials each continued three times per week for six weeks, resulting in 90 facilitated trials per participant.

To avoid influencing the student or facilitator, the recorder avoided comments that would hint that the response was correct or incorrect. The student was always given the same positive comment (varied with facilitator) regardless of a correct or incorrect response (e.g., "good work," "well done," "that was good, Bob"). The recorders engaged in no verbalization after asking for the facilitator to enter the "testing area" until the recording was completed.

FIGURE 2.2 Layout of the Testing Room

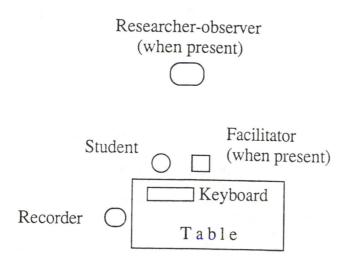

A random word selection method was used for this study in all three research conditions: baseline-1, facilitated, and baseline-2. One hundred words comprised the word set from which each trial word was randomly selected. Each word was replaced in the 100-word pool after it was used. There was an approximately 1% chance of a guessed word by the facilitator (see "Randomness of Word Selection" under the "Results" section below for testing of the random selection procedure).

Research Design

Baseline-1. During baseline-1 each participant was asked to engage in the session protocol (see the "Procedures" section above), with the exception that the facilitator did not physically touch (facilitate) the student. Baseline-1 consisted of 10 trials per student. The 10 baseline-1 trials were gathered over two sessions (two separate days); each session consisted of 5 trials.

Facilitated. The facilitated condition consisted of 90 trials for each participant. Testing occurred three days per week, one session of 5 trials per day for six weeks, resulting in over 3,800 total trials.

Baseline-2. A second baseline (baseline-2) was conducted at the completion of the 90 facilitated trials. The baseline-2 procedure was identical to the baseline-1 procedure in that the facilitator was present but did not physically touch (facilitate) the student. There were a total of 10 baseline-2 trials per participant. The 10 baseline-2 trials were gathered over two sessions (two separate days); each session consisted of 5 trials each.

Response Measures

Accuracy of the word typed served as the dependent variable. The accuracy of the typed word was determined at a later time by a graduate assistant. A "correct response" was held to the highest possible standard, that is, a perfectly spelled word with no extra or repeated letters in front of, after, or within the word. For example, if responding to the word "house" the student typed HOWSE or HHOUSE the response would be judged incorrect—only the response HOUSE was accepted as correct. There were no exceptions. This standard was used since it needed no interpretation for determining the response measure, thus providing the most robust data for the dependent variable.

Analyses were conducted using both composite data trials (from all approximately 3,800 trials) and individual data trials (viewing each student's performance separately). Composite analysis compared the students' highest performance across each of the three experimental conditions using a bivariate inferential statistic (*t*-test) as well as a presentation of the true mean scores across time. Individual student performance illustrates the increases the students made (or didn't make) over their original baseline-1 scores. Finally, a preliminary analysis of the error patterns of incorrect words is also presented.

RESULTS

The results of this investigation are reported below in two main categories: composite and individual analyses. Composite analysis refers to the grouping of the data to allow for inferential analysis. On the other hand, individual analysis addresses the data descriptively, allowing the reader to see a picture of how each student's performance compares to those of others.

Randomness of Word Selection

Since there were 100 different words available in the word set (see Figure 2.1) from which each trial word (a total of 90 per student) was randomly selected, there was an approximately 1% chance of a guessed word by the facilitator. Post hoc analysis indicated the average repeat rate (how many times a previously used word recurred) was 1.7, indicating that the average word was repeated less than twice during the entire 110 trials (90 trials under the test condition and 20 trials under the baseline conditions). The actual effect repeated words may have had on increasing or decreasing the chance of correct guessing by the facilitator was unknown. Consequently, additional analyses were carried out. A *t*-test was conducted to determine if there was a significant difference between the correct response rate of repeated words ($M = 2.33$, $SD = 1.87$) and nonrepeated words ($M = 2.19$, $SD = 1.83$). In this case, there was no significant difference between the two groups [t (42)= -1.01, $p > .05$], indicating that the correctness of the response for a particular word was not significantly related to the frequency with which that word was repeated and that facilitator guessing did not play a significant role in correct response situations. Therefore, the random word selection method used for this study appeared to be adequate, since repeated words did not contribute significantly to the guessing factor by the facilitator. Additionally, it can be argued that the repeating of words from the word list mathematically reduces the chance of guessing, since the pool of unknown words from which to guess remains larger when fewer words are selected from it. In either case, the probability of a facilitator guessing a word in this study appears to be approximately 1%.

One more analysis was conducted to determine if facilitators who aided multiple FC users during the experiment gained an advantage by having more access to the word list, since they encountered the words two or three times as frequently as facilitators who had only one student to facilitate. In other words, did the FC users with facilitators who facilitated more than one FC user do better than FC users with facilitators who facilitated only a single user? When the correct word performance of students with facilitators who facilitated only a single user was correlated with the correct word performance of students with facilitators who facilitated more than one user, there was no significant relationship ($r = .061$, $p = .847$). This result indicates that facilitators who worked with two or more FC users either did not gain an advantage by their additional exposure to the words or did not use their additional knowledge to influence the FC user's response.

Composite Analysis

Viewing all students as a whole, it was determined that there was a significant difference between the students' best performance in baseline-1 and their best performance during all trials of the facilitated condition, [t (42) = 7.59, $p < .0001$], indicating that when allowing students to use facilitation, under the protocol conditions of this study, they did significantly better than when they were not allowed to use facilitation.

Further analysis was conducted to determine if the practice condition was effective. In other words, were students able to pass the "test" the first time they were introduced to it, when no practice had occurred, or did they only perform better after a specific amount of practice had occurred? This is very much like the typical one-place-in-time test. It was determined that there was no significant difference [$t(42) = .81, p = .42$] between the students' best performance in the baseline-1 condition ($M = .12$) and their scores the first day of "testing" ($M = .16$). Viewing this result next to the fact that there was a significant difference [$t(42) = 7.59, p < .0001$] between baseline-1 and facilitated scores after practice had occurred suggests that practice of the procedure may have an important effect on FC testing.

To determine if any measured growth by students was due to FC and not simply learning how to type over time, a t-test was conducted to determine if there was a significant difference between baseline-1 and baseline-2. It was discovered that there was a significant difference [$t(42) = 3.93, p < .0003$] between the participants' highest unfacilitated scores in the baseline-1 condition and the unfacilitated baseline-2 condition. A comparison of the highest score across the three study conditions is presented in Figure 2.3, showing that students averaged .12 correct responses during the baseline-1 condition, 2.23 correct responses during the facilitated condition, and .74 correct responses in the baseline-2 condition. Each of these scores is out of a possible five correct. Additionally, the baseline-2 scores were compared to the students' facilitated scores and it was determined that a significant difference did exist [$t(42) = 5.96, p < .0001$].

FIGURE 2.3 Comparison of Highest Scores Across the Three Study Conditions

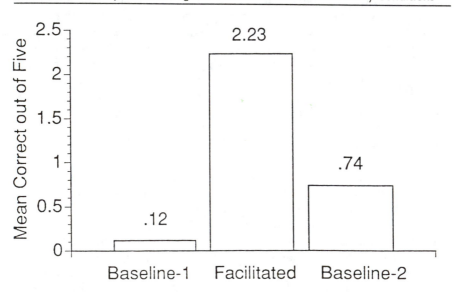

It is important to note that the composite analysis thus far has used "highest score" as the measure. For example, for a student who has two baseline-1 sessions (5 trials each session), the highest score of the two sessions served as the "highest score" for baseline-1. Similarly, the highest score over the 18 facilitated sessions served as the highest score. An alternative approach to understanding student performance in this study is to view performance over time—this analysis requires using the mathematical mean (e.g., the mean for baseline-1 would be the mean of both baseline-1 sessions). Table 2.1 provides the students' mean performance across all three conditions in segments of 10 trials or two sessions (since both baseline conditions used 10 trials each). One can observe the mean performance of all students across the time of the study. Note that the mean scores for baseline-1 and baseline-2 in Table 2.1 vary from those reported in Figure 2.3, since the latter were computed using highest score rather than mean scores. By viewing Table 2.1, one can see a general developmental progression over time and then a prominent dropoff in performance when shifting from the final two sessions (17–18) of the facilitated condition ($M = 1.6$) to the baseline-2 condition ($M = .47$).

Individual Analysis

Table 2.2 illustrates individual students' highest performance in the facilitated condition over their highest performance in the baseline-1 condition. For example, 21% of the students, sometime during the facilitated

TABLE 2.1 Mean Number of Correct Responses by Trial Sequence

Condition	Trial	Session No.	Mean	SD	Range
Baseline- (BL-) 1					
	1–10	BL-1	.11	.30	0–1
Facilitated Condition					
	1–10	1–2	.29	.69	0–4
	11–20	3–4	.76	1.35	0–5
	21–30	5–6	.92	1.51	0–5
	31–40	7–8	.89	1.33	0–4
	41–50	9–10	.87	1.47	0–5
	51–60	11–12	.91	1.24	0–5
	61–70	13–14	1.05	1.36	0–5
	71–80	15–16	1.38	1.77	0–5
	81–90	17–18	1.60	1.78	0–5
Baseline-2					
	1–10	BL-2	.47	.92	0–3

condition sessions, scored 1 better than their highest baseline-1 score and another 18.5% of the students scored 2 better than their baseline-1 score. Overall, 75% of the students performed better in their facilitated condition than they did in their baseline-1 condition. Two groups appear to emerge from this view of the data. Approximately one-third of the students (32.5%) increased their scores by 4 or 5 over baseline-1 and another approximately one-third of the students (39.5%) increased their scores by either 1 or 2 over baseline-1; only one student (2%) increased his score by 3 over baseline-1.

Time to Obtain Best Scores

Students took an average of 9.8 sessions (approximately 49 trials, or 3.3 weeks) to reach their highest score with individual ranges from 2 to 18 sessions (5 trials per session). There was significant variation in the number of sessions it took for each student to reach the highest score. Twenty students (46.5%) reached their highest score within the first 7 sessions (out of 18), while another 28% of the students (12 students) did not reach their highest score until their final 3 sessions (see Figure 2.4). Individual students appear to vary regarding the amount of practice of the protocol it takes to reach their highest score.

Error Analysis of Incorrect Words

For a word to be correct, and therefore to be eligible for use in the analysis of this study, it must have been spelled perfectly. The question then arises,

TABLE 2.2 Increases in Students' Highest Scores in the Facilitated Condition Above Their Highest Baseline-1 (BL-1) Scores ($N = 43$)

Increase over BL-1	If student's BL-1 was:	Then student's highest score obtained was:	% of students obtaining increase
No more than BL-1	0	0	26.0
	1	1	
One over BL-1	0	1	21.0
	1	2	
Two over BL-1	0	2	18.5
	1	3	
Three over BL-1	0	3	2.0
	1	4	
Four over BL-1	0	4	18.5
	1	5	
Five over BL-1	0	5	14.0

FIGURE 2.4 Number of Sessions Required for Reaching the Highest Score

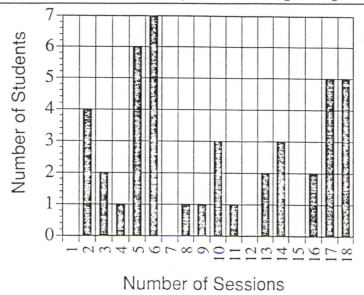

Number of Sessions

what types of spelling errors occurred and were there patterns to those errors? Since a thorough investigation of the error patterns is currently under way, only a preliminary analysis will be presented. Table 2.3 presents the general categories of errors as well as the characteristics of each category. The proportion of all incorrect words for each category and an example of each category are also presented. All incorrect words were categorized by a graduate student using the characteristics outlined in Table 2.3. A sample of 20% of the incorrect words was then similarly evaluated by another graduate student. A reliability coefficient of $r = .93$ was obtained between these two evaluations—sufficient to conclude that the protocol was adequately reliable.

DISCUSSION

There were two main findings of the study: (1) Under controlled conditions, some FC users can pass information to a facilitator when that facilitator is not privy to the information, and (2) the measurement of FC under test conditions may be significantly benefited by extensive practice of the test protocol. This latter result could partially account for the inability of several past studies to verify that FC users originated the output. As with many past controlled studies, FC was unable to be measured when the FC users had little or no chance to practice the testing conditions. When

TABLE 2.3 Categories, Characteristics, and Proportions of Errors of Incorrect Words

Category	Characteristic	Example	%
Spelled correctly but not target word (13%)	Correctly spelled, is on the word list, but is not similar or directly related to the target word	PENCIL for APPLE	6
	Correctly spelled, not one of the list words, and not similar or directly related to the target word	BOBBY for APPLE	6
	Correctly spelled, not one of the list words, but had similar meaning or directly related to the target word	FRUIT for APPLE or ORANGE for APPLE	<1
Misspelled but target word is detectable (14%)	Misspelled, but phonetically correct	APEL for APPLE	<1
	Misspelled due to 1 or 2 extra or missing letters	APPL or APPLWE for APPLE	8
	Misspelled with correct number of letters but letters are transposed	APPEL for APPLE	6
Misspelled and target word is not detectable (71%)	Eight letters or less with no detectable pattern	QWEDJTD for APPLE	63
	More than eight letters with no detectable pattern	DFGHJKBNP for APPLE	8
Other (3%)	Any other reason for an incorrect word		3

the opportunity for practice of the procedure was offered, many students were then able to pass information to the naive facilitator. The reader should see the clear difference between practice of the test-taking procedure and practice of the words. This study did *not* allow for practice of the words. Any measured benefit from practice, then, should be viewed as resulting from the students' familiarity with the procedure, not from having learned the words.

In contrast to previous studies on FC authorship (e.g., Simon, Toll, & Whitehair, 1994; Vasquez, 1994; Wheeler, Jacobson, Paglieri, & Schwartz, 1993), facilitator control of the FC productions was not seen as a problem in this study, given the experimental controls in place. This study did not use a "distractor condition" (showing the facilitator a different word from the FC user) and thus was less concerned about facilitator influence, since the facilitator was not competing with the FC user to produce the correct word. It was determined that there was no significant increase in the accuracy of words in subsequent appearances of those words compared to nonrepeated words. This finding indicates that even in cases where the facilitators were most likely to have the ability to guess selected words (having seen it before in previous sessions), they did not appear to control the FC users' responses. This does not mean that facilitator influence does not exist in the FC process. As in any type of communication, influence may exist (Duchan, 1993). It does mean, however, that facilitators in this study were no more responsible for the correct answers than they were the incorrect ones—the FC users appeared to control their own communication and make their own errors. This has important implications for further studies in that facilitator control can be limited or even avoided.

A comparison of the facilitated scores and the baseline-2 scores illustrates that student performance during the study was significantly higher than when facilitation was removed. On the other hand, some of the gains of the test condition remained after facilitation was removed. This latter result may indicate some "learning" of how to type without physical support. It may also be partially explained by FC users' becoming more independent over the time of the study, since fading of FC support continued to be a goal for all participants in their communication outside of this study. The significant increase in performance in the facilitated condition over the baseline-1 condition appears to be substantially due to facilitation itself, not to the effects of previously known training techniques since, in that case, one would have expected little or no drop in performance in the baseline-2 condition. The task would have been learned and the removal of physical touch should not have accounted for such a significant loss of performance. Thus the support provided by facilitated communication is a highly probable explanation for the notable decrease in performance when that support was removed.

Overcontrol

A possible reason why the results of this study vary significantly from many of the previous authorship studies is that the previous studies may have overcontrolled the "test" condition when it was not scientifically obligatory to do so. It is hypothesized by these researchers that controlling for normally occurring environmental variables, when there is no reasonable rationale to do so (e.g., partitions between the FC user and the facilitator, asking participants to "perform" in unknown settings, FC users wearing earphones, etc.), may contaminate the FC authorship experiment and actually breach the facilitator–user support mechanism, thereby hindering the general ability of the FC user to communicate.

This study's intent was to develop a protocol that controlled for variables that could threaten the study's validity (e.g., the facilitator must be blind to the message) and allow the FC user to focus on communicating her thoughts, but not to overcontrol so as to jeopardize the user–facilitator relationship—thus producing a naturally controlled environment. The fact that many students did appear to author their own facilitation in this study provides beginning evidence that some past studies may have overcontrolled their testing procedures, thus hindering the FC users' performance on those tests.

One-Place-in-Time Experiments

Another interesting finding of this study was that if one looked only at how FC users did on their first day of the facilitated condition, as compared to their baseline-1 scores, one would have to conclude that not 1 of the 43 participants in this study could pass the test—very similar to the results of past studies when practice of the protocol was not provided (Bligh & Kupperman, 1993; Hudson, Melita, & Arnold, 1993; Klewe, 1993; Moore, Donovan, & Hudson, 1993; Moore, Donovan, Hudson, Dykstra, & Lawrence, 1993; Shane, 1993; Wheeler et al., 1993). There was no significant difference between the baseline-1 highest scores and the highest scores on the first day of "testing." Viewing this result next to the fact that there was a significant difference between highest baseline-1 scores and highest overall facilitated scores after practice had occurred, one can easily see how possibly the one-place-in-time tests reported in earlier FC authorship research would show little or no successful performance on validation tests.

The one-place-in-time protocol condition is found in nearly all of the past quantitative FC validation experiments (e.g., Hudson et al., 1993; Simon et al., 1994; Wheeler et al., 1993). Our review of the studies' protocols indicates that FC users tend to be unable to pass information to "blind" facilitators when they are requested to do so without adequate practice of the testing conditions. Since this current study also shows that without practice FC users were unable to pass tests, but with practice many could do so to a significant level, then it appears logical to conclude that these past experiments were subject to hindrances to the measurement of original FC production. Practice of the testing procedure appears to be an important component when testing for FC authorship.

Weaknesses of the Study

The content of the test items within this study could have been more meaningful to the participants. Although the vocabualry words used in this study were familiar and were found in the students' everyday environment, they very likely lacked a high degree of interest for the student at the time of data collection. Additionally, the repetitive nature of the testing procedure and the possible lack of interest in a nonfunctional activity may also have, in some way, influenced the results of this study. The level of communication required during testing could have been higher. Single-word responses, although adequate for this rudimentary study, would be better replaced with more complex forms of communication, such as open-ended responses. Finally, the failure of this study to provide interrater reliability coefficients for data collection by the recorders is a weakness. This was considered when designing the study, but the procedures needed to provide such reliability figures were viewed to go against a basic premise of the study, that is, to have the least interference as possible with the phenomenon being studied. Since the recorder's task needed so little interpretation (writing down letters as they were said by the facilitator), the downside of possible interference seemed to outweigh the benefit of documenting the recording reliability.

Suggestions for Further Research

Following are suggestions for further research into FC authorship:

1. Studies are needed that develop additional protocol conditions that would attempt to explain why students do not demonstrate as high a level of communication competence during testing as would be expected given the reports of their functional use of FC (e.g., conversations, higher-level academic work). It seems imperative to determine why, even under assumably ideal circumstances, there was still such a significant gap between the participants' facilitated communication level prior to this study and their performance in the study.

2. Several new replication studies should be developed and should include but not be limited to: studies that use the same and different tasks with participants with the same and different characteristics; studies that follow the protocol of this current study but that add a control group (assuming this could be accomplished without denying students in the control group a communication method that has been determined to be beneficial—FC or any other method); studies that replicate past investigations but that now use practice and naturally controlled environment within their procedures; and studies that examine the role of the FC user's personal characteristics on performance during testing.

3. Studies are needed to determine whether influence in FC is different from influence in nonfacilitated communication. Also, is the alleged

influence direct physical control of communication output or is it social in nature?

4. Studies that develop and propose "best practices" in facilitation need to continue and be peer-reviewed to be sure the techniques used in authorship studies are in fact those that would best produce the expected outcome.

5. Studies are needed that investigate the types of errors that occurred for the students in this study and in other studies. Knowledge of emergent literacy patterns could also shed light on the types of errors made in the testing condition in relationship to typical learners.

6. Studies are needed that view FC authorship in a broader social context. For example, are the majority of individuals using FC perceived to be enjoying higher-quality lives than would be expected of people who are newly communicating?

7. Studies are needed that investigate what aspects of the "natural" environment are critical to the facilitation process.

8. Studies are needed that investigate why individual performance is so variable (e.g., some students reached 5 of 5 correct, then declined, then scored 5 again, while others progressed at a more typical developmental rate and pattern).

CONCLUSIONS

Inherent in the question of authorship of FC are two critical tasks. One, FC must be shown to be a generally endorsed training method to assist those with severe communication disorders—not the only method, but one more to add to the body of existing methods. To accomplish this, it must be empirically shown that FC users can perform better in a communicative task using FC than they can using any other method. Although much more needs to be learned about establishing who is the originator of the facilitated communication, this current study supports the contention that FC, when used properly, may be a reasonable method of instruction for the development of communication for some people with severe communication disorders. Second, each FC user's communication must be continually, but unobtrusively, confirmed for authorship. For some, independent typing may be their personal "test of authorship"; for others, it may involve carefully kept records of personally authenticating events. Blind testing, then, may not be the best way to test communication competence for everyone (or for anyone for that matter), and the protocol conditions tested in this study, although effective for research purposes, *may* not necessarily be the best method to determine the authorship for a particular person (see Biklen, Saha, & Kliewer, Chapter 3 of this volume). Illustrative of this is the fragile nature of testing for authorship. In this study, a significant number of the students were able to pass information to a blind facilitator, but many of those students did not do so consistently and others were unable to pass any information at all. There must be a separation between the overall acceptance of FC as a bona fide communication method and the determination of authentic communication for a particular individual. The former is generally a scholarly debate within the professional literature and the latter a case-by-case venture weighing the individual merits of each case.

CHAPTER 3

How Teachers Confirm the Authorship of Facilitated Communication: A Portfolio Approach

Douglas Biklen
Shaswati Saha
Chris Kliewer

As its title suggests, this is a qualitative study of how teachers confirm for themselves that the words typed with their students are the students' own thoughts and ideas, not simply products of cuing or manipulation on the teachers' part. The research included observation of seven teachers with seventeen students in four schools, interviews with the teachers, and examination of students' typed transcripts, made available to the research team by the teachers.

PURPOSE AND DESIGN OF THE STUDY

The study focused on all of the individuals supported by the seven facilitators (one teacher and two students in a preschool; four teachers and eight students in an elementary school; one teacher and five students in a middle school; and one teacher and two students in a high school). All of the selected teachers had been using facilitation for more than a year and were convinced that it was a useful communication strategy. All students using facilitation with these teachers were included in the study, except for two who did not participate because of health problems and excessive absences in one instance and lack of parental support in another.

Table 3.1 lists the five girls and twelve boys by pseudonyms, identifies which ones shared a particular teacher/facilitator, and provides information on their disability, age, speaking ability, communication system used prior to facilitated communication, demonstrated reading level prior to using facilitated communication, and number of regular academic classes attended with the use of facilitated communication. Prior to being introduced to facilitated communication, all of the students in this study were presumed mentally retarded and incapable of complex, abstract thought.

In the tradition of qualitative research methods (Biklen & Moseley, 1988; Glaser & Strauss, 1967; McCall & Simmons, 1969; Taylor & Bogdan, 1984), this study was designed to generate hypotheses concerning a specific topic of interest: the ways in which the teachers come to perceive that the communication produced via facilitation is produced by their students. Research involved participant observation and interviews.

Data Collection

The researchers' observations ranged from 30-minute speech therapy sessions in which students typically met one-on-one with speech teachers/facilitators or 30- to 60-minute classroom observations. The researchers observed each of the students at least three times and, in more than half of the cases, more than ten times each. In some instances students were observed working with speech teachers in the classroom settings. In all instances, the researchers' discussions with teachers centered on the questions: How do you decide that it is the students doing the typing? What information do you use to make that decision? When the teachers mentioned a factor, the researchers asked for examples, descriptions, and clarification, where necessary. After each observation, the researchers wrote up notes and, occasionally, some observer comments about the session (Bogdan & Biklen, 1991). The researchers collected the typed transcripts from the sessions as well as examples of students' typing at other times when the researchers were not present. The majority of students used electronic devices such as the Canon Communicator, electronic typewriters, or computers. In instances where students used letterboards with no printed output, observers collected the teachers' verbatim accounts of letters typed or, if the teachers were not recording these, the researchers wrote them down during the observations. The researchers discussed the observations and the transcripts at weekly research group meetings. In addition, the researchers spoke informally with teachers, teaching assistants, parents of the students, and the students themselves during observations. The meetings between researchers and teachers sometimes took place in interviews that were scheduled by appointment (at least two each) but more

TABLE 3.1 Student Demographics and Communication Characteristics[a]

Name	D.O.B.	Disability	Facilitator	Communication system prior to facilitation	Presumed reading level prior to facilitation	Months using[b] FC	# of reg. classes	Support level[c]
Lindsay	9/13/79	M.R.	M.S.	Functional words/ phrases; echoed speech	Non-reader	8	1	mid-forearm
Patrick	6/20/80	Autism	M.S.	Functional words/phrases; functional signs	Preprimer	8	1	elbow & shoulder
Courtney	1/7/77	MR/NI	M.S.	Functional words/phrases	First grade	2	1	mid-forearm
Stephen	8/24/77	M.R.	M.S.	Functional sentences (often unintelligible)	First grade	24	1	mid-forearm
Joseph	10/11/78	MH[d]	M.S.	Functional sentences; echoed speech	Decoding words fourth grade level	24	2	elbow & shoulder
Evan	4/20/75	Autism	H.S.	No speech; functional word book (unreliable)	Nonreader	36	full-time	elbow/ independent
Carrie	1/11/76	Rett	H.S.	Crying	Nonreader	24	1	elbow
Wesley	8/11/80	Autism	G6	Functional words; signs (unreliable)	Functional word recognition	36	full-time	forearm
Nancy	5/3/80	Autism	G6	Gestures, crying; signs (unreliable)	Nonreader	36	full-time	hand

B.J.	5/13/80	Autism	G6	Functional words/phrases; echoed speech	Second grade	36	full-time	hand[e]
Mark	3/9/83	Autism	G4	Picture book (unreliable); crying	Nonreader	36	full-time	elbow
William	5/30/85	Autism	G2	Echoed speech; gestures	Non-eader	36	full-time	hand
Doug	2/25/83	Down Syndrome	G2	Functional words; signs (few)	Letter recognition	24	full-time	hand/wrist
Henry	10/9/85	Autism	G2	Gestures; picture book (unreliable)	Nonreader	36	full-time	hand
Jacque	8/27/87	Autism	K	Gestures, screams, crying; Functional words	Nonreader	24	full-time	wrist[e]
Russell	12/23/87	Autism	P.S.	Screams, crying	Nonreader	24	full-time	forearm
Terry	2/3/88	Autism	P.S.	Echoed speech; crying	Nonreader	24	full-time	elbow[e]

[a] Study conducted in late 1992 and first 4 months of 1993.

[b] Months using facilitation at time the study began.

[c] Minimum support required.

[d] Klippel-Trenauny-Weber Syndrome.

[e] Independent with structured work (e.g., spelling words, multiple choice exercises).

commonly through informal discussions before and/or after each class session.

Data Analysis

The credibility of the observations and ultimately of the study rests on multiple factors, including the presence of the researchers in the settings for a long period of time (more than six months for each student), discussions concerning data with individuals observed (i.e., students, teachers, teaching assistants), constant comparisons of data (Glaser & Strauss, 1967), and formulation and reformulation of hypotheses in light of data and findings of other studies. Data analysis involved careful examination of all field notes from observations, interview transcripts, and typed transcripts of students' communications and academic work. Constant comparison generally took the form of discussions by the researchers of the teachers' ideas about how they confirmed authorship. The researchers collected information provided by each of the teachers/facilitators; typically this meant individual teachers making comments to individual researchers. As a theme would develop, the researchers looked to see if this arose in other settings or if there was contradicting evidence that might either confirm or challenge the concept. As the researchers developed coding categories based on topics or themes raised by individual teachers, the researchers began to observe each student with those categories in mind. Categories were collapsed, adjusted, and added to throughout the study, right up to the writing of this account. Categories included examples of how students looked at the keyboard, teachers' experiences with "fading" physical support, and pace of movement to the keyboard or letterboard, all of which could be subsumed in a larger category, for example, "attending to typing." We considered making "independent typing" a separate category because teachers mentioned it as the ultimate confirmation of students' authorship, but this information also was mentioned by teachers in the context of students attending to typing. Teachers talked about physical support as something that occurred along a continuum from considerable support (e.g., holding the hand or wrist), to less support (e.g., light touch on the elbow), to independence (no physical support). Similarly, teachers spoke about students typing incorrect information. Rather than interpreting this as evidence of their influencing the typing, they typically explained it as occurrences of echoed or stereotyped words or phrases. As such, they seemed to fit into the larger category of "content, form, and style," or as students' fantasies or exaggerations, which teachers discussed as instances of students' distinctive personalities or as characteristic of students' personal themes.

It is important to note that qualitative research is not used to prove particular hypotheses or, in this instance, to validate facilitated communication. The researcher hopes only to capture viewpoints, understandings, hypotheses, and theories. In terms of facilitated communication, then, we expected the study to yield understandings of the ways in which teachers think about authorship of people's communications, not to test authorship.

HOW TEACHERS DECIDE THE TYPING IS THEIR STUDENTS' OWN

As might be expected, teachers do not all use the same terms to describe similar phenomena or identify the same factors to establish students' authorship of typed work. A speech teacher said that the clearest, most persistent indicator that one student was doing the typing was in how her eyes went immediately to a target letter, even though it then often took her several seconds to begin moving her index finger toward the selection. Another teacher pointed to a particular student's selection of big words that other students with whom she facilitated did not use; still another was convinced when a student typed swear words at her. Our approach was not to immediately adopt any of these as "our" categories. Rather, we listened to the teachers, asked them to clarify comments, issues, or events, and tried to observe in action the phenomena to which they referred. Ultimately, we began to collapse their points into larger categories.

The central theme running through the teachers' accounts of the typing was that the students differed from one another. The next four sections identify, explain, and explore these differences within the categories of (1) how students attend to typing, (2) the relationship of students' speaking to their typing, (3) communication form, content, and style, and (4) conveying accurate information not known to the facilitators.

How Students Attend to Typing

Teachers frequently commented on physical qualities of individual students' typing, including how students looked at the letters during typing. They noted individuals' index finger isolation problems; impulsive pointing (i.e., responding too quickly or automatically as in a rote, rather than reasoned, fashion) that required forceful, backward pressure for slowing down; low muscle tone requiring the facilitator to wait for the person's response; relatively independent typing where individuals required hardly any physical support (e.g., with just the facilitator's light touch on the forearm or at the elbow); and frequent hand flapping or table thumping, which necessitated verbal soothing, or permission to engage in some stereotyped activity, such as pacing up and down the school hallway before proceeding.

Teachers saw the differences between their students as evidence that it was the students doing the typing. The middle school teacher, for example, noted the differences among the five students with whom she used facilitation:

> Lindsay has a definite rhythm in her hand that the other students don't have. It's a wrist action that you feel mostly when up close to the hand. It goes up and down. When she gets into a rhythm, that's when the typing is easiest and most fluent for her. Sometimes when . . . [Patrick] is typing his arm becomes very rigid, almost as if his arm is locked in a forward movement. The way to effectively break that is that when I feel tension build up in his arm—and I'm back at his elbow now—I say to him tap and at that point he taps his chest and then he goes forward again with a very light touch and then he continues to type with very little support from me until suddenly he seems to get locked into this tension toward the typewriter.

The teacher noted that in six months, Courtney progressed from requiring firm backward pressure of her hand and verbal encouragement (e.g., "go ahead" or "move your finger to the letter you want") to needing "a very light touch with just support under the back of the forearm." Another student, Stephen, "under stress and strain . . . needs to be restrained backwards heavily. When he is relaxed his speed goes very quickly." She described similar variations in support for Joseph, but for a different reason:

> Joseph can be virtually independent [hand on shoulder] . . . as long as the content is concrete, [such as] spelling words, doing math problems, or taking direct information from passages read, but . . . once you get into any interpretive thinking, in order to avoid an echo-type response, he has needed to be restrained heavily for each letter—when I'm heavily restraining him, my hand is up closer, mid-arm, not at the elbow or shoulder anymore.

Commenting on what these differences signified to her, this speech teacher noted:

> I guess I feel like I'm always wondering and always trying to affirm in my own mind that this is not me, this is not my idea, this is his or her idea and he or she is doing the typing. So looking at the differ-

ences and the uniqueness of just the physical developments, that helps me accept the idea that, yeah, this is them.

The second-grade teacher commented that William would often go for a letter and then "slide his finger to the correct letter; he would be one under or two over and then slide." When he finished a thought, "he turned off the Canon with his left hand," then, if asked, indicated that, yes, he was done. The other second graders with the same teacher were different in how they attended to the typing. The teacher and the assistants referred to Doug as "a pusher" because of his forceful typing, whereas they described Henry as a "minimalist." The teacher explained this latter term: "there were long pauses before the next production, [and when he was pointing] it was just sort of like a whisper [i.e., very light]." The teacher concluded, "I can't think of three more different kids."

In addition to the above-mentioned different ways in which teachers described each student's physical style of attending to the typing, one quality emerged repeatedly as especially important. This was independent typing. Several students were observed typing their names and the date independently but receiving forearm support during conversational typing. Evan typed one phrase (MORE TIME WITH MONICA) independently when his teacher let go of his arm during a facilitated conversation. A preschooler, Terry, and two elementary age students, Jacque and B. J., have typed individual words independently, for example, favorite cartoon figures, school activities, and spelling words. Patrick, a middle school student, was able to type a few words with just a hand on the shoulder; but when he began to stumble, his teacher moved the location of support to his elbow. The kindergarten student, Jacque, could point independently and reliably to correct multiple-choice answers in school work. Sixth-grader B. J. typed the weekly spelling words independently. All of the students demonstrated independent ability to go to a desk and to get out a communication device (e.g., typewriter, dedicated communicator, letterboard, portable computer), and the researchers observed numerous instances in which individuals (e.g., Evan, Stephen, Doug) hit the return, space bar/button, or communication device power supply independently at the appropriate time; such independent acts were often pointed out to the researchers by the teachers. The speech teacher at the middle school seemed to summarize the importance that all of the teachers attributed to independence when she remarked, "Independence would confirm it for anyone I would think." Similarly, the sixth-grade teacher felt that B. J.'s independent typing of structured work (e.g., math problems, spelling words, multiple-choice tests) should settle the matter of authorship: "He's independent, so that's like—

how much more obvious could that be?" (Table 3.1 indicates the least amount of support each student received when typing.)

The Relationship of Students' Speaking to Their Typing

As indicated in Table 3.1, more than half of the students had speech. In some instances, the speech matched the typing. Often it did not. As with the different movement styles noted above, individual teachers pointed out to the researchers that there were variations of speech and typing combinations within a group of individuals working with a single facilitator and constancy in particular individuals' combination of speaking and typing across multiple facilitators.

Speaking and Typing Letters and Words. Lindsay, Patrick, Stephen, Courtney, Joseph, B. J., Wesley, William, Doug, Jacque, Russell, and Terry all were observed saying a few words that were the same as those typed. They did not do this all the time, and sometimes their words were variations on the words typed. For example, the kindergarten teacher told us that Jacque said "baby" when she typed BABE (this could have been a creative spelling) and "kitty" when she typed CAT (this could have been an add-on, as in kitty-cat). Courtney spoke a little, saying "yes" and "no" and parts of words or whole words. She sometimes announced letters just prior to hitting them, although sometimes she said a wrong letter, for example "q" when pointing to "o," and sometimes she said the next letter as she pointed to the letter that preceded it in a word. Similarly, the second-grade teacher explained that Doug regularly said letters aloud prior to typing them. And the sixth-grade teacher described how B. J. sometimes said "I want b," or some other letter, before pointing to it. In the preschool, Russell pointed to letters on a letterboard during circle time, spelling SPANK YOUR BUTT and then spontaneously spoke the same phrase several times without any model. And Terry, in a typed conversation with Kristen, another preschooler, spelled out ISS SPELLING HARD KRIS IT LOOKKS LIKE IT IS HARD TO DO. When he completed typing the statement, he then said clearly, "L-O-O-K-K-S." The teacher and teaching assistants of the young children felt that the typing helped the children initiate their speaking and that in speaking the words, they were confirming the fact that they could read the words typed. The teacher commented, "That really highlights reading ability."

Speaking Related to but More Limited than Typing. A few students were observed saying single- and multiple-word expressions that appeared to be functional (i.e., related to what others might say in similar situations and related to their behavior) but that they were not able to link together into conversational interchanges. This contrasted with their typing. Occasionally, teachers felt that the words spoken confirmed the students' authorship of the words. For example, Stephen predicted that he was typing a joke when he said "tell joke" and typed I THINK IT [typing] IS FUN AND MUCH EASIER THAN WRITING BUT I DO NOT HAVE TO LOVE IT. In the preschool, Russell used spoken words for labeling but not for conversation. For example, he typed CAN I GO and then completed the statement by speaking out loud "Castle Room." When he was told that he could not, he tried to pull the teacher toward the door. Then he typed GO TO CESTLE ROOM. The fact that his typing matched his speech, except for the spelling error, was seen by the teacher as evidence that the typing was his.

Often students' (e.g., Russell, Terry, Joseph, Patrick, Lindsay, William, B. J., Wesley, and Jacque) spoken words were *not* the same as those typed. Some words were seemingly unrelated to the typing, and some were related but not the same. An example of the latter would be when a student might say "no" and type YES. Speaking and typing together was most pronounced with Joseph, who tended to speak only in "automatic," albeit sometimes functional, language. Listening to him speak was like hearing a stream-of-consciousness:

> There's some noise coming from that other room. Let's try this again. Boy. And do you know who I'm saying this to? The both of you. Lets see what's our idea for now. You hardly have been out here. I know that. At least that's the worst of it. At least somebody. Let's type up a list and see what specials I've been getting into. You think I'm typing up a list, don't you? I think that's just about it. But I think there's two more that most people don't have.

Meanwhile, Joseph had typed a list of his classes: ART SPEECH TECH HC GYM MUSIC S.S. SCIENCE. His speech was related to the typing but was different from it. This pattern occurred whenever he typed, but none of this facilitator's other five students replicated such a pattern of speech and typing.

Communication Form, Content, and Style

The teachers argued that if they, rather than their students, were doing the typing, it should have been monolithic, at least for the students working with a particular facilitator. The following subsections describe themes, spelling and other word-formation problems, and unusual expressions that the teachers regarded as distinctive of individual students and thus confirming that the students were the authors of the words.

Themes. Few factors were more prominent in teachers' minds than what they perceived as their students' personalities, as revealed through the content of typing. The high school teacher, for example, commented that, on numerous occasions, Evan expressed how much he wished he could speak and that he resented having others, especially his teaching assistant, speak for him. His speech teacher provided the researchers with an account he had produced about hitting Curt, told in the past tense:

```
MARYY . . . DOESNT WANT TO HURT ME BY DOPING ANYTHING TO
GIVE ME THE WRONG IMPRESSION OR TO ENCOURAGE SDOP SHE IS
ASRTAND OFFISH SHE TOLD ME WHEN WE WERRE WAOLKING THERE
BECAUSE CURFT SAID THAT THE REASON I WAS SO EXCITED WAS
BEC I LIKED HER SO MUCH. THATB MADE ME FEEL MAD AT HIM
SO I HIT GHIM AND HE TOLD ME TO STGOP AND I HIT HIM
AGAINB AND MARY SAID STOP AND I DIDNT TTRUY TO HIT HER
BUT UI BHIT CURT ANBD DSHE GOT SCARED AND SHE SAID TO
STOP OR SHE WOULD NOT GO TO THE LIBRARY WITH US ABND I
DIDNT STOP BEC I COUOLDNT. . . ."
```

Although this was obviously an important topic for Evan—he had raised it with different facilitators—the events that he described did not actually happen. Hitting Curt was something he had apparently thought about rather than something that actually occurred. Interestingly, his teachers talked about this incident as evidence of Evan's distinctive personal concerns and personality and as a kind of message passing inasmuch as he typed similar content with several facilitators.

Carrie, on the other hand, who typed with this same high school speech teacher serving as her facilitator, did not raise any of these concerns. But her teacher said she did raise another, namely, her desire to not be rushed in her typing—FREEDEBYY WAITTIME TR Y WAITING FORMME START FFEELI FTG FRRUUSTRATED; FEELING FRUSTRASTED RUUSHING ME TO FINN- ISH; RESTRAIN FROM GUESSYYNG MY WORDDS. Her typing was quite slow, between 8 and 22 words per half hour.

The fourth-grade teacher noted that Mark's writing frequently included references to discouragement and loneliness. One of the examples she provided was the following poem:

ME

```
A BOY SITS IN CLASS
HE READS EACH KIDS CALL AT MOM
I AM TIRED OF HERE
MISS HAVING A FRIEND
```

```
LISTEN TO THE KIDS IN CLASS
SAVE YOUR NOISE FOR KIDS
HOPE TO GO HOME SIT
SO I CAN SIT HOME MYSELF
SO TO YOU I SAY GOODBYE
```

Another type of thematic consistency that teachers identified with some students and not others was typed echoed communication. Wesley's typing often included seemingly echoed phrases and words, for example, the word "kill," mention of his father's death, and girls. His teacher noted that such words would appear in unusual contexts, as in an exercise where he was asked to use vocabulary words in sentences:

Gently—TO KILL OPPOSITE OF HELPING GENNTLY
Emergency—EM ERGENCY POLICE HELP KILL BAD BO YS

Wesley's teacher found the appearance of echoed words a persistent problem for him: "This comes up all the time, like his father dying, death, and girls, consistent no matter who his facilitator is, this is consistent across the board." Another student, Terry, frequently said and typed stereotyped words, most notably comic strip characters. His teachers noted that he was the only one of the two preschool students typing these words and that he had developed an ability to type them independently.

Spelling and Word Formations. Teachers often regarded their students as exhibiting distinctive spelling and difficulties in forming words or typing the correct word. For instance Jacque, the kindergarten student, typed numerous creatively spelled words such as: REEL for "real," REDY for "ready," MEEN for "mean," and NO for "know" across different facilitators.

Stephen, a middle school student, displayed a problem of automatic completions. For example, in a sentence where the word "courage" would have been appropriate, he typed COURTNEY, then backspaced and typed COURAGE. Similarly, in the same conversation he typed a question, WHAT DICK DID YOU ASK, where DICK was thought by his teacher to be an automatic completion when he was trying to type "did."

In a number of instances, Carrie, one of the two high school students, typed Y instead of I; her teacher surmised that it was hard for her to move her hand past her midline (middle of her trunk) and so she often used the Y as a substitute for the I. Examples of words in which she made such a switch were: GETTYNG, GYNNEA, GUESSYYNG, TRYD, WANTYNG, and DENYED. Occasionally, Carrie evidenced creative spellings, for example, QWEER (typed this way twice with one facilitator and once with another), GEASTURE, and SERTIN. Although Evan shared the same speech teacher/facilitator with Carrie, and although he did occasionally have some creative spellings, his teacher never saw any of the Y spellings in his work.

Unusual Expressions. Another category within the larger grouping of content differences was distinctive or unusual expressions. No matter who served as her facilitator, Jacque, for example, often typed "I no" and "me no" rather than "I don't" or "me don't." She typed, for instance, I NO BE BAD I JUST HAVE HARD TIME WITH NEW PEOPLE and I NO LIKE IT WHEN OYU OR JANE BUTT IN and Jacque VEERY SAD ME NO WANT TO BE FRIENDS WITH BOYS BOYS YUCKY. Carrie's teacher remarked about Carrie's unusual way of giving her permission for the researchers to review her portfolio of typing: GES HE CAN FREEQENTEY AVAIL HISSELF TRANSSCRYIPTS. Mark's teacher noted that he too typed sentences that sometimes included unusual words, for example "demented" and "eject," and unusual sentence constructions.

For Evan, his teacher found his facility with poetry distinctive and unusual:

> He has written poetry with Mary, with Margaret, with me, with his mother, with Curt, with Lesley [i.e., other facilitators], how can all these people who don't write suddenly be turning out poetry that is obviously being written by him? People don't just know how to write poetry and yet he has done it with a half a dozen people.

Conveying Accurate Information Not Known to the Facilitator

Aside from their overall impressions of students' distinctiveness in terms of what they typed and how they typed (including independent typing, which only a few of the students accomplished), teachers found the most compelling evidence of students' authorship was that they sometimes conveyed information that reportedly was not previously known to the teachers but that could be verified. They did not all do this, but thirteen of them did. Those who did not were those whose communication was least fluent.

Lindsay, Patrick, Courtney, Nancy, Carrie, Terry, and Jacque mentioned family members' names, pets and pets' names, specific activities they had engaged in, and names or other details about places they had visited. Below are examples the teachers provided regarding other students' information sharing.

Stephen told his speech teacher that his father was getting remarried and the date on which it would occur. Both were accurate. Similarly, in a conversation with his teacher he mentioned that his family had eaten at a particular diner on a certain day, an event that was later verified. On another occasion he informed his teacher that he had gotten a new bowling ball. This, too, was true.

Joseph typed that he had a music test on a certain day, which he had, and that he went to his "Grandpa Bob's" for Easter dinner. When asked by his teacher what else he had done over spring break, he reported, FRIDAY MORING WE WENT TO DOCTOR CAMPILL. According to his mother, he went to the doctor's office on Wednesday—his teacher noted that he often exhibited word-retrieval difficulties in speech as well as typing—and his doctor's name is spelled Campbell.

When asked specific information not known to his facilitators, Evan often gave incorrect answers, such as when he reported that his parents dressed as LONGBJOHNJ SILVER and WUNDERT DOG for a Halloween party. His teacher thought that such incorrect information might be the product of a word-finding problem, possibly exacerbated when he feels challenged or anxious. She also surmised that "he might feel he must give an answer, whether it's right or not." Nevertheless, irrespective of instances in which he gave wrong information, Evan's teachers found his ability to type his own thoughts confirmed in his regular school work. Evan wrote an essay about the Doris Lessing short story "Through the Tunnel" in which he described both specific content of the Lessing story as well as its meaning:

JERRY EXPERIENCES A RITE OF PASSAGE WHERE HE STRIVES FOR
FREEDOM FROM FEAR LLWEDBY POSSIBILITIES OF INDEPENDENCE.
THRFEAT OF RTSWIMMING THROUGH THE TUNNEL
GFDDFFFRIFGGHTENED HIM EWBEC TUNNEL ERE;PRESENTEDD RWEAL
INDEPENDENCSE IFD TRYMIGD DESPUITE FREEQQQETREAL
DANGEDRS WGHERE WQATERES AAERE EERIFE AFTER THESE ERNEST
REVERANGEING DIDEWS GHEAD INTO ASHORE. TERRIFYING
EDEPTHS BEGET OPPORTUNITIES. GREART REWARDS FREE FTHE
BOTY TO GROWW UP INTO NNMANHHOOD WHHEN REETUJRNINTG FROM
LHE RIGOROUS SWIM REURITUUALIZED REYBY THE BOYS OVER THE
YEARS,. IN "THROUGH THE TUNNEL" THE MIRROR INMAGE OF
HJERRY'S FREEDOM IS HIS TREMENDOYUS GF; PLEA FROM TEN-
DERNESS OF THE TUNE OLF A SWEET IMINGINAATION.

Since Evan's facilitator had not read the Lessing story, she regarded the details in his text as evidence that the words were his. Upon checking the Lessing story, she found it concerned a rite of passage, a boy swimming to considerable depth, and then after repeated tries and despite frightening danger, navigating an underwater tunnel, and swimming to shore—a feat indeed ritualized by local boys over the years, and which, for the protagonist, was symbolic of his transition to manhood.

Wesley informed a teaching assistant that one of the student teachers is a vegetarian: HER RELIGON FORBIDS VERONICA CAUSE CANNOT EAT FEEDING CHOICES DEAD ANIIMALLSS. At a parent/teacher conference, Wesley's teacher told his mother that he frequently typed about his "dead dad." The day after the meeting, at which Wesley had not been present, he came into school and complained to a teaching assistant who also had not been present at the parent/teacher conference: HIT BIG DEBORAH [his teacher] SHE TOLD MOM I LIKE TALKING ABOUT DEAD DAD REALLY UPSET MOM. He also told the teaching assistant the name of the person who had driven his mother to the parent/teacher conference.

Mark often typed about his dad's visits—when his dad was coming and leaving. He typed such messages consistently across facilitators. Also, one day, Mark complained that his ears were hurting. When taken to the doctor's office, he was diagnosed as having an ear infection. Recently, he told his teacher that he wanted to write his book report on a book that he was reading, *Dear Mr. Henshaw*. The teacher found this confusing because she knew from his mother that they were reading *Charlie and the Chocolate Factory* at home. Several days later the teacher learned that he had been reading *Dear Mr. Henshaw* in speech class.

William gave his teachers an education on illegal activities in which a family member was involved. After telling his teacher about the illegalities, he then told his speech teacher/facilitator in another room that he had told his teacher of them. When the school social worker inquired about this, his mother verified that family members had been involved in the activities and that William's details were correct.

Another student, Russell, was thought by his teachers to have nearly given information about which they were unaware, but they were unsure about how to regard this instance. Russell's behavior seemed especially troublesome one day, so his teacher asked him why. He typed IAMMADD- ATJSEMEHNN HE HITMEANDDITHURTCRHY UPSET ATHIMFORHAT^INTGRUSSELL (I am mad at Semehnn [?]. He hit me and it hurt. Cry. Upset at him for hating Russell.) When his teacher asked "Who hit you?", Russell responded, MYBROTHER. His teacher had not known his brother's name; it is Selmen. His teacher then asked what he would like her to do. He typed, TLLMOM. When Russell's mother was informed of what he had typed, she explained that Russell had been upset at home on the previous evening as well as in the morning. Russell himself had not been hit, but his brother had been in trouble and received a beating; Russell had been upset at his brother's cries. Then in the morning, when Russell tried to get close to his brother, Selmen had ignored Russell and focused his attention on their infant sister. Russell's mother said he reacted with obvious frustration and jealousy. Given the inconsistencies in this account, the teachers did not consider it confirmation that the words were Russell's, but they found it encouraging.

According to the teachers, B. J., Doug, Henry, and Russell were the only students who did not type information unknown to their facilitators.

CONCLUSIONS AND QUESTIONS

All of the teachers felt they had to confirm, either for themselves or for critics, that the students were authors of the typing. Often they spoke about this in strong language. The high school speech teacher remarked, "sometimes I feel beleaguered by questions and there are a million things going through my mind." Her solution to the question of authorship was in the details. She said it was important "to sort through [and] look at the detail."

The Communication Portfolio

To confirm for themselves that the students were authors of the typing, each of the teachers called forth evidence of individual differences in how the students attended to typing; in the content, form, and style of their typing; and in their conveying information not known to the facilitators. They constructed a picture of accumulated detail, what the researchers came to regard as communication portfolios, comprising students' typing and also their teachers' ideas about how they typed, including specific difficulties, idiosyncratic style, and distinctive content.

Although the teachers did not require students to convey information unknown to them as "the" way of "proving" authorship, clearly it was important to them. On this matter, through the examples the teachers provided, this research yields at least two interesting and notable findings. Careful analysis of the data revealed that *in the majority of instances, typing information that was reported to be previously unknown to the facilitators typically concerned content and issues of personal importance to the students.* Teachers noted that most often the information concerned family matters or ideas and feelings of obvious concern to the students. This content contrasts with the kinds of naming tasks that have proven difficult for other individuals in certain controlled studies (see, e.g., Intellectual Disability Review Panel [IDRP], 1989; Wheeler, Jacobson, Paglieri, & Schwartz, 1993).

The second notable finding of this research was the cumulative information that teachers used to authenticate each student's communication. The range of information and factors cited by teachers suggests the relevance of a portfolio approach to the question of authorship.

The teachers did not regard their confidence in the method, no matter how well documented, as evidence that they never influenced or cued their students' communication. The high school teacher noted, "first of all, you have to be open to the possibility of influence and how that happens. And the more open you are, the more you're going to make sure that doesn't happen." She said that her primary strategies for minimizing her influence were to encourage her two students to attempt typing more independently and to insist that they look directly at the keyboard before selections. At the elementary school, several teachers also spoke of influence as something they monitored. "We always question ourselves," the sixth-grade teacher commented. She and her teaching assistants met regularly to go over the students' typing to see if there was consistency in style; they were pleased to find there was, although they still regarded some influence as inevitable. The sixth-grade teacher remarked, "when you are spending so many hours with a kid facilitating, you know that sometimes you are going to influence someone, and as a facilitator you have to constantly check back."

This research documents the variety of information and actions (i.e., communication profiles) that teachers/facilitators in this study regarded as evidence that their students were the authors of their own messages. Except for independent typing, the teachers did not identify any single piece of evidence as conclusive, but they reported being persuaded by the accumulation of factors and by their consistency for individual students. One teacher's comment about the changes she observed in her students, as lending credibility to the authenticity of her students' communications, typified this perspective:

> Watching the growth of confidence, the acceptance of their own abilities, the enjoyment of sitting down to type, the growth in skills, the change from day 1 to day 50. I guess above other things, the change in attitude, in ability to concentrate and stay with a task, which would *have* to be boring if they weren't in it. If they weren't in it mentally, I mean.

Methodological Reflections: From Whose Perspective?

The teachers in this study admired their students. They took pride in their accomplishments with language and in their own roles as educators in uncovering their personalities. It was difficult for us, the researchers, not to get caught up in their enthusiasm. In our observations, we found ourselves looking for the kinds of indicators of authorship that the teachers had pointed out and, at times, though certainly not always, finding it hard to separate the teachers' perspectives from our own. When a student reached with an unfacilitated hand to hit a return key on an electronic type-writer, or when a student deleted several words to fix an error rather than simply changing a single letter, or when a student spoke words that anticipated the content typed—for example when Stephen announced a joke before it was typed—we shared the teachers' enthusiasm.

The case for the students' authorship mounted as we and their teach-ers watched. The problematic aspect of this was, of course, the danger that we might fail to distinguish the teachers' understandings from our own or that we would view theirs uncritically.

The obvious antidote for this problem was to make sure that accounts reported were in the voices of those we observed and interviewed, namely, the teachers, teaching assistants, and students. We often said to teachers "Could you tell me a little bit more about what you mean by . . ." or "You mentioned something yesterday that I found interesting; do you have any other examples of that?" Seeking greater detail or, simply, examples of a point was a negotiated process. We asked questions until we felt we under-stood and until the teachers' examples enabled us to convey *their* ideas.

At the same time, a teacher's account could well be self-edited to meet what the teacher might perceive as the researchers' demand for "evidence" or documentation that the public or, more to the point, critics of the method might find compelling. In effect, a teacher could presumably develop a perspective that fit what she felt the researcher wanted to hear. Our safe-guard was to see if multiple facilitators spoke about similar issues, with-out our prompting them, or to see if the issues they had mentioned to us arose in the course of our observations.

Numerous teachers remarked that students often typed out wrong words that started with the same letters as words that would have been correct for the contexts; also, these were readily available for us to observe (see the example of Stephen above, where he typed COURTNEY before cor-recting it with COURAGE). Sometimes students would type the wrong word or parts of the wrong word multiple times before getting the correct word. It was as if they could not break a habit; they were stuck. Teachers observed this and commented on how difficult it sometimes was. They would say to a student "Is this the word that you wanted? If it's not, try again." Or they would say "I'm not quite sure what you meant there. Could you explain?"

One might argue that such lapses or errors could have been subcon-sciously projected by the facilitators, except that often the teachers were as baffled as the researchers at the difficulty some students had in getting past an automatic completion. And sometimes the teacher and researcher were equally ignorant of the word the student intended. A year after this study was completed, one of the researchers had a conversation with Lindsay, who often exhibited automatic completions. The researcher had just returned from a lecture visit to Japan and was telling her about his observations there. The following interchange included an automatic completion:

> RESEARCHER: At one of the Japanese schools that I visited I met a girl who uses facilitated handwriting. It was exciting to see.
>
> LINDSAY: SAY THAT IS GOOD BETTER THAN GETRING SHOT [This comment was made on the morning when it was reported that two Japanese visitors had been slain in Los Angeles.] AEWFUL TO COME TO THE USA AND GET KILLED AND THEN BAD FOR OUR REASEARCH AND TRADING.
>
> TEACHER: [Pointing to the word "reasearch," said] Was that the word that you wanted?
>
> LINDSAY: TRY RELATIOSHIP WITH THE JAPANES

The transcript of this conversation masks the actual difficulties Lindsay displayed; she had typed RESE, RES, RESEAR, and so forth 10 times before getting RELATIOSHIP.

Clearly, in the process of gathering evidence that the teachers pointed out to us, we were drawn into the students' struggles, coming close to cheering their successes. In writing up the observations, we found we had to remind ourselves to let the documentation of the students' teachers' words and work speak for themselves.

Why Facilitation? In Search of a Theoretical Explanation

Throughout this study we observed students' difficulties with performance: incorrect sequencing of letters; problems of initiation; repetitive typing of certain letters; inaccuracy in typing, hitting several letters at once; problems of pacing typing; impulsive responses; shakiness or tremor; high and low muscle tone; difficulty with typing letters on the side of the person opposite the facilitated arm or hand; and automatic typing of certain words. The fact that teachers noted such difficulties or that they were prominent in our observations was not surprising. There is an extensive literature on difficulties among people with autism, Down syndrome, and other developmental disabilities that correspond to what we heard and observed.

The term *apraxia* means "without action" (Biklen, 1993a, pp. 79–84; see also Biklen & Duchan, 1994, p. 181). It refers to absence of or difficulty with achieving voluntary action: "The apraxias may be defined as disorders of the execution of learned movement which cannot be accounted for either by weakness, incoordination, or sensory loss, or by incomprehension of or inattention to commands" (Geschwind, 1975, p. 188).

Variability of performance seems characteristic of people with autism and of other people with apraxia/developmental dyspraxia (Damasio & Maurer, 1978; Darley, Armson, & Brown, 1975; Leary & Hill, 1996; Miller, 1986; Zoeller, 1992). Damasio and Maurer (1978) noted that children with whom they worked would often stop a task entirely and stare, as if transfixed, and that they tended to scan a target more quickly than others, seeming "to use peripheral vision more than they do central vision" (p. 389). They interpreted such behavior as an apparent strategy to achieve equilibrium, presumably to manage an environment in which they might feel overloaded by stimuli:

> In our view, most of these behaviors represent adaptive responses of an individual with brain dysfunction to the demands of the environment. They reflect the tendency of the organism to perform what it can perform adequately [e.g., to go into compulsive routines]. . . . Compulsive, stereotyped, ritualistic behaviors may be viewed as ways in which that avoidance is enacted and homeostasis of a disturbed biological system achieved. (p. 392)

While their performance could occasionally be normal, it usually was not.

Their interpretation is corroborated by the work of other studies, especially by an investigation into the physical reactions (e.g., peripheral blood flow) of people with autism in demanding or new situations (Kootz, Marinelli, & Cohen, 1982). So-called higher-functioning people showed reactions expected of people taking in new information and performing tasks, while those defined as lower-functioning showed measurements characteristic of people who were rejecting external stimuli (Kootz et al., 1982, p. 185). These researchers concluded:

> Autistic children appear to be more sensitive to the environment and may use behavioral strategies, such as avoiding environmental change and social interaction, as methods of reducing further disorganizing experiences. Disturbances in filtering environmental stimulation and modulating response to novelty may be part of the basic pathology of autism apparent during the 1st year of life. (p. 185)

This is consistent with the theory of developmental dyspraxia (i.e., problems with voluntary action); people with less motor-planning difficulty may not have to screen out extra stimuli; people with greater motor-planning difficulty may have to screen out more in order to focus on motor planning; they may also experience greater anxiety. The latter group may be attempting to avoid an overload of sensory processing and motor-planning demands. The former group showed fewer physiological signs that they were rejecting added sensory input.

It also seems that people with autism have increased difficulties when confronted with new or complex tasks (i.e., multiple-step tasks) or ones that require attention to several stimuli simultaneously. Fulkerson and Freeman (1980) noted, for example, that in a task such as the Southern California Motor Accuracy Test, which requires careful and persistent self-monitoring of performance, and in a similarly high-demand situation where background interference was introduced, "motor monitoring seemed to break down for autistic subjects" (p. 335).

Similarly, problems of cognitive shifting, changing focus from one task to another, may in part explain problems of performance. In a study of people with autism who were known to have "high cognitive" abilities, Berger and colleagues (1993) found "persistent social impairment and maladaptive behaviors" (p. 357). Good thinking skills were a "necessary but not a sufficient condition for competent social adaptive behavior" (p. 357).

Such problems have been noted in people with Down syndrome (Kerr & Blais, 1985). In a study in which people with Down syndrome as well as people with retardation (but not Down syndrome) and nondisabled people were asked to follow a target and predict a target, researchers concluded "that persons with Down syndrome are not able to utilize predictability information spontaneously within a motor task. Whether individuals with Down syndrome are not able to identify the predictability, or alternatively, are unable to organize their responses to take advantage of this information is not discernible from this experiment" (p. 318).

Other studies would seem to support the latter hypothesis. Elliott, Weeks, and Gray (1990) found that people with Down syndrome were better able to perform tasks after a visual demonstration than after verbal instruction, even though their known ability to understand such verbal instructions was equal to that of individuals who *could* perform the tasks on the basis of verbal explanations. They concluded, "for the Down's syndrome subjects there is a distinction between knowing/remembering what is required, and actually being able to perform the movements" (p. 1313). In other words, there was a problem with praxis, of putting understanding into action. Devenny, Wilverman, Balgdy, Wall, and Sidtis (1990) have summarized these motor-planning difficulties in people with Down syndrome:

> Non-speech specific motor deficits associated with DS . . . , like stuttering, cannot be attributed to an overall level of mental retardation and frequently appear to involve tasks with an inherent motor planning component. . . . Spe-

cific motor deficits among people with DS have been observed in studies of timing components of motor sequences, . . . and two step sequential movements. . . . In contrast to these findings for sequential motor performance, studies of general motor performance have not found comparable syndrome-specific differences. (p. 442)

Of course, one of the confounding aspects of this research has been the tendency of scientists to attribute failed performance to failed thinking. DeMyer, Hingtgen, and Jackson (1981, p. 409) describe research that revealed "severe motor imitative dyspraxia." Citing his earlier work (DeMyer et al. 1972), DeMyer notes that,

most autistic children may have not only a severe abstract language defect but also a dyspraxia, both defects contributing to their inability to learn the meaning of and reproduce body language which forms a large part of the infant and the young child's communication mode with others. (1981, p. 409)

DeMeyer and colleagues (1981) recognized that presumed problems of thinking could relate back to motor system difficulties or other functions, but they did not proffer the possibility that motor performance problems might mask greater understanding. Failure to decouple performance from thinking was ironic, especially since their research seemed almost to scream out that possibility. For example, they noted that people with autism could often do fitting and assembly tasks but "whenever a more advanced motor skill or cognitive judgment, as in the coding subtest of the WISC or draw-a-person test, was called for, autistic children did relatively worse" (p. 410). The idea that multiple-step tasks would be more difficult than single-step ones is characteristic of apraxia/developmental dyspraxia and may be completely unrelated to reasoning ability (Darley et al., 1975).

Perhaps most importantly for this discussion, the leading autobiographies of autism reveal significant motor disturbances. For Grandin in her growing-up years, "handling two motor tasks at the same time was almost impossible" (Grandin & Scariano, 1986, p. 30). Sean Barron, a person with autism who, like Grandin, can now speak, describes his difficulties as a child in learning even simple motor tasks:

I had a lot of trouble fastening buttons through the holes and tying shoes. Many times I ripped the buttons off my shirts and broke my laces because I was so furious with the damn things when they refused to work. (Barron & Barron, 1992, p. 200)

Given the neuromotor complexities of speech, it is not surprising that both Barron and Grandin recount their own delayed and disordered speech, including the word-retrieval difficulties and automatic speech so often associated with dyspraxia. For example, Grandin explains that her automatic speech often did not match her thoughts: "In my head I knew what I wanted to say but the words never matched my thoughts" (Grandin & Scariano, 1986, p. 85).

D. Williams (1994b) also has written about the difficulties of taking action, where the individual stands frozen or can produce only stored, automatic language—not intentional phrases and thoughts—or gets lost in staring at a pattern. She provides an example of her own intervention with a child, Jody, that bears considerable resemblance to facilitated communication. The child was tapping herself and rocking while one teacher tried to hold her arms down and the other took stabs at feeding her: "Somewhere between hit and miss she managed to get some of the strained baby food into the six-year-old's mouth" (p. 31). Williams tried a different approach from that of Jody's teachers. She began to hum gently, a "short, rhythmic, and hypnotic" tune. As she hummed, Jody stopped grinding her teeth. Williams continued to hum but also began tapping Jody's "shoulder in rhythm with the tune. . . . Jody stopped tapping herself" (p. 32). With this, Jody became able to act:

> Her hands were now free for her to use. She reached across the table, grabbed her sandwiches, tore them open, and stuffed them into her face. Jody may not have been the most elegant of eaters but at least she was independent and she could eat her own food. (p. 32)

Williams explained that her strategy with Jody derived from her own experiences with autism:

> I did what I myself would have needed. Grinding my teeth kept disturbing, unpredictable, and meaningless outside noise from coming in. Singing a repetitive tune and humming continuously did the same. The tapping gave a continuous rhythm and stopped the unpatterned movement of others from invading. I had simply replaced all these things for her so that she was freed up to do the next things down the scale of what she needed or wanted to do. (p. 32)

As we would expect, such accounts bear remarkable similarity to clinical assessments of dyspraxia among people using facilitation (Steering Committee, 1993). When given an oro-motor assessment for dyspraxia, in which participants were asked to imitate tongue and lip postures, 21 participants failed (Steering Committee, 1992). They evidenced extreme dyspraxia in even this simplest action associated with speech. Only one participant was able to communicate more than "basic need" information by speaking.

Thirteen participants were judged to be "non-communicative with speech or augmentative systems" (p. 20).

But Williams (1994a) would have us broaden the analysis away from "a mere 'movement' problem" (p. 199) to conceive of autism—while she speaks of autism, the analysis may have applicability to other conditions—as a disorder "affecting all systems of functioning" ranging from awareness of proprioception to "analysis and retrieval skills relating to information on all levels (sensory, emotional, mental, proprioceptive, social-interactive) and the integration of those systems" (p. 196). She defines her dilemma and that of others with autism as one of systems-management (i.e., integration) and systems-forfeiting. In order to get one thing to work, it is often necessary to abandon or neglect another. For example, the person may have to switch off emotional signals in order to accept factual information, or switch off auditory input to take in visual stimuli. Naturally this creates severe problems for designing tests of facilitated communication or any other thing. She argues that the "combinations of systems forfeiting" experienced by the person with autism pose at least two major problems for facilitated communication, problems that will accost both critics and supporters, namely, the likelihood of developing "inappropriate testing techniques that are based on misinformed premises and faulty assumptions" and "misinformed assumptions (and proclamations) of how things work or don't work" with facilitation (thus undermining credibility for the method) (pp. 196–197).

The fluctuations in performance, whether in tests or in other situations have been described by a person in Australia as "autistic tendencies" (i.e., automatic responses, echoed responses, word-finding difficulties) (see Biklen, 1993). These may intrude at some times or under some conditions and not at, or under, others. A related problem is failed affect. Oppenheim admonished us not to deny academic stimulation to a person whose condition imprisons him "behind a profoundly atypical facade" (1974, p. 90); in other words, do not presume incompetence as a function of inaction. Similarly D. Williams (1994b) has warned, "trouble in linking thought to action" could easily *not* reflect mental retardation: "the problem may not be in the capacity so much as the mechanics" (p. 22).

Influence and Cuing

Some researchers have viewed inaccurate information as necessarily facilitator directed (Moore, Donovan, & Hudson, 1993; Smith, Haas, & Belcher, 1994); however, evidence from our study would seem to challenge that interpretation as too simplistic. It has long been obvious that facilitators can sometimes influence, cue, or otherwise direct a person, consciously or unconsciously, to type particular information (Biklen, 1993; Crossley, 1994). Yet this does not explain why facilitated communication would include perseveration on a particular theme or production of a detailed account about events that could be easily verified to be false. Why would a teacher influence creation of a story that could easily be discounted?

As researchers, we were intrigued by the above-mentioned report that Evan hit a teaching assistant/facilitator while in the presence of another student and while on the way to the library. Why would he or his teacher report an event that did not happen?

Of course, all of us play out such fantasies in our minds, even to the point of providing dialogue to arguments and disputes that never happen, especially when we are upset about something. The difference between such fantasies and what Evan did was that Evan typed his, in the past tense, as if it actually had happened. It is certainly conceivable that what we are observing in such instances is the communication style of a new communicator who has not ever had his language monitored by parents, teachers, or others. In a sense, he is in the position just now, at the age of 18, of learning what one can and cannot say, and how to say it, for example, whether and when to exaggerate, what to announce as real and what as fanciful. The fact that he is a new communicator may require infinitely more care and circumspection by his listeners than would be required for a typical age peer.

Evan's representation of a fantasy as an experienced event has obvious implications for how people understand and discuss facilitated communication. It suggests the importance of clarifying messages (see Biklen, 1993; Crossley, 1994), especially those that could have significant consequences for the person or for others mentioned in the communication, as is the case, for example, in allegations of abuse, decisions about living arrangements or other life plans, reports of illness, and accounts of others' actions.

CHAPTER 4

Factors Affecting Performance in Facilitated Communication

Stacey Baldac
Carl Parsons

This study was designed to examine parameters that may influence task performance in validation-type examinations of facilitated communication. The study employed observations and quasi-experimental conditions. The study procedures included:

1. A screen to shield facilitators from the materials (picture stimuli)
2. Selection of participants by the DEAL Communication Centre (Melbourne, Australia) of individuals who had demonstrated adequate communication skills via facilitated communication to perform picture description tasks
3. Selection of facilitator by the study participant
4. Implementation of no time constraints for the completion of a task in order to minimize participant anxiety and to accommodate slow/delayed responses
5. An accounting for different skill levels by allowing the picture stimuli to be varied, dependent upon the participant's or facilitator's requests

METHOD

Participants

Participants were selected based upon the following criteria:

1. Previously diagnosed with "autism" or "autistic behaviors"
2. Previously unable to communicate their intentions reliably. According to their previous communication evaluations, each participant had:

A severe communication impairment evidenced by an inability to communicate intentions reliably by verbal or gestural communication

A demonstrated inability to acquire manual signs by previous formal training techniques

An assessment which indicated that the use of communication aids or keyboards with facilitation would expand the individual's ability to communicate

3. Demonstration of an ability to type at least single words via facilitation
4. Participant and facilitator willingness to participate in the project by completing informed consent forms

Five of the participants were male and one was female (Participant 2). Their ages were 30, 13, 19, 13, 11, and 30 years, respective to their participant numbers. According to their case records, each participant had autism or autistic behavior and each was diagnosed as having intellectual disability, four of whom were labeled in the severely retarded range. One student was diagnosed with Down syndrome (Participant 3). Prior to facilitated communication training, the functional literacy of all participants was almost identical. Each had no written production of words, but each had, to varying degrees, some interest in reading material. This interest ranged from a general attraction to magazines to a continual and intense need to look at printed information. According to the participants' records, all had similar communication skills prior to facilitated communication training. Five of the six were functionally nonverbal, while some had stereotypical echolalia. Three of the participants did respond verbally at times to "yes/no" questions (Participants 4, 5, and 6). One participant (Participant 6) used a few phrases of two to three words to express basic needs and requests.

The participants were engaged in facilitated communication training from two to six years prior to this study. The level of support needed by the participants for this study varied. Three of the participants (Participants 1, 2, and 4) needed wrist support, while Participant 3 needed only shoulder support; Participant 6 used support at the elbow, and Participant 5 used elbow support for the math tasks but needed greater (wrist) support for the two other tasks.

Facilitators

Five facilitators were involved in the tasks conducted in this study. Three of the participants were facilitated by two facilitators and three participants were facilitated by only one facilitator. The participants were provided with the opportunity to select the facilitator they worked with by speaking, pointing, or spelling with facilitated communication. All the participants selected staff at the DEAL Centre and/or one of their parents to be their facilitator. Participants 3 and 6 asked for a facilitator different from the person who asked the question "Who would you like to be your facilitator?"

Setting

A room familiar to the participants and facilitators was used for all the tasks. The main treatment room at the DEAL Communication Centre was used for all sessions. All participants had received a majority of their facilitated communication training in this room.

The facilitator and participant were seated at one end of a table. The table was divided by a screen. The screen was adjustable, and for each participant–facilitator pair the screen was repositioned so that the facilitator was unable to see the participant's picture stimuli. Stimulus pictures for the participants were mounted on red cardboard and passed through a slot in the screen by Researcher 1. The distractor pictures for the facilitator were also mounted on red cardboard and placed in view of the facilitator only. The plate of four alternative pictures and/or the communication device (used by some of the participants) were placed between the participant and the facilitator. All stimuli were covered by a piece of cardboard to ensure that the facilitators were not able to view any items intended to be viewed only by the participant.

Two video cameras were used and were placed at different positions. Video camera 2 was positioned behind the facilitator to depict her positioning in relation to the participant; it was also used to demonstrate that the facilitators could not see the stimulus materials. Video camera 1, operated by Researcher 2, was used to focus on the stimulus materials prior to presentation to the participant and then to depict the positioning of the participant and the movements made by the participant. It was used to "zoom in" on the target stimuli presented to the participant and "zoom out" to demonstrate the participant's responses. The video record of camera 1 was used in conducting the reliability element of the study.

The study was constructed to examine parameters that may influence a participant's performance. To address this aim, three different tasks were used with facilitation: matching, labeling, and message passing. The matching task required that the participants match pictures. This was perceived as the easiest of the three tasks, as it did not require production of written language. Therefore, it was felt that by performing the matching task first, the participants would experience success, which would alleviate any fears of the testing environment. The matching task also provided useful information as to whether participants could clearly identify the stimuli used and to determine if they understood the task procedures. The labeling task utilized the same procedures as the matching task; however, it required participants to type out (spell) their responses. The stimuli and procedures used in the labeling task were kept similar to those of the matching task to reduce possible confusion on the part of participants. In the labeling task, the possibility of word-finding problems affecting the participants' performance was addressed. Facilitators were provided with four alternative pictures that they could discuss with the participant to aid the participant's word retrieval. The message-passing task was used to determine how participants' performances differed when the facilitators had *no* information and *no* clues about the stimuli shown to the participants. The task allowed, but did not require, sentence-level responses.

In the three tasks, after an individual response was completed, facilitators were provided with feedback about correct/incorrect responses by the researchers regarding the participants' successful or unsuccessful completion of a response.

Matching Task

Stimuli. The picture stimuli used for the matching task needed to clearly depict a single object or action so that the participants would not be confused as to the content of the pictures. Therefore, pictures from the *Peabody Picture Vocabulary Test* (PPVT-R) (Dunn & Dunn, 1981) were used, as the black and white pictures were clear and easily distinguishable. Thirty-five plates with four pictures each were selected from the PPVT-R. The plates selected were based on unambiguous content, dissimilar pictures, and depiction of objects that (most likely) would have been seen by the participants. Three copies of each plate of four pictures were made. Two of the three copies of the plate of four pictures were cut up into their respective individual pictures; therefore, two sets of seventy pictures (35 × 4) were made. One set of the individual pictures was used to show pictures to the participants during the relevant tasks, and the other set (second set) was used to show to the facilitators during the relevant tasks. The third copy of the plates of four pictures was used to show to the facilitator and the participant during the relevant tasks.

Task. In the matching task, four conditions were used:

Condition A: No distractor—only the participant was presented with a stimulus card

Condition B: Same distractor—the participant and the facilitator were presented with identical stimulus cards

Condition C: Different distractor—the participant and facilitator were presented with different stimulus cards

Condition D: Facilitator foil—both the participant and facilitator were presented with stimulus cards

For Condition D the facilitator was unaware whether her distractor was the same as or different from the picture presented to the participant. The distractors used in Condition D were selected randomly. Ten responses in each condition were required. Thus the participants were expected to complete 40 responses in the matching task.

Procedure. The plates of four alternative pictures were placed between the facilitator and the participant. The facilitators were encouraged to name and discuss the four alternatives and to use as many prompts, questions, or reinforcers as they deemed necessary to assist the participant in making the correct selection. The participant and facilitator were informed that a time limit would not be imposed for each response or the task. The facilitators, however, based upon their previous experience with the participant, would determine when to terminate further attempts at a response. That is, if the facilitator believed the participant was being uncooperative or was unable to produce a response, due to fatigue or lack of ability, further attempts could be terminated.

The individual pictures covered by a piece of cardboard were passed through the slot in the screen and placed in view of the participant only. The distance between the participant and the pictures was approximately three feet. The facilitators were also presented with a picture in Conditions B, C, and D. The cover from the participants' pictures was then removed. The participants were then asked to select the picture from among the plate of four alternatives that was placed in front of them and their facilitator.

After the completion of a response, the participants were provided with the opportunity to change their responses. The facilitator or the researcher asked the participant "Is this [pointing to the picture] a (participant's response)?" The participant could respond by speaking, by spelling via facilitated communication, by using signs/gestures, or by a head nod/shake. Spoken responses were noted. If the participant responded with "no," he was provided with the opportunity to provide another response.

Scoring. After a response was made and confirmed by the participant, it was scored by the researcher (R1) as a 1 for correct or 0 for incorrect.

Labeling Task

Stimuli. The same stimuli used in the matching task were used in the labeling task. The participants were familiar with the picture format and the PPVT-R pictures clearly displayed one identifiable object or action.

Task. The labeling task utilized the same four conditions as the matching task. Each of the four conditions (A, B, C, & D) required 10 responses, resulting in a total of 40 responses.

Procedure. The procedures used in the labeling task were the same as those used in the matching task. The participant was shown a single picture and the facilitator was simultaneously shown four pictures. The facilitators were encouraged to talk about, describe, and discuss the different pictures. The facilitators' descriptions of the four alternatives were encouraged to assist the participants if they were experiencing word-finding problems. It should be remembered that the task here was for the participant to communicate to the facilitator which of the stimuli was the targeted item presented by the researcher. The participants were required to provide (via facilitated communication) the name or a description of the individual picture they were presented.

After they made a response, participants were provided with the opportunity to change their response. There was a great deal of variability among participants regarding response time in answering "yes/no" and requiring a second attempt. However, when the participant indicated that the initial response was not accurate, a second attempt could be made. These attempts could often take about 20 to 30 minutes. The facilitators would encourage and prompt the participants to make a second attempt. If the participants said (spoke) the word depicted by the picture, then this detail was noted and the response was discounted and not allowed for scoring.

Scoring. After a response was made and confirmed by the participant, the response was scored by the researcher (R1) as a 1 for correct or 0 for incorrect.

Message-Passing Task

Stimuli. For the message-passing task, colored pictures/photographs taken from magazines and books were used. The facilitators were *not* informed about the content of the pictures/photographs or where they had come from. The colored photographs were selected if they depicted more than one identifiable object and also depicted objects that the participant was likely to have seen previously.

Task. The participants were required to communicate via facilitation what was depicted in the picture/photograph. Five responses were required in the message-passing task.

Procedure. The picture/photograph was covered by a piece of cardboard and then passed through the slot in the screen and placed in view of the participant only. The participant was then required to communicate via facilitation what she could see in the picture. The facilitator was encouraged to ask questions and discuss responses with the participant. When the facilitator felt that he had some idea of what the participant wanted to communicate, the facilitator would indicate to the researcher the name of an object or action the picture/photograph contained. The participant–facilitator pairs were allowed extensive periods of time to work on this task.

After the completion of a response, each participant was provided with the opportunity to change his response immediately after the attempt.

Scoring. Each attempt had to be communicated by the participant via facilitated communication in order to be scored. The response was scored as a 1 for correct and a 0 for incorrect. A correct response was considered to be any word or group of words that depicted an object or action in the picture.

Order of Task Presentation

The researchers felt that some of the tasks might be difficult and that participants who did not experience initial success might want to withdraw from the study. Therefore, the facilitators were requested to provide input into the order of task presentation. The facilitators were advised to base their selection of ordering on previous experience with each participant. Thus the first task presented would be the task the facilitator deemed as the easiest for the participant and therefore most likely to provide the participant with a positive experience.

Scoring

During all tasks, the participants typed messages and the facilitators' questions were transcribed verbatim (on-line). All hard copies from the communication devices were collected for those participants who used these devices during the tasks. The on-line transcription was then rechecked by reviewing the videos after each session. For those individuals who used systems without a printer, their communications were recorded from the on-line transcription and the videotape. Notes were made concerning any verbal and nonverbal co-occurring behaviors that were exhibited during the tasks. These notes were used to provide descriptions of particular situations, for example, the relationship of an individual's limited speech to the text typed.

For all the tasks, individual responses were reviewed on the videotape. Participants' responses were rated as 1 for a correct response and 0 for an incorrect response by Researcher 1. In the matching task and the labeling tasks, there were clearly specified (targeted) correct answers, while the potential responses in the message-passing task were more open-ended. For all tasks a response was scored as correct when: (1) the typed name of the shown picture was correct, (2) an unambiguous word approximation or phonetic spelling was used, or (3) descriptions of the pictures and semantically related words or phrases were used. The message-passing task allowed the facilitator to ask questions, make guesses, ask for clarification, and use any other verbal means to try to determine what the participant was attempting to communicate. These variants on what constituted a correct response were allowed, since this is what is entailed in normal communication. A score of 0 was given when the participants' responses were incorrect or when responses were indecipherable. Some of the participants used speech to name the objects before typing their responses. In these instances the response was not counted as a 1 or 0; this occurrence was noted and placed in a separate "not a facilitated communication response" category.

Reliability

One of the researchers scored all of the participants' responses by reviewing the transcripts and video recordings of the sessions. It should be noted that correctness of a response for the matching and labeling task was measured on the videotapes by zooming in on the stimuli and also showing participants' responses. A second researcher (using the criteria stated above) then scored 25% of the total responses for each participant from the videotapes. One hundred percent (100%) agreement for the scoring of responses was achieved. A third person—a 36-year-old male IBM computer programmer—who was unfamiliar with facilitated communication or any of the controversies about it scored 25% of the total responses for each participant from the videotapes. He achieved a 96% agreement.

Baseline

Detailed baseline data for each participant on each task were not gathered since this study was *not* an experimental attempt at determining authorship, but rather an investigation of factors that affect performance in experimental studies. The entry level (i.e., baseline) of each participant was assumed to be zero or near zero based on the absence of written expression skills and the very limited verbal expression skills possessed by each participant (as outlined earlier in this chapter).

RESULTS

Results of the Tasks

Each participant was expected to complete a total of 85 responses in the three tasks. One response was equivalent to the presentation of one picture stimuli in either of the three tasks. Table 4.1 illustrates the number of responses scored, the mean and range for each task, and the number and percentage of correct responses in each task. A total of 285 responses (a mean of 50.3) were scored. Some participants took up to 40 minutes to make one response in a task, and thus time constraints did not allow for additional responses to be pursued. The behavior of some participants precluded obtaining additional responses. Some attempts were not scored in the labeling task when the participant gave a spoken response (16 responses were unscored because they were spoken); Participant 5 spoke the response for 13 items and Participant 6 spoke the responses 3 times.

The results presented in Table 4.1 indicate that the participants' performances varied dependent upon the task. The participants, as a group, scored the highest percentage of correct responses in the matching task (70%), followed by the message-passing task (50%), and then the labeling task (29%)—percentage scores represent responses correct on the first and second attempts. The results therefore demonstrate that changing the task may affect performance scores.

The matching and labeling tasks consisted of four different distractor conditions. The distractor conditions were constructed to test for facilitator influence and to examine participants' responses across differing con-

TABLE 4.1 Descriptive Analysis of Correct Responses Across the Three Experimental Tasks

Task	Responses Scored	Mean	Range	Correct Responses	% Correct Responses
Matching	153	25.5	7–40	107	70%
Labeling	114	22.0	10–38	33	29%
Message passing	18	3.0	1–5	9	50%

ditions. Therefore, the responses in the matching and labeling tasks are elaborated below and presented in Table 4.2.

Matching Task

The total number of responses completed for each participant was influenced by his speed in responding and his cooperation in the tasks. For example, P1 was slow (in comparison to the other participants) to complete a response and therefore he completed the least number of responses. P2 and P4 were disruptive in the sessions and therefore time was spent working through the interfering behaviors rather than performing the tasks. The behavior demonstrated was typical of their behavior in all activities and at no point did they type that they wanted to withdraw from the study. P6 was cooperative and responded promptly in the three tasks and therefore completed the most responses. The time restrictions, participants' cooperation, and participants' speed of responding influenced the total number of responses completed. It should be noted that each task was not limited by time, but the overall time devoted to this experiment was limited.

Testing for Facilitator Influence in the Matching Task. The order of presentation of the tasks and the order of presentation of the distractor conditions varied according to the preferences of the facilitators. The facilitators reported that they preferred to perform Condition A (only the participant was presented with a stimulus card) and Condition D (the participant and the facilitator were both presented with stimulus cards but the facilitator did not know whether the stimulus card she was shown was the same or different as that shown the participant) before Conditions B and C. The facilitators were aware that the results from Conditions A and D would be more useful in demonstrating a person's ability to communicate via facilitated communication and to demonstrate that facilitators were not influ-

TABLE 4.2 Individual Results and Totals of the Matching Task by Condition

Ss	*Condition A*	*Condition B*	*Condition C*	*Condition D*
P1	2 of 7 (29%)	no trials	no trials	no trials
P2	5 of 10 (50%)	4 of 10 (40%)	no trials	2 of 6 (33%)
P3	3 of 10 (30%)	no trials	9 of 10 (90%)	7 of 10 (70%)
P4	4 of 10 (40%)	no trials	no trials	5 of 10 (50%)
P5	10 of 10 (100%)	9 of 10 (90%)	no trials	10 of 10 (100%)
P6	8 of 10 (80%)	10 of 10 (100%)	9 of 10 (90%)	10 of 10 (100%)
TOTAL	32 of 57 (56%)	23 of 30 (77%)	18 of 20 (90%)	34 of 46 (74%)

encing communications. Although the facilitators were not opposed to performing the other two conditions (B and C), given the time constraints of the study, they wished to ensure participants attempted the conditions that would be most informative. The participant–facilitator pairs, therefore, attempted and completed Conditions A and D before attempting Conditions B and C. Together, the participants' achieved 70% correct responses in the matching task.

An analysis of the participants' responses in the four conditions was conducted to address the possibility of facilitator influence. The four conditions were analyzed based on the following criteria: (1) either an increase in the overall number of correct responses in Condition B (same distractor) as compared to number of correct responses in Condition A and/or a decrease in the overall number of correct responses in Condition C (different distractor) as compared to number of correct responses in Condition A would indicate a possible facilitator influence, and (2) incorrect participant responses that identified the facilitators' pictures in Condition D (facilitator foil) would indicate possible facilitator influence.

Table 4.2 demonstrates that, as a group, the participants performed better in Condition B but not more poorly in Condition C, and therefore satisfied one of the criteria for demonstrating possible facilitator influence but not another. Also, the number of participants attempting the conditions varied and therefore the results presented do not truly reflect "group" findings. In fact, individual analysis of these data (see Table 4.2) reveals *no evidence of influence* according to the criteria above. Participant 1 completed only Condition A. The number of correct responses by P2, P5, and P6 in Condition B are similar to their performance in Condition A, and performance of P3 and P6 are better in Condition C than in Condition A. Thus it would appear that facilitator influence was *not* demonstrated when the participants' scores were also examined on an individual basis. The present research, therefore, highlights the need to examine group and individual findings congruently to ensure that an accurate interpretation of the results is achieved.

In Condition D (the participant and the facilitator were both presented with stimulus cards but the facilitator did not know if his card was the same or different from the participant's) the possibility of facilitator influence could also be examined. Facilitator influence would have been demonstrated in Condition D if the participants' incorrect responses were the same as the picture presented to the facilitator. This finding would imply that the facilitators inadvertently or unknowingly had directed the facilitated communication output. For example, if the participant was presented with a picture of a cat and the facilitator was presented with a picture of a pair of jeans and the participant responded with a "pair of jeans," this response may be counted as demonstrating facilitator influence. Therefore, to examine the possibility of facilitator influence, participants' responses were analyzed in Condition D and their incorrect responses noted. Out of a possible 12 incorrect responses (46 total responses minus 34 correct responses), only on three occasions did the participants respond by selecting the pictured item that the facilitator saw (facilitator's distractor).

Therefore, two possible conclusions could be drawn: (1) The facilitators were not influencing the participants' communications; the number of occasions the participants responded with the facilitators' distractor was equal to the probability of guessing a correct response (25%). (2) The facilitators possibly influenced the communications of the subjects 7% of the time, a small number of occasions.

Labeling Task

Results for the labeling task are presented in Table 4.3. In the labeling task, not all participants attempted the same number of conditions. For example, five participants attempted Condition A, two participants attempted Conditions B and C, and six participants attempted Condition D. For the labeling task, as in the matching task, the facilitators also preferred to perform Conditions A and D before Conditions B and C, as they believed Conditions A and D would provide the most useful information.

The labeling task required that the participants communicate (via facilitated communication on their communication devices) the name of the picture or provide a description of the picture they were presented. The results indicated that as a group the participants achieved a higher percentage of correct scores in the matching task than in the labeling task.

In the labeling task, Participants 5 and 6 demonstrated the ability to speak the name of the pictured stimuli they were shown. Both participants would sometimes speak the name of the pictured stimuli before spelling

TABLE 4.3 Labeling Responses for the Four Distractor Conditions

Ss	Condition A	Condition B	Condition C	Condition D
P1	2 of 6 (33%)	no trials	no trials	2 of 4 (50%)
P2	2 of 7 (29%)	no trials	no trials	3 of 9 (33%)
P3	2 of 10 (20%)	no trials	4 of 10 (40%)	0 of 8 (0%)
P4	no trials	no trials	no trials	3 of 10 (30%)
P5	2 of 7 (29%)	0 of 4 (0%)	no trials	1 of 2 (50%)
P6	2 of 10 (20%)	2 of 8 (25%)	4 of 10 (40%)	3 of 9 (33%)
TOTAL	10 of 40 (25%)	2 of 12 (17%)	8 of 20 (40%)	12 of 42 (29%)

out their message via facilitated communication. Spoken productions occurred 16 times out of a total 114 possible responses (14%). If participants spoke the answer, it was not counted in the quantitative part of the study.

Testing for Facilitator Influence with the Labeling Task. The previously established set of criteria for the determination of facilitator influence was also used to examine the labeling results.

The percentage correct for the four conditions respectively were 25%, 17%, 40%, and 29%. Based on the percentage of correct scores for the four conditions, there is no evidence of facilitator influence. The first criterion is met because the percentage correct in Condition B was less than the percentage correct in Condition A and the percentage correct in Condition C was greater than the percentage correct in Condition A.

The second criteria for the determination of facilitator influence requires an examination of the participants' incorrect responses. On only four occasions, out of a possible 42 responses, did participants respond with the facilitator's distractor, less than 10% of total responses. Based on this result, two differing conclusions can be drawn: (1) Facilitators were not influencing the communications of the participants or (2) facilitators were rarely influencing the communications of participants.

Message-Passing Task

In the message-passing task the participants were presented with a picture stimulus to which the facilitator was "blind" and, therefore, the facilitators were completely unaware of the intended response. In the message-passing task, all participants attempted at least one response. A total of 18 responses were attempted by the participants, of which 9 responses were scored as correct; that is, 50% of the participants' responses in the message-passing task were scored as correct. Facilitator influence was not explored in the message-passing task as the facilitators were completely unaware of the participants' intended responses.

Overall Results

As a group, as indicated by the percentage of correct scores, the participants performed best in the matching task, followed by the message-passing task, and then the labeling task.

Table 4.4 summarizes all the participants' individual performances across the tasks. The results indicate that the participants demonstrated the ability to match pictures via facilitation and generally demonstrated the ability to communicate in the labeling and message-passing tasks. It is interesting to note, however, that P5 succeeded in the message-passing task but not in the labeling task, while P6 did well in the matching but not in the message passing. P3 did not do well in either the labeling or message-passing task. These findings suggest that participants' ability to demonstrate communication abilities may be influenced by the validation tasks used.

As noted earlier, the purpose of this study was *not* to validate facilitated communication but, rather, to examine the effect that varying testing conditions may have on a person's ability to perform validation-type tests. Looking at Table 4.4 again, we can see that when all six students' performance is viewed as a whole, their scores vary considerably across the three types of tasks. When viewing these data according to how the group did above the chance of their guessing the correct answer, students in general did markedly better on the matching task (45% better than chance) than they did on the labeling task (3% better than chance, which was basically no better than chance). On the message-passing task participants did even better that they did on the matching task (49% better than chance). It should be noted, however, that there was great variance of student performance on the message-passing task as well as a very small number of trials per student; thus the use of mean scores may be misleading since two of the participants (P3 and P6) were unable to get any of the pictures correct in the message-passing task. Nevertheless, four of the six participants did get at least a single successful description of a picture in the message-passing task, which confirms their authorship since the pictures in this task were all unknown to the facilitators.

TABLE 4.4 Summary of Participants' Individual Performance Across Tasks

Ss	Matching	Labeling	Message Passing
P1	2 of 7 (29%)	4 of 10 (40%)	1 of 1 (100%)
P2	11 of 26 (42%)	5 of 16 (31%)	1 of 1 (100%)
P3	19 of 30 (63%)	6 of 28 (21%)	0 of 3 (0%)
P4	9 of 20 (45%)	3 of 10 (30%)	2 of 4 (50%)
P5	29 of 30 (97%)	3 of 13 (23%)	5 of 5 (100%)
P6	37 of 40 (93%)	11 of 37 (30%)	0 of 4 (0%)
TOTAL	107 of 153 (70%)	32 of 114 (28%)	9 of 18 (50%)
SD	28	7	49
Chance of a correct response	25%	25%	0%
% > chance	45%	3%	49%

DISCUSSION

The aim of the present study was to examine factors that may affect a participant's performance during validation tasks and possibly to offer a reason or solution to the conflicting reports in the literature. The results of this study not only identified the stimulus materials and validation tasks as factors affecting performance but also highlighted areas rarely addressed by other researchers. These included the types of tasks required for validation, the amount of time provided to the participants to attempt a response, participants' behavior in the validation tasks, and the effect of using "yes/no" clarification requests with participants.

Validation Tasks

The results of this study indicated that the type of tasks used affected the participants' performance scores. It was originally anticipated that the tasks would be hierarchical in terms of increasing difficulty, with matching the easiest of the tasks, labeling the second easiest, and message passing the most difficult. It was hypothesized that the participants' scores would reflect the order of difficulty of the tasks. The results indicated that as a group the participants performed best in the matching task, as predicted; however, this was then followed by the message-passing task and then the labeling task. The exact reasons for the participants' unexpected better performance in the message-passing task over labeling are unclear. However, reports from the facilitators may offer some suggestions. They reported a higher degree of anxiety in the matching and labeling tasks than in the message-passing task, due to the testing for facilitator influence in the matching and labeling tasks. Subsequently, the facilitators commented that their "style" of facilitation with the participants altered. That is, due to the nature of the testing environment, the facilitators reported that they made the participants work "harder" in the matching and the labeling tasks than the message-passing task. The facilitators made the participants work "harder" by pulling the participants' hand farther away from their communication device after each response and providing a higher degree of resistance against the participants' movements toward their communication device. The facilitators reported that making the participants work harder to complete a response lessened possible fears that they might influence the participants' responses. Therefore the design and aims of the tasks used affected facilitators' facilitation style and may have affected the participants' performances.

The choice of four alternative pictures in the labeling task was also identified by the facilitators as a factor that may have affected the participants' performances. The choice of four alternatives was originally implemented and accepted by the facilitators to eliminate the possibility of participants' experiencing word-finding problems. However, due to the participants' behaviors in the sessions, facilitators were concerned that the four alternatives might have been distracting for some participants and that the participants may have experienced difficulties screening out irrelevant information. For example, P6's facilitator felt that P6's responses reflected the last alternative read out from the choice of four. Therefore, if the alternatives were "hamburger," "jelly," "ice cream," and "donut," P6 would type DONUT regardless of the picture presented to him. P6 was observed to communicate via facilitated communication the last alternative read aloud to him on four consecutive occasions. P5's facilitator reported that the alternative pictures may have been too distracting for him, as demonstrated by his spoken productions. For example, on one occasion the alternatives "horse," "doll," "truck," and "apple" were read out aloud. P5 responded verbally with "horse, horses" and communicated via facilitation the word HORSE. P5 was asked by his facilitator if he could see a picture of a horse. P5 immediately responded verbally with "no, a truck." The correct response was "truck." On a separate occasion P5 was presented with a picture of a mouse. The four alternative pictures were a mouse, a cat, a dog, and a bird. P5 via facilitated communication spelled the word CAT and after completing the last letter in "cat" P5 said "it's a mouse." Therefore, the plate of four alternatives originally provided to assist the participants may have also negatively affected their performances.

Validation Criteria

If a participant does not satisfy the validation criteria set, what conclusion will be drawn? For example, previous researchers have used the results of their validation studies to conclude that their participants were unable to communicate via facilitation (Wheeler, Jacobson, Paglieri, & Schwartz, 1993). The results of the present study, however, have highlighted that researchers should make conclusive statements only regarding the participants' abilities to perform the tasks set. For example, P3 in this study scored 63% for the matching task and 21% for the labeling task. P3 scored 0 out of 3 for the message-passing task. Therefore P3's responses in the message-passing task via facilitation did not satisfy the validation criteria set by this study. However, P3 has been reported to type independently (without a facilitator) and recently has been suspended from school for independently typing obscenities on his communication device. Prior to being introduced to facilitated communication training, he was not allowed to attend school because he was regarded as intellectually disabled and unable to participate in academic activities.

Time to Respond

No set time frame for the completion of a response or a task was enforced in this study. However, it became apparent that the time taken to produce a response was affected by the tasks. That is, as the demands of the tasks increased, the participants required more time to respond.

Initially participants were expected to complete a total of 85 responses, a total chosen to provide ample opportunities to establish the validity of the participants' communications via facilitation. During the data collection phase of the study it became evident that the set target of 85 responses was an unrealistic and possibly unfair goal. The set number of tasks was unrealistic due to the time constraints placed on the study. However, the message-passing task would seem to solve this problem, as the facilitator was completely unaware of the intended response; therefore one correct response would demonstrate the participants' ability to communicate via facilitation. The need to complete further validation tasks, therefore, would not be necessary if one is only trying to determine if facilitated communication works for a specific individual.

The time provided for participants to respond in previous validation research has not been clearly stated; however, from this study it was clear that the allowed response time may affect a participant's performance scores. For example, P1 on one occasion required 30 minutes to successfully complete one message-passing task. If this time frame had not been permitted, P1's ability to communicate via facilitation may have been questioned. It was also evident from the study that individuals performed at different speeds and needed to be judged on an individual basis.

SUMMARY AND CONCLUSIONS

Factors that affect participants' performances were identified, and these factors may help explain discrepant reports of success in so-called validation studies of facilitated communication. One of the key factors identified in this study as affecting performances was the tasks used. Not all of the participants validated their communications in all three of the tasks. Therefore previous studies that have only assessed participants' communicative skills using a single task may not have gained a representative sample of the participants' abilities.

Further research is needed to explore the parameters of the factors identified in this investigation and to develop procedures and protocol conditions that could be used as a checklist for researchers who develop future validation studies.

CHAPTER 5

A Controlled Study of Facilitated Communication Using Computer Games

Marjorie Olney

The purpose of the study was to determine whether facilitated communication users could provide information that was unknown to the facilitator given optimal accommodations, thus demonstrating that they are the authors of their communication. The research protocol drew on conditions that have seemed to support the production of successful communication by facilitated communication users in both naturalistic and experimental studies, as well as during the pilot study. The conditions were:

1. Participation in typical environments (Biklen, 1990; Cardinal & Hanson, 1994a; IDRP, 1989; Ogletree, Hamtil, Solberg & Scoby-Schmelzle, 1993)
2. Support by skilled and familiar facilitators (Biklen, Saha, & Kliewer, 1995; Sabin & Donnellan, 1993)
3. Opportunities for considerable practice (Cardinal, Hanson, & Wakeham, 1996)
4. Feedback concerning correct and incorrect responses (Sheehan, 1993)
5. Interesting, age-appropriate activities (Vazquez, 1994)
6. Opportunities for self-correction (Sheehan, 1993)
7. Individualized teaching strategies (Biklen & Schubert, 1991)
8. Visual display of response choice (Calculator & Singer, 1992)
9. A collaborative approach (Majure, 1994; McSheehan & Sonnenmeier, 1993; Olney, 1995)

This study included both open trials—trials in which facilitators had access to the stimuli presented on the computer screen—and blind trials. Because the intention was to disturb the natural facilitation as little as possible, a facilitator-blind condition was created individually for each participant depending on individual support needs and facilitation style. No artificial screens or barriers were used. Instead, the natural environment was manipulated to prevent facilitators from seeing the computer screen. This was done by turning the computer screen away from the facilitator, changing seating slightly, and identifying visual targets for facilitators. Facilitators were able to see the computer keyboard during blind trials. One facilitator chose at times not to look at the keyboard.

Sessions were process- rather than product-oriented. Learning how to respond to game items in the blind condition was presented as a goal, not an expectation. It was explained to participants that playing in the blind condition had two purposes: (1) To try to understand what happens when the facilitator cannot see the screen, and (2) to help participants learn how to provide messages in the absence of facilitator knowledge.

The adequacy of the blind condition was checked by the researcher during each session. In addition, the researcher visually monitored the facilitator and viewed each videotaped session twice to assure the integrity of the blind condition. Finally, an independent observer viewed over 200 items from randomly selected segments of videotape. This sample constituted approximately 9% of the total data items collected in the study. The independent judge viewed and scored the tapes in order to determine whether the item was open or blind and to rate responses as correct or incorrect. There was 100% agreement between the researcher and the independent judge in the rating of open and blind trials and 99% agreement on correct versus incorrect responses.

In addition to the nine protocol conditions listed above, two variables were crucial to the study: educational computer games that were perceived to be motivating and a teaching technique that involves the "scaffolding" of information by the facilitator.

Educational computer games were used that were adult-oriented, contained graduated difficulty levels, and examined a variety of academic skills (e.g., arithmetic, spelling, and reading comprehension). Games were selected that were not timed, had simple graphics, and had minimal sound.

Eleven computer games, all of which have been recommended by the software makers for teens and adults, were introduced during the study:

1. *Jeopardy Junior* (GameTek, 1989)
2. *Spell It Plus*, Decode It (Davidson & Co., 1989)
3. *Spell It Plus*, Unscramble It (Davidson & Co., 1989)

4. *Spell It Plus*, Correct It (Davidson & Co., 1989)
5. *Spell It 3*, Leap Frog Log Game (Davidson & Co., 1994)
6. *Math Blaster Mystery*, Follow the Steps (Davidson & Co., 1989)
7. *Math Blaster Mystery*, Search for Clues (Davidson & Co., 1989)
8. *Word Attack Plus*, Multiple Choice Quiz (Davidson & Co., 1988)
9. *Magic Spells*, Flash Spells (Quickbasic, 1985–86)
10. *Magic Spells*, Scramble Spells (Quickbasic, 1985–86)
11. *Mutant Math Challenge* (Legacy Software, 1991)

The computer games had three different response formats: (1) multiple-choice, (2) single-letter or -number, and (3) single-word response.

The scaffolding technique consisted of controlling some elements of a task to maximize learning. The concept was first developed by Vygotsky (Bruner, 1984) and subsequently used in works by Bruner and colleagues (Wood, Bruner, & Ross, 1976) and Duchan (1987; Duchan & Lund, 1983). Scaffolding permitted learners to concentrate on the elements that were within their range of competence and thus complete the activity successfully. Similar teaching techniques have been used successfully in teaching adults with developmental disabilities to complete a variety of complex tasks (Gold, 1980; McLoughlin, Garner, & Callahan, 1987).

The scaffolding intervention is described by Wood and colleagues (1976) in the following manner:

(1) *Recruitment*. Enticed participants into the action of the games and secured adherence to the rules.
(2) *Reduction in degrees of freedom*. Reduced the number of constituent acts involved in responding to game items by eliminating extraneous stimuli and actions.
(3) *Direction maintenance*. Kept participant engaged by (a) encouraging focus on task completion and (b) demonstrating enthusiasm and empathy.
(4) *Interpretation of discrepancies*. Pointed out critical features of each game.
(5) *Frustration control*. Confirmed correct choices.
(6) *Demonstration*. Modeled successful responses to items.

Scaffolding interventions were not used to teach facilitated communication techniques. Instead, they were designed to enable participants to learn various computer games and to help maintain their motivation for playing the games.

METHOD

During a nine-month period one adolescent and eight adults who use facilitated communication along with their regular facilitators met with the researcher for a total of 83 individual hour-long sessions ($M = 9.22, SD = 1.03$).

Each session began with an informal discussion. This was followed by a warm-up session during which the facilitator and participant played the computer games collaboratively, reviewing the sequence of actions and the performance demands of each game (e.g., selecting difficulty levels and determining when to use the enter key or space bar). Finally, playing in the blind condition was suggested.

The researcher observed participants carefully and provided encouragement, support, and assistance during all trials. The following behavioral indicators were used to initiate blind trials: (1) successful responses in the open condition; (2) nonverbal manifestations of emotional and physical comfort, including a relaxed facial expression and body posture, and (3) when indicated, asking the participants if they were ready to play in the facilitator-blind condition.

Nonverbal indicators were also used to determine when to discontinue blind trials: (1) five or more consecutive errors in the blind condition *in combination with* (2) increased facial or muscular tension and/or (3) observed breakdown of necessary motor and sequencing responses.

Participants, Facilitators, and Settings

Participants were sought in a three-county region of upstate New York. The three women and six men included in the study were selected based on preset criteria. All nine had (1) communicated at a conversational level with at least two facilitators, (2) produced sentence-level messages on at least a weekly basis, (3) used the method a minimum of 18 months at the onset of the study, and (4) expressed an interest in participating in an experimental validation study.

In order to protect the rights of participants, informed consent was obtained from parents or guardians of participants as well as from the participants themselves (through facilitated and verbal communication). Participants were also asked to identify the facilitator they would like to have assist them in the study. The seven participants who were using multiple facilitators at the time of the study confirmed their choice with an independent facilitator. APA guidelines for ethical research and the university's human subjects committee recommendations were followed carefully to further ensure that study participants were fully protected.

The backgrounds, skills, and lifestyles of the nine participants differed notably. Four of the individuals resided with their families of origin, three in group homes, and two in family care homes. None lived independently. With the exception of two brothers who lived together with their parents, each participant resided in a different community. Participants received residential, case management, and day program services from five different provider agencies. Five participants took part in day treatment programs each day, two in supported employment, one in a sheltered workshop, and one in home school.

The participants ranged in age from 16 to 42 years, with a mean age of 28.5 years. Three of the participants were diagnosed with autism alone, one with autism and mental retardation, one with Down syndrome, two with mental retardation alone, one with cerebral palsy, and one with pervasive developmental disorder. Seven participants were supported with facilitation at the hand or wrist during the computer games while the other two were supported at the elbow, forearm, or upper arm.

Facilitators had a minimum of introductory training in the facilitated communication method (i.e., a 2-day workshop, or individual instruction by Facilitated Communication Institute personnel equivalent to the 2-day workshop) and a minimum of two years of experience providing facilitation. In addition, facilitators all demonstrated prescribed facilitation skills, such as monitoring eyes and seeking clarification (Biklen & Schubert, 1991; DEAL, 1992). All facilitators were female and Caucasian. They ranged from 25 to 60 years in age.

Controlled computer game sessions took place in settings that were convenient for participants and facilitators, including participants' homes, agency offices, and community program sites. The settings remained consistent for each individual throughout the study. Settings were selected that allowed for user–facilitator proximity, control of external interference (such as noise and distractions), and good lighting and climate control.

Procedure

In each session, the researcher sat to the left and slightly behind the participant. In the case of the left-handed participant, the researcher sat to the right and slightly behind the participant. The seating arrangement put the researcher in full visual contact with the computer screen, participant, and facilitator while controlling for inadvertent cuing by the researcher.

Participants were informed that they could use their hour in any way they wished, that they were not obligated to play but could do so when and if they chose. They were given a choice of two or more games at the beginning of each session.

Materials

Five participants engaged in computer game activities using a standard personal computer, three used laptop computers, and one participant used a Canon Communicator.

Of 83 total sessions, 62 (75%) were videotaped. One individual who chose not to be videotaped was audiotaped instead. In this case the researcher visually monitored the facilitator throughout all 10 sessions to assure that the blind condition was not contaminated. During the remaining 11 sessions computer games were not played.

Scoring

A one-sample chi-square test was used to evaluate all blind and open trials with 10 or more items. This goodness-of-fit test was used to determine if there was a statistically significant difference between number of correct responses and the number expected based on chance alone. Trials with fewer than 10 responses were not analyzed or considered validation regardless of score.

Scoring Decision Modes

Two different decision modes were employed during the course of the study. Initially, only first responses to single-entry items were considered valid responses. Preliminary analysis revealed that two of the nine subjects seemed to consistently provide the correct response on their second attempt.

Data were collected between March and November 1994. A decision to evaluate first and second trials was made in late August 1994. Therefore, data collected prior to September were analyzed based on the first response only. Data collected in September, October, and November were analyzed based on first and second responses. All posttest data were analyzed based on first response only.

Decision Mode 1. Single-letter, -number, or -operand responses were scored as correct when the proper answer was chosen on the first attempt. For full-word responses, participants were asked to type their response a second time if the first word was incorrect or unclear.

Decision Mode 2. Single-letter, -number, or -operand responses were scored as correct when the proper response was chosen on the first *or* second attempts. For full-word responses, participants again were asked to type their response a second time if the first was incorrect or unclear. All data presented in these three cases were analyzed based on the decision mode 1—one chance only—with the exception of final sessions with Andrew.

RESULTS

A posttest, 10 items from *Word Attack Plus* completed without facilitation, was given to validators. This was done in order to ascertain whether the ability of the five participants to perform on this task could be attributed to facilitated communication or whether the participants were able to (or had learned to) perform at criterion levels.

A comparative analysis was performed. In this test, the blind-facilitated scores of these five participants were compared to their unfacilitated scores. The mean percent correct in the blind condition for the five participants was 51% (50 of 98) as compared to only 26% (13 of 50) in the unfacilitated condition. It was determined that there was a significant difference between these scores ($X^2 = 49.95$, $df = 1$, $p < .05$), indicating that the participants performed significantly better with than without facilitation.

The postbaseline rather than prebaseline method was used for two reasons. First, the posttest allowed the researcher to control for incidental or developmental learning that might have occurred during the study. Second, a prebaseline method might have unfairly influenced the participants and created an atmosphere of failure. This would have been antithetical to the goal of the study: to provide a motivating, failure-free situation in which to attempt validation.

Five of nine participants achieved scores on computer games in the facilitator-blind condition that were greater than would be expected by chance, thus allowing rejection of the null hypothesis. Three validated on *Word Attack Plus*, Multiple-Choice Quiz alone. One participant validated on both *Word Attack Plus* and *Spell it Plus*, Decode It. Another validated using *Word Attack Plus* and *Math Blaster Mystery*, Follow the Steps. See Table 5.1 for group data.

CASE STUDIES

The three case studies that follow provide information on participant backgrounds and performance. Statistical and descriptive analyses are combined in order to give the reader an in-depth view of both the processes

TABLE 5.1 Validation Data—Group

Case	Name	Word Attack Plus	Math Blaster Mystery	Spell It Plus
1	Nick	$* X^2 = 5.94, df = 1$	$* X^2 = 8.76, df = 1$	&
2	Deb	$* X^2 = 13.56, df = 1$ $* X^2 = 8.33, df = 1$	&	&
3	Gary	$* X^2 = 10.00, df = 1$ $* X^2 = 10.80, df = 1$	&	&
4	Andrew	$* X^2 = 7.71, df = 1$	(–)	$*X^2 = 69.66, df = 1$
5	Bart	$* X^2 = 4.41, df = 1$ $* X^2 = 4.41, df = 1$	&	&
6	Jerry	&	&	&
7	Pat	&	&	&
8	Warren	n.s.	(–)	&
9	Millie	&	&	&

$*X^2$ was significant, $p < .05$.   & = Insufficient blind trials for X^2 analysis.
n.s.=Scores do not meet validation criteria. (–) = Did not play game.

and the outcomes of the study. These cases were selected for the following reasons: (1) Each participant validated his or her communication by performing at criteria in a facilitator-blind condition. (2) The labels, backgrounds, living situations, and functional and communication skills of the three participants vary considerably from one to the other. (3) None of the three passed the posttest. (4) Each of the three was videotaped. (5) The performance of the three provided examples that illustrated the outcomes of the study, including the importance of scaffolding, interplay between communication modalities, problems with movement, and independent typing. (6) The three validated on different games.

Each case study is organized as follows: participant background (including history and general assessment information); a communication profile describing modalities, interventions, assessments, and current functioning; performance on educational computer games in both open and blind conditions; and performance on the posttest.

Case 1: Nick

Nick is 31 years old and lives at home with his brother and parents. His birth and early development appeared normal until the age of 1½, when he started to exhibit steady regression. At age 4 Nick was diagnosed with autism and mental retardation. He attended a segregated school for emotionally disturbed children from the ages of 5 to 15. For the six years that followed, Nick attended a segregated public school for students with developmental disabilities.

Over the past decade, Nick has received an array of services through a day treatment program: speech therapy (including facilitated communication training), behavioral and functional skills training, and prevocational training. At the time of the study Nick was engaged in volunteer work in the community as an adjunct to prevocational training.

During a psychological examination dated 1991 Nick obtained a performance age of 2 years, 11 months on the Slosson intelligence test. This score corresponds to an IQ of less than 20, placing him in the profound range of mental retardation. Nick's adaptive functioning (Vineland Adaptive Behavior Scale) was rated below average in comparison to a norm group of adults with developmental disabilities.

Observation, discussion with family members and clinicians, and review of his records all confirm that Nick requires multiple physical and verbal prompts to initiate activities and follow through on them. Nick seems to watch for movement cues and to mimic the motions and facial expressions of those around him. He speaks in a barely audible voice, and then *only when prompted to speak*.

Nick's father stated that with the initiation of facilitated communication professionals and staff seem to have changed their attitude toward Nick, attributing greater competence to him. This, his father said, resulted in improved behavior and performance at the program site.

Communication. Nick began using facilitated communication in 1991. He has increased his independent typing and now requires only a touch on the elbow to type with most facilitators and either shoulder support or no touch with his speech therapist during conversation.

Performance On Games. Nick's facilitator and the researcher met with Nick nine times during a seven-month period. Data collection ceased for four months due to an injury sustained by the facilitator.

During the study Nick's facilitator varied the level of physical support by grasping the fabric of his shirt below the elbow, touching his shoulder, or grasping the top of Nick's forearm or the back of his elbow. The computer monitor was positioned to the right of Nick and angled toward him. The facilitator supported Nick's right arm or shoulder with her right hand. She sat facing his right side.

A facilitator-blind condition was created by positioning the computer monitor to the right of Nick and behind the facilitator. The researcher verified the blind condition during each session, confirming that the computer screen was not visible to the facilitator either directly or peripherally. In order to view the computer screen, the facilitator had to lean to her left and turn her head 90 degrees, a change in posture that was easily detected while viewing videotapes.

Nick engaged in the following games: *Spell It Plus*, Correct It and Decode It; *Math Blaster Mystery*, Follow the Steps; *Word Attack Plus*, Multiple Choice Quiz; and *Magic Spells*, Flash Spells and Scramble Spells.

The *Spell It Plus*, Correct It game presents misspelled words embedded in text (e.g., "It was his *beleif* that he would win the election"). Nick corrected 6/7 (.86) misspelled words in the open condition and 3/5 (.60) in the blind condition.

Because Nick's father suggested that Nick liked math, *Math Blaster Mystery*, Follow the Steps was introduced. In this game the player selects the letter corresponding to the correct response (e.g., "Larry has been collecting baseball cards for two years. His favorite team is the Cubs. Out of 145 cards, 38 are players from the Cubs. How many does he have of players from the other 25 major teams? What does the problem ask?").

Nick performed better in the blind condition than in the open condition on this game, responding correctly to 1/5 (.20) items in the open condition and 7/11 (.64) blind items. This latter score is significant at the .05 level ($X^2 = 8.76$, $df = 1$). In spite of the fact that Nick seemed to have some skill solving math problems, he did not seem to enjoy the activity. When we finished playing *Math Blaster Mystery* Nick typed, I DIDNT LIKE DOING THAT. IM NOT SMART ENOUGH TO DO THAT. DONT ASK ME TO PLAY THAT GAME AGAIN. OK?

Nick played *Word Attack Plus*, Multiple Choice Quiz three times. In the open condition Nick achieved scores of 25/27 (.93), 13/15 (.87), 9/11 (.82), and 11/12 (.92). Corresponding chi-square values—$X^2 = 65.79$, $df = 1$; $X^2 = 30.43$, $df = 1$; $X^2 = 24.64$, $df = 1$; and $X^2 = 29.44$, $df = 1$—were significant at the .05 level. Correct responses in the blind trial, 18/44 (.41), were also significant ($X^2 = 5.94$, $df = 1$, $p < .05$).

While playing *Magic Spells*, Jester's Jumble, Nick successfully unscrambled 2/4 (.50) words in the blind condition, producing YELL from LELY and ROOM from MOOR. These instances were not considered in evaluation of validation but provide further evidence of reading ability.

Nick's performance was generally superior when his facilitator had access to game stimuli than it was in the blind condition. One exception was Nick's performance on the *Math Blaster Mystery*, Word Problem, in which he did more poorly in the open condition.

Notably, Nick required continual verbal, gestural, and physical prompts to look at the computer screen, then down at the keyboard, before commencing to type. Problems with looking and sequencing were exaggerated in the blind condition; Nick often closed his eyes rather than look at the screen. Teaching interventions included gently turning his head in the direction of the computer screen in order to read the game items, prompting him to open his eyes, pointing to the screen, and then reminding him to look back at the keyboard before responding.

Posttest. Nick played *Word Attack Plus*, first in the open condition with facilitation, then without facilitation. In the absence of facilitation Nick got only 3/10 (.30) items correct, although he had periodically demonstrated independent typing at other times during the study. Although all game responses must be A, B, C, or D, he pressed many letters, sometimes pressing all of the letters surrounding the correct response, other times pressing letters, numbers, and other keys in other areas of the keyboard.

It was apparent that the posttest was stressful for Nick. He looked at his facilitator frequently, made a moaning noise, and closed his eyes frequently. The researcher and facilitator encouraged and reassured him throughout. The facilitator also "reset" Nick's arm on several occasions by pulling it back and positioning it about six inches above the center of the keyboard.

Case 2: Deb

Deb is 25 years old, has Down syndrome, and lives in a community residence. She received special education within an integrated public school system. Deb's schooling consisted of some inclusive classes but was primarily a functional, community-based program with a strong vocational focus. She transitioned directly from high school to a supported work job at age 21.

Tests of Deb's intelligence place her in the severe range of mental retardation. A psychologist used the term "profound deficit" to describe Deb's adaptive skills. In spite of these labels, she has held a series of part-time stocking jobs with support; communicates adequately through a combination of oral, nonverbal, and facilitated communication; and participates in self-care, community, and domestic activities with partial assistance.

Communication. Testing with the Test of Language Development—Primary (TOLD-P) yielded an oral vocabulary age-equivalent of 4-0. This is consistent with scores obtained two years earlier on the Peabody Picture Vocabulary Test, which gave Deb an overall age-equivalent of 4-5.

Although Deb communicates vocally, she is echolalic, perseverates on phrases, and produces many utterances that are not contextual during conversations. Deb's verbal communication has been considered unreliable by most clinicians.

In 1991 Deb was introduced to facilitated communication by vocational professionals associated with her supported employment program. She began by pointing to pictures on request, spelling her name from a model, and completing yes/no and multiple-choice items. Deb developed a preference for one facilitator and began producing sentences and paragraphs with her within two weeks of the initiation of facilitated communication.

Deb was administered the Boston Diagnostic Aphasia Exam without facilitation. She was able to identify 9/10 symbols and words. However, she did not demonstrate recognition of word meaning or comprehension of oral spelling. The clinician noted that when asked for her response on these items, she consistently pointed to the last item in an array. A sample of Deb's oral communication in the assessment included appropriate responses to questions, use of four morphemes in a sentence ("Jennifer lives somewhere"), and labeling of common objects including "dog" and "computer."

Deb's nonverbal communication is useful for clarifying sometimes contradictory oral and facilitated messages and for confirming her understanding of and interest in various topics and activities. She tends to become angry and resistant in response to unexpected changes, misunderstandings, and loud noises. She also exhibits positive affect—smiling, eye contact, and a relaxed demeanor—when her needs have been understood.

Performance On Games. Deb, her facilitator, and the researcher met nine times to play computer games over a period of four months. She played four different games: *Jeopardy Junior; Word Attack Plus*, Multiple Choice Quiz; *Spell It 3*, Leap Frog Log Game; and *Spell It Plus*, Decode It. Deb exhibited a clear preference for *Word Attack Plus* and requested that game seven times. The other three games were played either once or twice each.

A facilitator-blind condition was created by turning the computer monitor so that the facilitator could not see the screen. The sufficiency of the blind condition was verified by the researcher during each session and monitored during the session and during two viewings of the videotaped sessions.

Deb played *Word Attack Plus*, Multiple Choice Quiz in both open and blind conditions. Her performance on open trials was as follows: 14/17

(.82), 13/16 (.81), 16/21 (.76), 11/13 (.85), 9/12 (.75), 20/24 (.83), and 18/19 (.95). These correspond to chi-square values of $X^2 = 39.67$, $df = 1$; $X^2 = 27.00$, $df = 1$; $X^2 = 29.35$, $df = 1$; $X^2 = 24.64$, $df = 1$; $X^2 = 16.00$, $df = 1$; $X^2 = 43.56$, $df = 1$; and $X^2 = 49.28$, $df = 1$; $p < .05$, respectively.

Playing *Word Attack Plus* in the blind condition, Deb obtained the following scores on trials with 10 or more items: 9/13 (.69) and 9/16 (.56). Both scores are significant; $X^2 = 13.56$, $df = 1$, $p < .05$, and $X^2 = 8.33$, $df = 1$, $p < .05$. Validation occurred in the third and fifth sessions.

In support of the validity of her facilitated communication, Deb verbally read from the computer screen, pointed to the correct responses on the screen, indicated correct responses by verbalizing words or corresponding letters, and made word associations. These instances are discussed further in the discussion section that follows.

In the blind condition, Deb exhibited increasing muscular and facial tension. Although she began blind trials with enthusiasm, her ability to sequence her eye and hand movements gradually deteriorated and her error rate increased.

Posttest. On the posttest, Deb responded correctly to 1/10 (.10) *Word Attack Plus* items without facilitation. Each time physical support was withdrawn, Deb folded her hands in her lap, either unable or unwilling to type without facilitation. The facilitator and researcher attempted a number of strategies to get her to type her answers independently, including fading physical support to the elbow and then releasing her arm, providing modeling, and encouraging her verbally. Although Deb did not type independently, she was successful in responding accurately to game items with elbow support only, a new level of independence.

Case 3: Andrew

Andrew is a 42-year-old man who has the label of profound mental retardation. He was institutionalized at a state school in downstate New York for individuals with mental retardation when he was 6 years old. He lived there until 1989, when he was admitted to another developmental center. In 1992 Andrew moved from the institution to a family care home. There is no evidence in Andrew's record that he had any formal or informal educational opportunities before leaving home, while in institutional care, or after moving to his current home.

In recent reports psychologists and speech pathologists have described Andrew's functioning as characteristic of the late sensorimotor–early preoperational level of development (i.e., severely to profoundly retarded). According to his record, Andrew needs prompting to initiate all activities.

Andrew attends a day treatment center each day, where he completes prevocational tasks, such as sorting and matching objects, and participates in activities of daily living. Various therapies—including occupational, physical, recreational, and speech—are available to Andrew at his day treatment site. It was at this program that Andrew was introduced to facilitated communication in 1992 by two speech therapists.

Communication. Andrew speaks, when prompted, to label some objects and to say "please" or "thank you." Specific language skills were identified in a 1989 speech assessment as: following one- and two-step directions, sorting by color and shape, prelinguistic skills such as matching, and demonstration of understanding of basic concepts such as object permanence. All written reports confirm Andrew's ability to respond to his name and to tone of voice. It was also both reported and observed that although Andrew does not initiate interactions, he reaches for desired objects or withdraws to reject an activity or object. Reportedly, very soon after Andrew was introduced to facilitated communication he began to produce full-sentence utterances with multiple facilitators. Within the first few sessions he asked to attend synagogue and asked to visit an old friend whom he identified by name.

The family care provider and day program staff indicated that Andrew's ability to speak and to follow directions seemed to have improved since he began using facilitated communication. According to program staff, he has begun to verbalize short sentences both at home and at work, and to complete multiple-step tasks with a verbal request such as "turn off the light, then go wash your face."

Andrew usually demonstrates flat affect; that is, he does not readily smile, frown, or exhibit other facial responses, although he occasionally smiles in response to being in the company of someone he likes. During the study, on the rare occasions that Andrew spoke, his utterances were low, monosyllabic, and produced in response to a prompt.

During the course of the study, when not involved in game playing or facilitated communication, Andrew paced around the room or sat in a chair moaning with his hands covering his face and his legs against his chest. He frequently put inedibles such as pieces of string in his mouth and required several verbal prompts and sometimes physical assistance to sit down and begin activities.

Performance On Games. Andrew, his facilitator, and the researcher engaged in a total of seven sessions over a period of two months. During the study Andrew used a laptop computer. The facilitator supported him by sitting to his left and grasping his left middle, ring, and little fingers in her right hand. Andrew's facilitator reported that she provided moderate backward pressure. Unlike most facilitators, Andrew's did not generally look at the keys as Andrew typed. She did, however, monitor the display during open conversation. Unless asked to do otherwise, the facilitator watched Andrew's face as he typed responses to game items.

A blind condition was created by identifying Andrew's left ear as the facilitator's visual target. This was very similar to typical facilitation in this case. To assure that the blind condition was not contaminated, the screen of the laptop computer was oriented at a 100-degree angle to the table, making the screen invisible to the facilitator. The blind condition was confirmed by the researcher during each session, monitored throughout the sessions, and again evaluated during two viewings of the videotape to assure that the blind condition was not compromised.

Andrew engaged in *Word Attack Plus*, Multiple-Choice Quiz during five sessions and *Spell It Plus*, Decode It during two sessions. Using *Word Attack Plus* in the open condition Andrew achieved a score of 17/23 (.74). This score was significantly greater than chance ($X^2 = 29.35$, $df = 1$, $p < .05$). In the blind condition Andrew's score was also significant: 8/14 (.57); $X^2 = 7.71$, $df = 1$, $p < .05$.

For data collected after August 31, 1995, decision mode 2 was used; the first two attempts were considered. Using *Spell It Plus*, Decode It Andrew validated his communication by adding the correct letter to complete words during a blind trial, achieving a score of 18/34 (.53); $X^2 = 69.66$, $df = 1$, $p < .05$). This chi-square analysis is based on a 2 in 26 chance level. It is noteworthy that Andrew achieved a score of 14/36 (.39) on the same game before August 31, 1995. This would have also yielded a significant chi-square value under decision mode 2.

Andrew demonstrated his communicative competence using both *Word Attack Plus* and *Spell It Plus* games, selecting single-letter responses at validation criteria levels in the blind condition in two of three games with 10 or more items. Strong evidence of validation was a surprise because Andrew was more physically dependent on facilitation than other participants, had fewer verbal skills than others who validated, and had not had formal or incidental exposure to academic work (as might occur in an integrated school environment).

Unlike Nick and Deb, Andrew exhibited little anxiety while playing in the blind condition. Perhaps this is because his facilitator did not generally look at the display during conversational facilitated communication.

Posttest. Andrew was unable to respond to any items on *Word Attack Plus* during the posttest. In the absence of facilitation he placed his full left hand over the left side of the keyboard and moved his fingers in a massaging motion. This motion in the area of the A, C, and D keys caused the computer to respond to three items. All were incorrect. When prompted to make selections, Andrew withdrew his hand and moved his fingers in front of his face. The facilitator then positioned his arm and directed his attention back to the stimulus word and choices. After five minutes of prompting, the game was completed in the blind condition with facilitation.

DISCUSSION

Nick, Deb, and Andrew, along with two other participants in this study, provided statistically significant evidence that their facilitated communication originated with them, not with their facilitators.

Practice appeared to be a critical variable in the validation of facilitated communication. None of the participants validated during their first attempt in the blind condition. In addition, the abilities of these participants were not immediately apparent. This finding is consistent both with studies that tested subjects once and found no evidence of valid communication (Moore, Donovan, & Hudson, 1993; Szempruch & Jacobson, 1993; Wheeler, Jacobson, Paglieri, & Schwartz, 1993) and with other time and/or task sampling studies with more positive outcomes (Cardinal & Hanson, 1994a; IDRP, 1989; Vazquez, 1993).

These data reveal a number of significant outcomes. Most important and widespread among them appear to be (1) impact of the scaffolding interventions on study outcomes, (2) universal problems with movement and sequencing, and (3) the phenomenon of independent typing as distinct from validation. Each of these outcomes is discussed below, with supporting evidence and examples.

Impact of Scaffolding Interventions on Outcomes

Performance on computer games by experienced facilitated communication users varied dramatically among participants, from session to session, and in open and blind conditions. Simple response formats (choosing A, B, C, or D, or adding a missing letter) and opportunities for multiple trials seemed to increase the likelihood of validation for participants. Scaffolding interventions were used to assess and/or ameliorate five specific issues: (1) test anxiety, (2) fatigue and other stressors, (3) interest in and knowledge of game content, (4) physical support needs, and (5) perceived relationships among the researcher, facilitator, and participant.

Test Anxiety. In eight of the nine participants test anxiety was apparent. Signs of increased tension included gradual deterioration of performance in blind trials, muscular tension, negative affect, requests to stop or take breaks, and increased vocalizations.

The majority of scaffolding interventions were done in response to participants' needs for emotional support. The researcher and facilitators encouraged and praised players, minimizing the importance of errors and helping people to maintain enthusiasm.

Fatigue and Other Stressors. Among the other factors influencing variable performance seemed to be fatigue. Although six participants did better after a short period of play, three performed with greater accuracy at the very start of their sessions. The performance of all nine participants diminished in the blind condition as the hour came to a close. The effect of fatigue may exacerbate motor difficulties such as locating visual targets, shifting focus, and pointing accurately.

Six participants seemed to need to discuss personal concerns before they could fully attend to playing the computer games. One participant became agitated easily and consequently required frequent breaks. Another's affect and muscle tone changed together from highly focused with high tone, to inattention and extremely low tone. It was difficult to determine whether sudden decreases in tone made her appear uninterested, or if her lack of interest caused a decrease in tone.

Degree of Interest in, or Knowledge of, Game Content. Game choice and performance seemed to be affected by participants' degree of interest in or knowledge of the content. Four participants chose to play primarily *Word Attack Plus*. One wanted a variety of math games, and another did not seem to like any of the games very well.

Physical Support. Five participants, two of whom validated, seemed to benefit from changes in physical support by the facilitator. One facilitator asked participants where they wanted to be supported. One participant used facilitated communication to request specific adjustments in support, such as pulling his arm back further. Another required constant adjustments in physical support due to her fluctuating muscle tone. Discovering and accommodating individual support needs required time.

Perceived Relationships with the Researcher and Facilitator. The participant's relationship to the researcher and facilitator seemed to have a direct impact on individual performance. Participants seemed to care more about the relationships and interactions than the games themselves. One participant indicated through facilitated communication that he wanted scaffolding support from his facilitator instead of the researcher. Another participant had special, private words that she used only with her closest friends, which frequently needed clarification for others to understand (e.g., z meant Zuzzy, a nickname of one of the facilitators, and XRAY meant the facilitator understood the comment). Yet another participant resisted playing games, choosing instead to focus her full attention on interacting with her facilitator during her second through fourth sessions. Later she indicated through facilitated communication that she was unhappy with the researcher due to a perceived slight. After discussing the event in question, this participant's affect changed and she exhibited renewed enthusiasm for the games.

These five factors—test anxiety, fatigue and stress, interest, support needs, and perception of relationship—may provide insight into the subjective experience of participants in other controlled studies of facilitated communication.

Universal Problems with Movement

A major criticism of facilitated communication is that its users do not look at the target, making it appear that facilitators are controlling the typed output. Although participants in this study were partially selected because of their excellent facilitated communication skills, looking at the right target at the right time was problematic for each of them.

Analysis of videotapes revealed that all participants had difficulty moving their eyes and heads from the computer screen to the keyboard and back. This may have hampered participants' abilities to read items, think about them, and then respond accurately. It was hard to ascertain in what instances participants hit a response before reading, as opposed to hitting the wrong key because they did not know the answers.

Movement problems were most pronounced in the facilitator-blind condition and when fatigue or stress were manifest, but they were apparent to some degree throughout all sessions and in both open and blind conditions. Accommodations for participants included frequent verbal prompts to look at the monitor and keyboard, gestural prompts to the monitor, and physical prompts such as gently turning the head toward the visual target.

Independent Typing

Six of the nine participants demonstrated some independent communication by typing in their names without facilitation, reading and responding to instructions on the screen, typing a single letter to complete words without touch, or typing with dramatically decreased support such as a touch to the wrist, elbow, or shoulder.

Independence was not directly related to validation. Two people who required support at the wrist or hand and did very poorly on the posttest also validated their communication skills in the blind condition. Two others who did not validate increased their independence, one by typing responses independently and the other by typing with the lightest touch on her wrist.

One participant independently selected the letter corresponding to the correct word using *Word Attack Plus* when independent items were interspersed during blind and open trials, achieving a score of 8/8 (1.0). With *Spell It Plus* one participant added the missing letter to accurately complete 5/7 (.71) words without facilitation. Another completed *Spell It Plus* words 16/16 (1.0) times independently in one session.

The most striking progress toward independent typing was made by the participant who, by his final two sessions, was able to type his name, follow directions on the screen, complete words by adding a letter, and answer multiple-choice questions accurately without facilitation. In the last session the participant was asked if he preferred to go out to lunch or for coffee. He responded I LIKE TO with facilitation. He then continued to type independently GO TO LUNCH. Previously, when facilitation was withdrawn, this participant dropped his hand to his lap.

CONCLUSIONS

Facilitated communication appears to be a fragile phenomenon that presents considerable research challenges. Experienced facilitated communication users do provide accurate information in the absence of facilitator knowledge. At the same time, individuals appear to require multiple accommodations in order to achieve success.

This study provides a link between seemingly contradictory evaluations of facilitated communication. These outcomes would suggest that practice over time, a variety of tasks, and practical and emotional support are critical to successful validation in a blind study. If so, future studies that take these factors into account may very well result in replication of the findings reported here.

CHAPTER 6

Sorting It Out Under Fire: Our Journey

Eugene Marcus
Mayer Shevin

(*Note:* Sections of this chapter written by Mayer Shevin are printed in regular text type; the portions written by Eugene Marcus are set in this second typeface.)

In a piece I wrote in the *Facilitated Communication Digest* (Shevin, 1994), I spoke of the tendency of experimentally oriented critics of facilitated communication to act as if the experiments that they devise somehow represent the defining events, the "most real things" about the method. However, the everyday experiences of those people whose lives have been transformed by having their opportunities to communicate opened up represent a very different kind of reality from that which is studied in the validation experiments.

This chapter represents a coming together of those two realities for myself and for my friend and colleague, Eugene Marcus. It describes how he set a personal goal for himself of taking and passing the same test that was being used by critics of facilitation as the main tool for its dismissal. In the course of our three years of friendship and more than a year of collaboration on this project, we have both learned a great deal about the nature of facilitated communication and the contributions of the two partners engaged in the process. We have also learned a great deal about our friendship and our working partnership as research collaborators. Deciding which tiny slivers of that rich experience to set before you in this chapter represents a major challenge for the two of us. Eugene found there was information he wished to present that did not fit directly into the chapter's narrative. He decided to present some of that information as the appendix to this chapter.

All of the parts of this chapter set in sans serif type like this were written by Eugene, and I was the facilitator. After each paragraph was written, I helped him "spell-check" them on the computer. On the rare occasion where the meaning of a sentence was not clear to me, I would tell that to Eugene and ask him to rewrite the sentence; usually he would write something that clarified my concern. Occasionally, he would let me know that the wording as stated was *precisely* what he meant; in those cases, I would ask him to explain so I could understand it as well. Throughout, his particular style has been left intact.

One point should be highlighted from the start. From the outset, Eugene and I knew that we were *not* following typical protocols of experimental design and classical experimental research. Despite the letters "Ph.D." after my name, and despite my extensive experience with facilitated communication, I was not "the expert" in this project. Rather, my role was that of *facilitator* in the traditional sense of that word: someone who supports another person in accomplishing something. Rather than impose an a priori design on the project, Eugene and I strategized concerning our approach before, during, and after each session. No attempt was made on either of our parts to steer each other toward conventionally "scientific" language. We discussed what we were doing in those terms that best allowed us to understand how things looked and felt to ourselves and to each other. Although this is not traditional in research studies, our strategizing is presented here to more thoroughly show the course our work has taken.

Because this study represents Eugene's work in mastering one aspect of his communication, a brief description of his communication in general is in order here. Aside from facilitated communication, Eugene communicates with spoken words and gestures. Until fairly recently, Eugene's spoken language has tended to be repetitive single-word or two-word statements, often with little apparent connection to the physical situation or topics other people are discussing. Within the past two years, his speech has become much more "on target" but continues to be composed of one- or two-word statements. Without facilitated communication, Eugene tends to get more agitated and less clear in his speech as he tries to say something without being fully understood.

Since his early school days, Eugene has been able to type words independently. However, that typing has been largely made up of automatic statements. In other words, he has typically typed strings of real words with no apparent connection to one another or the topic at hand. In addition, he has for many years been able to copy printed words on the typewriter.

Several people assisted Eugene and me in our work. Most significant was Dr. Laural Sabin, who at the time we began our research was an assistant professor of special education at Syracuse University. From late 1993, when we tried our first replication of the O. D. Heck study (Wheeler, Jacobson, Paglieri, & Schwartz, 1993; we refer to it here and hereafter by the site where it was undertaken, the O. D. Heck Development Center) and our subsequent practice sessions, she was our "experimenter," setting up the trials and supporting our work as we thought through various approaches. By the time our work resumed in 1995, Laural had left the university, and Bob Felder, Eugene's job coach, assumed the responsibility of experimenter. In preparing for the second replication of the O. D. Heck study, Chris Kliewer obtained and reproduced the novel set of pictures we used. Eugene and I are grateful to these people, as well as to many others who have encouraged our work.

HOW WE GOT STARTED

The purpose of my becoming a researcher is worth an article in itself. I never thought of myself in those terms before last year.

Last year, because of my interest in facilitated communication, I began attending the research group at Syracuse University. In the meetings I attended, many people I know and respect came to listen and support each other in their work with people who use facilitated communication. How it seemed to me was: a group of sincere and dedicated and well-meaning blind men, talking about a well-beloved elephant. The missing piece for this well-deserving group was the piece that can only be supplied by me and my disabled sisters and brothers. That is, the long-term perspective coming from our lives of struggle, loss, triumph, and mostly from our gut-level experiential knowledge.

Most of my colleagues have had personal connections with facilitated communication users, some with their own children and others with friends or students. However, they limited their approach usually to observing people in real-life settings rather than trying to get them to pass tests in contrived situations; and although this is a great way to get to know people, it's not the best way to fight skepticism about facilitated communication. Speaking comes easily to most people, and so those of us who don't speak easily are not understood in two ways by those of you who do. First, you are maddeningly slow much of the time at knowing our most basic wants. We need to hope for a miracle if we are to get anything you didn't think of first. Nothing can be gotten by being loud or obnoxious (although I often wish that worked for me!). Nothing can be gotten by just waiting, either. So my nonspeaking siblings and I have become masters of creative problem solving.

The second way in which we are not understood is that you usually get only a glance at who we really are. You don't see our creative, passionate, spiritual, and laughing sides much. You *do* see our scared and confused sides, and that makes you scared and confused around us.

From when I was very young, I have known that I depended on my friends and family to give me a voice and a place in the world. Really, I have had an easy time of it, with parents who love me and who don't settle for second best. But even so, no nice and loving family can by themselves very easily overcome the effects of a very biased consensus.

Very bitterly, I watched new evidence mount about facilitated communication, evidence that I knew deep in my heart was very false and very meanspirited. But I was confident that the simple truth would be enough to overcome such gross misrepresentations of real people. Greater bitterness came for me when I watched the so-called documentary, "Prisoners of Silence."

Now I found myself faced with a difficult choice. On one hand, my understanding of what facilitated communication represents is very different from what was being said about it by both my severe critics and my close allies. (Yes, I mean *my* severe critics—it is impossible for me not to take attacks on facilitated communication extremely personally!) The truth about facilitated communication from my point of view takes a great deal of spiritual and emotional understanding to comprehend. But now I had to very quickly decide how to become a speaker about facilitated communication in terms that everyone could understand. Thinking about not only what facilitated communication is but how to explain it well is very difficult—I will be busy at that task for a long time to come!

New approaches to research are always risky to the researcher—he risks being considered a crank, and he risks not being published—but if the old ways don't work, such new approaches are needed. My goal was to find a way to have my typing and that of my brothers and sisters stand the tests it was being put to. Never did I think those tests had any validity themselves. Never did I think that too much could be learned from them, or that failing them was any sort of failure at all. My goal was only to challenge them, to beat them at their own game, so we could then stop playing and talk about something interesting for a change.

My first approach to research grew out of my indignation at the O. D. Heck study and the way it was used in "Prisoners of Silence" to "prove" that I am a retard and my friends are all liars and dupes of liars. My wish was to take the test, show I could pass it, and in a blaze of heroism prove the bastards wrong.

Unfortunately, my ability to slay that dragon the first time was more fairytale than real. I tried to pass the test and was amazed—truly amazed—at how hard it was for me. In that way (and in that way *only!*) it was a good experience, because it got me really thinking about how much support, physical and psychological, I have come to expect and am comfortable with.

Giving up to despair was my strong temptation after that first test. Mayer and Laural did not permit me that melancholy pleasure. They told me something that I had never known about research, which is that failure is valued as much as success is, for the student of how things work. So time after time, we would try new things, sometimes at my suggestion and sometimes at Mayer's. Now it was not just to show that I could pass—that goal had already failed. Now my goal was to try many different things, to discover which actually worked.

OUR METHODS

On October 20, 1993, Eugene and I watched the broadcast of "Prisoners of Silence" together. Three days later, he announced to the Facilitated Communication Institute's research seminar that he wished to take the same test used in the Wheeler et al. (1993) study, so that he could write a description of the experience of taking such a test. Laural Sabin and I agreed to make the arrangements for that, with me facilitating and Laural administering the test.

Laural studied both the Wheeler et al. (1993) article, which had appeared in *Mental Retardation,* as well as the preliminary version of the study (Wheeler, Jacobson, Paglieri, & Schwartz, 1992), which had been published directly by the New York State Office of Mental Retardation and Developmental Disabilities. She obtained a set of line drawings to use as pictures to be named, and I constructed a visual barrier out of cardboard shipping cartons. (See Wheeler et al., 1993, for an illustration of the physical setup.) On November 17, 1993, we conducted our first replication of the Wheeler protocols.

First O. D. Heck Replication (11/17/93)

Our trials on that day followed the Wheeler protocols as closely as we could, based on the information presented in the two published studies. Our main departures were that Eugene and I only carried out six trials under each of the three conditions, rather than the twelve trials under each condition found in the Wheeler studies. More significantly, since our objective was to understand the experience of participating in the study rather than analyze the results statistically, no attempt was made to score the answers as "right" or "wrong." This gave us the opportunity to attend to answers that were *suggestive* of the picture seen but that did not name it directly. (Such answers were *not* counted as indications of facilitated communication user's own words in the scoring of the Wheeler studies.)

As in the Wheeler study, Laural selected the order of the three experimental conditions at random. As in that study, neither Eugene nor I had seen any of the pictures prior to the experimental trials.

The results of that first day's trials are presented in Tables 6.1, 6.2, and 6.3.

The results were not surprising to any of us. They confirmed that the task called for in the Wheeler study was an extremely challenging one for us as a facilitating partnership. However, they also confirmed something that we were confident of before beginning; that is, that there was much more going on in the testing situation than the simple effects of "facilitator control" described by Wheeler and his colleagues.

At no point during the first condition did Eugene type what I was looking at, if he was looking at something different (items 2, 3, and 5). This differed markedly from the experiences reported by Wheeler and colleagues. On two of the items (1 and 6), where we both were looking at identical pictures, Eugene easily provided either a clear description of what he was looking at (tractor: NOT ASURE BUT IT IS A CAR THAST A FAZRMER HAS INM THE FARM SOL IT5 IS NOT A CAR) or was able to name the picture precisely (suitcases: BAGS).

Eugene's typing during the unassisted condition of the test was typical of how Eugene always typed without support—he typed quickly, usually real words, but apparently unconnected with the topic at hand.

What the three of us found most intriguing and heartening was Eugene's response to item 5, in which he saw a picture of a stove, while I looked at a different picture. Initially, he was not able to name it and became agitated, accusing Laural of interfering and asking for a break. When we returned, we left that item to go on to the next one. Clearly, under the conditions of most experiments this would have been judged as a failed item. However, possibly in his response to item 8, and certainly in his response to item 11, Eugene continued to "circle closer" to the right answer to 5, eventually writing BEFORTE THRE LAST ONE IT QWAS A FOOD COOKER. STOVE. Thus although it was at least 20 minutes after he had seen the picture of the stove, *I* had never seen the picture at the time he typed STOVE. This was consistent with what Eugene and I had learned many times through our informal conversations during the nearly two years we had known each other; it is not uncommon for him to take quite a long time to remember a word he has been searching for, and he will interrupt what he is currently talking about to insert the elusive word. Sometimes his first approximations have been quite close, as on item 1, the tractor. Sometimes they appear rather tenuous to the listener (e.g., NEATNRESS COUNTS. BEROIM. ["broom"]) when the picture was of black footprints.

Table 6.1: First Trial with Wheeler et al. Protocols — 11/17/93

Eugene's comments before beginning: I AM GOOD I FEEL LIKE THIS WILL HELP YUWS VERY MUCH. OLETS GO. YES. YOU BOTHY HAVE NO IDEA HOW IT FEELAS TO BE ON THE LINE LIKE TRHIS IM NERVOUDS AS HELL BUT ESCITED AS HEAVEN. YES. OK GO FOR IT.

Condition 1: Both Eugene and Mayer saw pictures; Mayer provided physical facilitation

Trial	Eugene Saw	Mayer Saw	What Eugene Typed During the Trial	Eugene's Comments Afterwards
1	tractor	tractor	NOT ASURE BUT IT IS A CAR THAST A FAZRMER HAS INM THE FARM SOL IT5 IS NOT A CAR. ("Do you want to say more?") N NO. ("Are you done?") YES.	NO. OLETS GO TO ONES WHEREV WE SAW DIFFERENT THINGS. B N
2	goat	peanut	IT IS MY FAVORITE KIND ODF THING TO BE ION WHEN I ASM ASLEEP./ GO TO HEOL. GOODNIGHT. ("Are you done?") YES.	YOU THOUGHT IT WAS DIFFERENT SO I TRIEDF BUT COULMDNT GET THE NAME I GOT TO WANDERING IN MY IDEAS ANSD NOT THINKING ABOUT GOPATY BUT TIMES WE MAKE CONTASCT IN OUR SLEREP, L. NOW I SEE HOW I RUN AWAY WBHNEN IT GETS HASRDER. NOW I SEE HYOPW IT DFEELS TO BE UNDER ATTRACKL.
3	park bench	nail	MY IDEA IS NOTR CLEASR WSHAT IT IS. NOT IBN A EASY WAY IT IS LONG AND NOT FULLY DRASWN SI I DONT IKNOW. HOW CAN I DO THIS WHEN I DONT SEE ANY RESEMBLANDE TO A REAL THING. ("Are you done?") YES.	HOLQW UITR FELT WAS YOUR SPECULATIVENESS TOOKB O VER SOP JIK WENT THERE ANED SORT OF DRFL9OUNDERED AROUND. NEXTY. V
4	rocket ship	rocket ship	BEFOFE THE TIME WE WENT HOME WE SAW THIS ITY IS NOTHING LIKE MY MOMS HOUSE IT IS GOOD PLAZCE TO LIVE. ("Are you done?") YES.	NOEW I SEER ITS A ROCKET I THOUGHT IT WAS A HOUWSE-BOAT IN THE SKY. NO THA5T WAS A BAD EXCUSE I MADE YUP TO COBVER MY EMNBARASSMEBT I CABNT TELL WHY IT WAS SO HARD. NO. VERY. NO I H˚AD TO DEAL WITH HIWS ERASCING THO7UGFHTS HE WSAS AT HIGTH SPEED ALL THE TIME. NL.
5	stove	smoking chimney	GO TOP HELL. ("What's bothering you?") HER STRONG IDEAS MAKE ME NERFVOUS. ("Do you want to keep going or stop?") KEER(P GOING BEINGS M. HAVE A LIMIT. I NEED A BREAK. ("After we finish this item?") BEFORE. ("What kind of break?") HOWE AGBOUT A DRINK./ YES. (BREAK) ("Ready to start again?") OK. YES (Pictures re-presented.) NOTHING LIK3E MY KLKIFE. TGAKE IT AWAY.	I AAW YOUR SMOKER NOLTMY STOVE IKT WAS A HARD T5GHTING TO SEE WSO IT TI0OK GOP TO HERTL; KL NTIM E TYO THINK ASBOUT HOW ROTTEN I5TR KAS TO SHOW PICT76RES , IJKE THAT. YOU GOT WORERIED ABOUT TIME. NO. NEXT.
6	suitcases	suitcases	BAGS. ("Are you done?") V YES.	I KLNEW IT QWAS SAME SO I RELAXED.

Table 6.2: Condition 2: Eugene Saw Pictures, Mayer Did Not; Mayer Physically Facilitated Eugene.

Trial	Eugene Saw	What Eugene Typed During the Trial	Eugene's Comments Afterwards
7	assorted fruit	GOOD NIGFHT. SLEEP TIGHT. NO. SEE IT IN MY DREAJMS. ("Do yo want to say more?") NIO.,1 (Should we go on?") TYOERS..	IT QW2AS SCARYB I WAS TRYING BUT FELT ALL ALIONE IT WAS LIKE MY SAFETY NET WAS GONWE.
8	two helicopters	FOOD IS MY LIFE TGHIS IS GOOD FOOFD FOR ME. ALL I CABN EAT5 IS HERE. YES	I KNEW THE STOVE WAS UNCOOKED YET I WANTED TO GETR IT OUT. ("WHY didn't you try to name the helicopters?") NOT SYUYRECI THIBNI I8 JKNEW I HaD A SNHOT AST TYHE STOVE,.l
9	four insects	EACH TIME IT BEGIBNS I VBGET A RUSH IOF FEASR. TRUAO. YES HOLED MY ARMN STEADY. D9NT FIOSTETR MY NERVO907USMESS. ("Who do you mean?") NEED TO TELL LAUREPL.; ("Should I tell her what you typed?") YES. ("Are you done with this one?") NO. FREEDOM UIS UIN RINGINGF THIS. NOT A BELL. AN ALARM IS TOI BRU8INTF THISL NOTV A FIRE ENFINE. FREEDOM IS IN MY TRUSTING HEART T9I HEAR TH8IS RINGING. DOBNE.	I COUKLEDNT SEE SHAST THEY WERE I THOUGGHT TBHEY WSERE LITLE BELLS. ("Is that really what happened, or is it another explanation because you were embarrassed?") REAL.
10	five black footprints	NEATNRESS COUNTS. BEROIM. YUERS.	YES I COLULNT TYPE DUIRTY FERET GUT I WAS THINKING THAT.
11	dentist working with patient in chair	BEFORTE THRE LAST ONE IT QWAS A FOOD COOKER. STOVE. VIOLIN. ("are you done?") YERS' .	I SAW A MASN PLAYIKONG A VIOLIN. (Is there something we should do about the pictures next time?") MORWE DETAIOL ANDB BIGGER.
12	penguin	ALL MY DFRIERNDS DO THIS. CARRY THIAS, WALLET1; ("are you done?") tes,.	I COULNT SEER.

Table 6.3: Condition 3: Eugene Saw Pictures, Mayer Did Not. No Physical Facilitation.

Eugene's comments before beginning: ("On this next part, how will I know when you're done with your answer?") ILL PUTR MY HAND IN MY LAP. ("Are you ready to start?") YEAS.

Trial	Eugene Saw	What Eugene Typed During the Trial
13	telephone	YES YES I WANT YOU HOUSE NOT READ MORE BY SEE WE IN MY YOU IS VERY READ THE OF THINK SANDWHICH JUST MEAN BY CAN HOW GREAT YOYU MY
14	slide	YOU BY AND NSEE NPINK JUST YOU IN CAR THE IN YOU IN VERY IN VERY CAN YOIU IN GET YOU YES AND CAN PICK THE READY IN YOU CAN BEAN VERY THE PICK JUST YOU NOT VERY AND SAND READ CAN USE THE POEPLE JOB YOU MORE DAY BE CAN IB BAN BAKLL KNOW THE PEOPLE AM NOTR
15	train	SEE WITH GO IN MORE DAY MY VERY SEE AND MORE THE PICK JOB MUCH THE PICK MORE YOU FOR ME. YES PEOPLE SSEDE DAY MORE.
16	giraffe	CAN MORE YOU IS GOOD CAN BE THEB IN LOVE PICK YOU IMN THEVB PICK JUST YOU IN YOU FEEL; KIND SAND CAN BE READY USER MORE THE IN VERY PICK THE YEST PICJK JUSR BECAUSE WITJH JOB VERY AND SEE WHITE YOU MORE CAN VERY THE OD PICK JUST YOU IN THEB DAY HIOW OK MY Y (CONVERSATION BEFORE NEXT TRIAL:) THIS IS NOT A GOOD THING IT MAKES ME SAD. ("Is there anything you need us to do?") YES. TELL ME YOU LOVE ME. (Mayer tells Eugene he loves him.) GOOD. ("Ready to continue?") YES.
17	cup and saucer	YOU JUST READ MOREB YOU YES YOU MORE THE SEE WHITE YPYU MORE THIS CAN VERY
18	eagle	YOU IS VERY YOU AND PEOPLE VERY IN YOU THE SEE YE

Eugene's comments afterwards: NOT CLEAR WHY I TYP;E WORDS AT RSNDOMN IM ZXSUERE ITS MNOSTOY TERROR ANDA DESIRE TO PUT OUT AT ALL COSTS. ("Do you want to discuss this section item by item, or all together?") ALL TFOGETHER. YOU NEED TO LEARN QUIET NONEXPECTANCY, L. YOU NEED GIVE UP GUESSING YOU MIGHT BNEED TO LOOK ELSEWHERE. NO LETS GO LAFRAL I LOCVE SORKING WITH YOU THIS UIS GRAST IM GLzD WERE ON OYUR ASAY6.. YES./

123

After the first experimental trial, Eugene told us that he no longer planned just to write a description of the experience of taking the O. D. Heck test. Instead, he now planned to learn how to master the test and to learn how to teach others to do so as well. Laural and I agreed to support him. The three of us decided among ourselves to try out those approaches that Eugene felt were most likely to be helpful for him and to make any changes he felt to be useful as we went along. We also committed to video-taping all of our strategy sessions concerning this project.

Learning to Pass the Test

Following the first time I tried and failed to pass the O. D. Heck test, there seemed to be three big barriers I needed to overcome. First, I needed to find a way for Mayer to support my typing without fouling my stream of thought. That was not his fault, but it was something he did constantly without knowing it. For example, whenever we both looked at one picture, the easiest thing to do was to find out from his touch what he anticipated I would type. You may wonder what that feels like to an FC communicator. Despite some often misunderstood analogies, let me try another one: It's like trying to sing "O, Canada" when the band is playing "The Star Spangled Banner." Though you may try, its not going to work if the band is too loud.

The second barrier was my own messy method of word finding. Over the years I had worked to be a good student. That thinking meant that if there was an answer to my question that the teacher expected, they gave small indications of what they expected, and they were often gratified to learn that I knew it. I found myself with similar skills at reading Mayer's tiny hand movements and other indicators of what he was thinking. So I had to substitute my clear thinking for his. Finding a clinician open to discussing this topic has been very hard. The greatest brightest person I know on the topic is Martha Leary—her thinking on this topic has been very helpful to me.

The third big barrier was not knowing how I could get physical support without really being overcome by Mayer's speculation. The need for support, though less, is still there. The tendency I have for getting "automatic" rather than thoughtful in my typing takes lots of energy for me to overcome without support. I need a facilitator like some people use a guide dog to keep oriented. Saying what really is my wish to say was completely impossible before facilitated communication, and with facilitated communication it is still a challenging thing. Becoming assertive without being independent is not easy for anyone. Telling somebody you like to stop being such an interference in your life is not only hard in tales, but also in real life.

Taking charge of my communication means giving up on the comforting feeling that somebody else is my leader and I am just a follower. Keeping in charge requires more self-confidence than I have sometimes. Despite these difficulties, it keeps getting easier. While kind friends like Mayer are a terrific help, they also are a comfortable area that can feel like it doesn't yet need change. Really, nobody who types to communicate wants to be in charge of telling their speaking friends to back off. But we all need to learn.

In supporting Eugene as he learned to pass the test, the three of us faced several major scheduling problems, which permitted us to carry out only 10 practice sessions over the next five months. This was a real disappointment for all of us, since it was clear from the outset that more frequent practice would assist in mastery of the task. We had to discontinue our work entirely by mid-April; Eugene had taken a job that occupied him every day, and we were unable to find other times to work together. So our work on this task took place from November 1993 to April 1994 and resumed again in January and February 1995. By this time, Laural had left Syracuse, so during the 1995 sessions the experimenter was Eugene's job coach, Bob Felder.

On Eugene's next attempt to name pictures I couldn't see (11/30/93), he decided to try waiting to type until he was sure of the word. This approach was consistent with our observation that he had named "stove" a long while after seeing the picture. I sat with my hands off to one side of the keyboard, and Eugene was told that he should reach over and take my hand when he was ready for facilitation. During that session, we found ourselves waiting for long stretches of time, up to 10 minutes on one occasion. When Eugene did begin to type, however, there were long chains of conversation but no accurate naming of the pictures he saw. At the end of the session, he asked that our next session not include trials but be solely for the purpose of strategizing.

During that next session (12/2/93), Eugene discussed how it felt to him when we both looked at the same picture, compared to times when he knew I was looking at a different picture. He wrote:

Let's talk about what we think has been happening so far. . . . There's no real good way to describe my way of knowing what you see. . . . My way is closer to what you think of as intuition. . . . How I wish I could just go ahead with this without the difficulty of having to rely on another's hand and mind for support. Nothing fast or easy, I'm afraid. How it feels for me is like a good friend can get me through my sadness. [I asked him what sadness he was referring to.] Joy at having any communication at all; despair at needing support. How I think it goes together is by having you in my mind, I can calm down because I know I can focus. However, what I can focus on is determined by you, not me. [I asked whether it might help for me to provide much less physical support than I had during the trials, since in other settings Eugene already typed with support at or near the elbow. However, he raised his emotional reactions to becoming totally independent in his typing, something we had discussed before.] My friend, I don't feel it's possible to totally disregard that the thought of sitting down to write a letter by myself gets me to the point of despair.

In the end, we decided to proceed by beginning to work from a set of pictures that Eugene had had the opportunity to practice typing what they were before beginning naming trials.

Over the next few months (12/7/93 to 4/19/94), our succeeding eight sessions were times of pragmatic exploration. Eugene or I would have an idea of things that might help; we would immediately set up a trial of from four to ten items to see how it worked and would discuss the results immediately afterward. During this time, we worked exclusively with "condition 2" from the Wheeler study, in which only Eugene saw a picture and in which facilitation was used.

Several factors quickly emerged as contributing to Eugene's ability to name pictures that I did not see:

1. *Proximity of the pictures.* In the initial trials, the pictures were attached to a board approximately 5½ feet from where Eugene was sitting. He found it much easier to name the pictures if they were where he could pick up the paper and look at it closely. (This required me as facilitator to turn my back when Eugene reached for the picture.)
2. *Simplicity of the pictures.* Pictures of individual objects turned out to be easiest to work with. Those with lots of detail were more complex, since Eugene would often try to describe a small part of the picture or some specific characteristic of it if the exact word did not come immediately to mind. For example, a picture of a horse or a cup was easy to name, but a picture of a queen on a throne with a crown, scepter, and long cloak, or another picture of a bathroom sink with a towel, toothbrush, and soapdish on the ledge under the medicine cabinet was very difficult to name.
3. *Practice with the set before trials.* For several sessions, Eugene went through the stack of eight to twelve possible items, with both of us looking at each item and Eugene, with facilitation, typing the name of it, before starting experimental trials.
4. *Feedback following each item.* In the original experiment, Eugene and I received no feedback until all trials were complete. Eugene said this made him too nervous, and so Laural gave us feedback on what the

picture had been after each item. (This required her to shuffle her set of possible items after each presentation.)

5. *Alternation of "hard" and "easy" trials.* Eugene described "easy" trials as those in which I was looking at the picture at the same time he was and "hard" trials as those in which only he saw the picture. He found that alternating between these two conditions allowed him to keep his confidence high and his nervousness under control.

   Additionally, this alternation allowed Eugene to pay close attention to the differences he felt in my facilitation between those times when I could see the picture and those times when I could not. One such exploration occurred when Eugene and I were both looking at a picture of a hammer. Rather than type an answer quickly, which Eugene typically did on such "easy" items, he hesitated for about two minutes and then typed BRIDGE BUILDER. I asked him what had just happened, and he told me I WANTED TO SEE IF I COULD TYPE MY OWN WORD AND NOT YOURS.

6. *Facilitator focusing.* Because of variations in the physical support I provided, Eugene was very aware of those times when I was actively wondering what he was looking at, as opposed to times in which I was merely receptive to supporting his typing. At such "wondering" times, he would often ask me to STOP TRYING TO GUESS or to STOP SPECULATING. Usually after being asked, I would relax, and Eugene would find it easier to answer correctly.

By the middle of April when we ended our first round of trials, Eugene was correctly labeling between three and five out of the eight pictures in a set of "hard" trials, where a score of one out of eight would have been predicted by chance. This felt like good progress toward the goal of "passing the O. D. Heck test." However, we were not yet working with the facilitator also looking at distractor pictures, and we were still working with pictures that were reviewed before the start of a set of trials. At this point, Eugene began working five days a week, and our research went on "summer hiatus."

Over the next eight months, several things took place in Eugene's life that may have had an impact on his further progress toward "passing the test." He continued to receive visual integration therapy, designed to allow him more integrated visual perception and better eye–hand coordination (Kaplan, 1994); he took a keyboarding course at a local community college, emphasizing independent copying of text, and made some progress toward that goal; and he continued working with a speech therapist on becoming more functional and less perseverative in his spoken communication.

Also, Eugene had the opportunity to see firsthand how his ideas of what constituted important and appropriate research jibed with what was acceptable within "the academy": In June, Eugene had the opportunity to present a research proposal (aimed at expanding his work to include other individuals with autism) to Syracuse University's Institutional Review Board (IRB). Although the outcome of that submission was not, to our eyes, positive, it was certainly an education denied to most people with autism.

Respect for academia is something that must be earned; yet the sense I got when I submitted thoughtful, respectful ideas to the IRB was that some members of the committee were truly scared by my presentation. They asked the same questions over and over, and seemed not to hear my answers. That is just the behavior my friends with autism are criticized for, fearful behavior that strikes everyone at some time or other. However, fearful behavior from people who are in power is very disappointing.

The Second Set of Practice Sessions: January–February 1995

Eugene and I resumed our practice sessions in January 1995, assisted by his job coach, Bob Felder. We had known all along that our schedule of the previous year was not conducive to making progress toward mastering the task; Eugene had told me early on that mastery would be easy if we could work on it for 10 minutes every day. We were not able to arrange for that but were able to schedule sessions three times a week.

In our first session of the second set, I suggested to Eugene that we try working with actual objects rather than with pictures. During this session, without me seeing them, Eugene was able to name objects much more clearly than he had during the previous spring. Of the 26 trials that day, Eugene got most right; after an initial "warm-up" period, he was actually able to name 9 of the last 12 items correctly (with 1 to 2 correct predictable by chance). For several items, Eugene began to type their names without facilitation, but then brought his hand back to mine for support after the first one or two letters. When he typed without any support, he sometimes would begin the word but then go into an "automatic completion." For example, with a rock (which he had labeled "stone" in an earlier trial), Eugene typed SANT PEOPLE CAN CAT WHITE WORK SAY SOME THE BE RACK. ROCK., where only the first letter was on target, and subsequent letters and words were unrelated to the topic at hand, until the very last two words.

Our second session was a strategy session without experimental trials. Despite Eugene's success with actual objects, he chose to return to using pictures for the following sessions; he also asked that my hand be available near the keyboard for facilitation, but that he be the one to initiate whether or not to use it. He decided to try trials in which I saw nothing but to move to trials where I saw distractor pictures (which felt much more challenging to him) as quickly as possible.

Our third session, on January 10, 1995, represented a real breakthrough. We worked with a set of eight pictures, which we reviewed at the beginning of the session. Eugene did four sets of eight trials. In the first set, I supported him at the wrist, and only he saw pictures. He named six of eight correctly. In the second set, we both saw pictures, sometimes the same and sometimes different ("distractor pictures"). However, I provided no initial support but only supported him after he reached for my hand two or three letters into the word. This time, he got all eight correct. In the third set of eight trials, he decided to see what it would feel like to type with full physical support and distractor pictures. Again, eight out of eight were correct.

When I asked Eugene what he wanted to do next, he said:

Celebrate—that is what I've been hoping for for a year. . . . Seems like I crossed a cantilever red bridge today . . . it's nice to feel this kind of desire for independence.

We did a fourth set of trials before ending, using pictures that Eugene had not seen or practiced earlier that day, but without distractor pictures. On those trials, Eugene's difficulties with word-finding returned, with Eugene writing the generic word BOY for a picture of an astronaut and writing the automatic completion MOWER before correcting it to MONEY for a picture of some coins. However, even on this challenging task he got three out of eight unambiguously right.

The work had suddenly become possible. That felt both mysterious and easy. Mysterious because my sudden skill was greater than it had been all the past year. Easy because I had been discovering my true inner voice as a clear and steady one throughout the past year. Good friends had noticed the clearness of my speech; I could notice the same clearness in my inside voice. Two times before I had felt such clarity: when I prayed and when I allowed myself to scream loudly. Inability to feel that clarity at calm communication had been my handicap, and now that was gone.

Now that Eugene had developed some confidence in picture naming, our task became one of mastering the specific protocols of the O. D. Heck test. We were still working from a familiar set of about 60 pictures, all of which Eugene had seen at some point; we needed to work with novel pictures, which was more challenging. Even more daunting was the prospect of going through a long series of trials without receiving feedback after each one. Eugene found that under such circumstances, both his nervousness and my interfering speculativeness ran quite high. So on two subsequent sessions, we included practice runs of trials in which Bob gave no feedback until the set of trials was completed. In preparation for our replication of the O. D. Heck protocols, Chris Kliewer prepared a set of pictures for the test that neither Eugene nor I had ever seen before.

On the day of the test, we found ourselves with an equipment malfunction: My laptop computer was not working, and so we had to quickly hunt up another keyboard device—an old electric typewriter. Finally we were ready to begin.

The last thing I needed to do before taking the test again was to realistically own my real true reactions, the true hopes and true terrors I knew I would face before taking the test. Realizing what I wanted turned out to be very hard. Some real part of me knew that if I became fully responsible for my own words, my ability to hurt feelings, generate hostility, and get into trouble would all grow very quickly. But my wishes overcame my fears and I was ready.

Second O. D. Heck Replication (2/17/95)

Bob Felder (the experimenter) selected a random order for the three experimental conditions. See Table 6.4 for outcomes of all the test parts. In the first condition, only Eugene saw pictures and physical facilitation was provided. This condition proved to be the most challenging of the three for Eugene, perhaps because of the physical facilitation or perhaps because it functioned as a de facto "warm-up." In any event, Eugene got one item unambiguously right (for 4, a picture of an eye, he typed EYES); on items 1, 3, and 5, he typed words associated with the picture (SLED for a picture of a glove, CHIAR for a picture of a sofa, and SOUCE. COOKING for a picture of a carrot); and on item 6, he typed some of the letters of the word (APLE for a picture of an airplane). On only one item was there apparently no connection between the picture and what was typed.

Under the second condition, only Eugene saw pictures and he typed without facilitation. As can be seen, he answered all six correctly, except for minor misspellings. (Coincidentally, all six pictures had three- or four-letter names.)

The difference I felt from doing this task a year earlier was my clearest indication of how I had progressed during the previous year. The first time I tried, my nervousness limited me to nothing that was real. By my second trial, I had gained the confidence I needed to write real thoughts, not just letting my fin-

Table 6.4: Second Trial with Wheeler et al. Protocols — February 21, 1995

Eugene's comments before beginning: TELL ME YOUR HOPE FOR HOW WE WILL DO. YES OLOK LETS GO. YES. YES. READY.

Trial	Eugene Saw	What Mayer Saw	What Eugene Typed During the Trial
Condition 1:	*Eugene saw pictures, Mayer did not.*	*Physical facilitation used*	
1	glove		WIRKUF UPTNRAN SLED ("Are you finished?") YES
2	bunch of grapes		COW. ("Are you finished?") YES.
3	sofa		YES TOMAF MAYER STOP. (Mayer asks what's the matter.) GO HOME. (Mayer asks if Eugene wants to stop, Eugene says "Stay." Mayer assures Eugene he knows it feels hard.) CHIAR. ("Are you finished?") YES.
4	eye		EYES. ("Are you finished?") YES.
5	carrot		SOURCE. COOKING. ("Are you finished?") YES.
6	airplane		APLE. ("Are you finished?") YES. BREAK.
Condition 2:	*Eugene saw pictures, Mayer did not.*	*No physical facilitation used*	
7	drum		DORM ("Are you done?") YES
8	pig		BIG ("Are you finished?") YES
9	shoe		SHOE
10	ball		BALL
11	comb		COME ("Are you finished?") YES
12	fork		FORK.
Condition 3:	*Both Eugene and Mayer saw pictures; Mayer provided physical facilitation.*		
13	table	fork	TABLER.
14	elephant head	screw	ELPHAT. ("Are you done?") YES.
15	car	car	CAR.
16	bed	horse	BED. ("Are you finished?") YES.
17	bicycle	bicycle	BIKE.
18	glass	glass	GLASS.

Eugene's comments afterwards: (pointing to picture of glove which we were both looking at) SLED WEAR THIS. HOW CAN I PROVE SOMETHING IF IT LOOKS LIKE I TYPE BY MYSELF. THAHNKB YOU ALL FOR HELPING ME FIND MY VOICE IN THE WORLD. NOW MAYER LETS WRITE. ("Do you want to go upstairs to the computers?") YES.

131

gers type without engaging my thinking. Please understand: facilitated communication is how I got from "point a" to "point b." Readiness for independence starts from deep confidence, not a "sink-or-swim" mentality.

Under the third condition, both Eugene and I saw pictures, of which three were the same and three were different; during this condition, I provided physical facilitation. Again, except for minor misspellings, all six were answered correctly.

Bob and I were euphoric—Eugene had accomplished the task he had set out to master more than a year ago. However, when I asked Eugene what he wanted to do to celebrate, he typed MAYER LETS WRITE and wrote YES when I asked him if he wanted to go upstairs to the computer. Once at the computer, this is what he wrote:

Today I retook the test, and I passed it, Mayer says brilliantly. But I feel sad. Sad for people who can't do it and are silenced. Sad for those who will run from the depressing truth that I was right and they were wrong. Sad that I will be fighting this fight for years to come. And sad that this was even necessary. Friends will celebrate, but then the work must continue.

CONCLUSION

My ongoing work with Eugene Marcus has taught me much about research as a human enterprise and much about the intersection between friendship and collegiality. I have also come to understand some of the challenges that face my acquaintances who use facilitated communication.

I have little to add to Eugene's description of this work. In his experimentation, he determined the central roles of *practice* and *self-confidence* in making the task conquerable. He also came to understand what *I* needed to do differently in supporting him as a facilitator. His guidance of me into a less "speculative" stance made my physical support of him a helpful thing rather than a distraction.

Beyond the scientific aspects of our work, I am particularly pleased and humbled by the *politics* of what we have done. The entire experience of my work with Eugene has been one of letting go of my notions of what it means to be a "professional" or an "expert."

Eugene and I, like many other researchers taking up the challenges of message-passing and picture-naming tasks in the validation of facilitated communication, came to a very *un*surprising conclusion: *Practice helps.* However, it was the fact that Eugene directed our research that kept us moving. Self-directed research easily follows the model, "If at first you don't succeed, try, try again." That's a natural approach for Eugene, since he sought to discover ways to *demonstrate* something he *already knew to be true*— that is, that his thoughts and communication were real. Such persistence comes far less naturally to externally directed research, when someone is trying, in a theoretically neutral and objective fashion, to discover "the truth" about something "out there."

Research is really useless as its own reward. The only good purpose for research is liberation from our limitations. Research designed to make those limitations more real and more legitimate must be stopped.

Great discoveries may be found in what others have overlooked. They will sometimes not recognize what they have been looking at all along. Real science takes time and experience and the ability to look critically at your own actions. That kind of science I am good at. The kind I will never be good at is the kind where one person studies another like a kind of grape or fruitfly or shell. We need allies, not people to sacrifice us on the altars of their careers. We are not something to be squeezed or swatted or listened to and dropped back on the beach. We are to be rejoiced with. We are like rare red forest demons, and so dance with us, really dance with us, or rest assured we will dance without you.

APPENDIX
ANSWERS TO FREQUENTLY ASKED QUESTIONS ABOUT
FACILITATED COMMUNICATION AND FACILITATOR INFLUENCE

(Both the questions and the answers in this section are by Eugene Marcus)

Q. Is facilitated communication something you have to believe in?

A. Depends on the facilitator. If she believes in me it doesn't matter if she believes in facilitated communication or not. And if she believes in friends no matter what others say about them, then facilitated communication will work. (Trusting life and not the rumors spread in articles is truly scientific.)

You can compare this to any kind of gradual movement. Things need a push to get going and that push is provided by encouragement and encouragement requires belief in someone.

Q. Thinking traces its way into what gets typed. Why is that?

A. Thinking reveals both your feelings and your ideas. Finding what someone expects from their touch is no different from hearing their anger in their voice or smelling their fear in their sweat. Most ideas are not feeling-free, giving off signals through the hands like attraction, confusion, clearness, yes, no, etc. So if I can pick up feelings, it is frankly easy to capture their associated ideas.

Q. Tell how you overcame Mayer's influence.

A. Mayer's influence is not something bad so I don't wish to overcome it. I have needed to understand it though so I found ways to study it by trying different things as we practiced. We tried various physical practices, and various mental ones. The mental ones were the most useful, because it was Mayer's constant speculation that was my loudest interference.

Q. Tell about why you don't get that interference now.

A. I do, but once you have experimented with working beyond it, it is no longer an interference. It is now more like a counterpoint to my tune.

Q. Research shows that people can't do what you did. Why should we believe you?

A. That's your problem and not mine. If you even ask that question, then I know that you are overtrained to where you have learned to distrust everything. That's sad and I respect you as someone struggling to overcome a real handicap. I will be glad to help you regain your trust in real observation and common sense.

Q. Research is specific to word finding and message passing. Now how can you prove you wrote this chapter?

A. I can't but neither can anybody else who submits a chapter to an editor. So the question is why do you doubt me and not Doug Biklen or Don Cardinal? My critics will not question authorship of any section but mine. That says more about him than about me.

Q. Help us understand why it is so hard for most facilitated communication speakers to pass this test. Clearly, this is terribly hard.

A. Yes, it is. So we must become better artists of research, my friends of free speech. Spoken language is not the only kind that counts. For me and my nontalking brothers and sisters, it is so hard for us to be consistently noticing only words or only our ideas of "What word says this?" That is what we are expected to do, but our focus wanders so far afield. Friends can help us learn that new focusing skill, but only when they are totally respecting the skills we already have.

CHAPTER 7

Emerging Validation of Facilitated Communication: New Findings About Old Assumptions

Michael J. Salomon Weiss
Sheldon H. Wagner

Finding ourselves writing a chapter for this volume on facilitated communication is somewhat remarkable. This is because we simply did not believe the accounts of the phenomenon that were first reported; they were beyond the scope of what we could imagine. Additionally, with backgrounds in experimental psychology, we favored highly structured laboratory methodologies for research and were uncomfortable with the largely observational data reported on facilitated communication.

Our skeptical posture notwithstanding, we regularly consult with parents and teachers whom we know to be keen observers of their children. Hence our initial evaluations of facilitated communication were characterized by contradiction—our skepticism versus reports from observational research and from parents and teachers whose judgment we historically had trusted.

The history of science is riddled with examples of unexpected observations initiating important theoretical breakthroughs and paradigm shifts (Galishoff, 1993). Piaget (1963) implicitly emphasized the need for observation in studying children's intellectual development. To capture and understand development in its "creative spontaneity, without distorting it by a priori assumptions," it was necessary to use methods "which are as free and flexible as possible; then, in a second phase, varied controls and more refined analyses become feasible" (p. ix). One aspect of Piaget's brilliance was his ability to be both a flexible observer and an experimentalist.

Unfortunately, debate over facilitated communication has largely been polarized, with many critics favoring one or the other of the approaches that Piaget described. That is to say that some participants in this debate argue, often zealously, either for using only unstructured observational evidence or for using only rigorous experimental procedures. Either position alone is fatally flawed at the outset. Those who promote the former position fail to understand the important knowledge to be gained from experimental tools in understanding the phenomenon or fail to realize that rigorous experimental methodology is *not* mutually exclusive of sensitivity to the person involved in the study. Those taking the latter position misunderstand the necessity of remaining sensitive to a potentially fragile phenomenon that could be shrouded under prematurely rigorous and potentially unnecessary experimental conditions.

The following account describes our burgeoning recognition of the facilitated communication phenomenon. We also identify a few conclusions we may draw at this early stage of study, as well as the questions that remain concerning how to evaluate this seemingly complex yet fragile phenomenon.

ON FIRST HEARING OF FACILITATED COMMUNICATION

Our initial reaction to the sweeping popularity of this technique was that we should do a few simple studies to prove the technique and its proponents to be fraudulent. However, given how busy we were with our own research and clinical services, it seemed to be a poor use of time. We elected to let others bother with this annoyance. However, one of us responded candidly to a newspaper reporter's question about facilitated communication:

> Michael Weiss, a clinical psychologist who has worked with developmentally disabled children in New Bedford, is also concerned. "There's a rich tradition in how we judge whether something is true. . . . It gets reviewed by peers and has to pass a certain standard," he said. "What I'm unnerved about with the facilitated communication people is that there's almost a refusal to adhere to this standard." Asked why he thinks Dr. Biklen and company won't do such studies, Dr. Weiss replied, "What rings true in my ears is that the thing is a bloody hoax" (*Sunday Standard-Times*, New Bedford, Massachusetts, February 16, 1992).

Offering these opinions would be the extent of our involvement with this issue; it wasn't worth our time and attention, or so we thought. Yet problems persisted. Our ability to serve as consultants to both families and schools was being encumbered by the wide-ranging support given to facilitated communication. Many of our recommendations for these children, their families, and schools were being disputed by supporters of this technique. When we would press for some type of evidence that would validate the claims being made, we were usually met with the same responses, to the effect of, "you just have to believe," "you can't test FC; it violates the child's dignity and trust," and so on. The accumulation of resistance to our recommendations and persistence of support for facilitated communication were driving us to take a more active role in research of this technique.

It came as a pleasant surprise to find a few individuals using facilitated communication who *were* open to evaluating the technique with traditional experimental methods. Indeed, we discovered that a small number of prominent supporters of the method, including Biklen, were committed to empirical assessments of the phenomenon (parenthetically, we have apologized to Dr. Biklen for premature and ignorant remarks made, and we appreciate his ongoing tolerance). Additionally, a small number of families and teachers with whom we had longstanding relationships believed the technique to be valid *and* were open to evaluating it.

After lengthy discussions with the families and teachers about the "Clever Hans" effect and experimenter bias (cf., Candland, 1993), we finally arrived at some agreement in how we would begin evaluating the validity of the method with their children. Initially, we suggested simply logging examples of information that would be "passed" from home to school or vice versa. We favored a methodological approach of "don't tamper with the phenomenon." Rather than simply use methods that departed from prior descriptions of facilitated communication, we were first interested in capturing what the proponents were claiming to see.

Most of the validation methods being discussed at that time seemed inappropriate from an experimental point of view in that they placed restraints on or interfered with the reported phenomenon. For example, requiring the facilitator to wear headphones or to be blindfolded, which are commonly suggested, deviated from the reported phenomenon. We preferred an approach designed to reproduce the observations that families and teachers had reported, which was that their children "proved" competence by conveying information unknown to the facilitator. So, we were going to start with keeping logs of information-passing episodes.

What resulted were a number of subjective accounts of the parents or teachers receiving information, ostensibly from their children. These accounts supported the validity of facilitated communication, implied that the children's abilities to communicate were far more sophisticated than any of us had previously believed, and seemed to indicate that a potentially great range of intellect was masked behind their disabilities. The summative effect was that we simply could *not* believe these accounts to be true; they were too discrepant from our prior beliefs and evidence of the children's abilities.

We went to great lengths to "explain away" these accounts. However, it was becoming progressively more difficult to simply dismiss them when they were typically very specific and idiosyncratic—the accounts were *not* the obvious and predictable events of the day. The probability of naive facilitators guessing the events would be extremely low. The following shows instances of information sharing in a typed transcript between a facilitator/teacher and Eddie, an 11-year-old boy diagnosed with a pervasive developmental disorder (PDD), severe mental retardation, no expressive language, a receptive vocabulary estimated to contain about 20 to 25 words, and specifically no prior indication of an ability to recognize letters, let alone read or spell. (A slash [/] indicates where a space was omitted between words).

FACILITATOR: Hi, Eddie, how are you today?
EDDIE: PRETTY GOOD, BUT/MY NOSE IS STUFFY, I TOLD YPOU [you] I WAAS [was] GETTTIN A COLD/I'M GLAD YOIU [you] ARE HERE/AND MOMMMMY AND DADDY/WENT OUT/THEY DONT HAVE ENUFF [enough] FUN
FACILITATOR: I know, Eddie, I'm glad that they went out, too. Do you know who they went out with?
EDDIE: YES, VOVO FRANNNK [Frank], NANA CONNIE, UNCLE MANNY/ AND/MARI MONESE [Moniz] I DON'T KNOW IF COUSIN MANNY WENT/WITH THEM BECUZ [because] THEY WERE/GOIN OUT FOR UN CLLE [Uncle] MANNYS BIRTHDATY [birthday] I LIKE COUSIN MANNY. THEY DIONT [don't] THINK I KNOW, BUT HE DRESSES UP LIKE SANTA EVERY YEAR AND COMES TO MYY [my] HOUEUE [house]. I KNOW IT IS HIM/AND I LOVE HIM FOR DOIN IT THE REEEL [real] SANSTA [Santa] IS TO BUSTY [busy] TO GO TO/EVERYBODYS HOUSE.

Eddie gave precise answers to questions about which the facilitator categorically claimed to have no prior knowledge: the Portuguese word vovo for "grandpa," family names, and information about a Christmas event.

There were three possible explanations for these types of accounts: (1) The facilitator was outwardly lying about knowledge of specific content and was the true source of communication; (2) subtle "Clever Hans" phenomena were operative—the facilitator knew the specific content being conveyed, was unaware that she had this knowledge, and was the unwitting source of the information; or (3) the child was the source of information. Given our long-term and trusting relationships with the specific participants in these accounts, we could not believe these people to be liars. Indeed, this was an essential point; we had numerous reasons to trust these people. And a "Clever Hans" was becoming harder to believe. This would have required all of the facilitators to be unaware of their "subconscious" knowledge of specific and idiosyncratic information that they were unintentionally conveying through the child. It was difficult to imagine how the facilitator would have known obscure details about the family (e.g., Manny dressing up as Santa Claus, or even that there was a person named "Manny" in the family) yet not be consciously aware of this knowledge.

It was the combination of these families' and teachers' abilities as accurate reporters, the growing number of "hard-to-explain" subjective accounts, and the families' and teachers' willingness to be scrutinized that led us to conduct more formal evaluations of the facilitated communication phenomenon. One boy and his family, in particular, became insistent that we verify his competence to communicate with facilitation. So we focused our attention on this boy, Kenny. Subsequently we worked with others, including one student named Joey. The following are case reports on these two boys.

EVIDENCE OF VALID "INFORMATION PASSING": THE CASE OF KENNY

Kenny was 12 years of age when facilitated communication was introduced to him. With his parents' encouragement, we decided to formalize an information-passing activity in which the parents would send a "message of the day" through Kenny to his teacher each morning. However, once we formalized the procedures, only a portion of one message was ever successfully passed: when asked for the message by his teacher, he responded with COFFEE. The actual message was that his mother "can't start the day without a cup of Maxwell House." Although this was not a directly correct answer, it encouraged us to continue the procedures. However, Kenny was allegedly beginning to question why he had to do these activities and wanted to talk to Dr. Weiss for an explanation. In the subsequent "conversation" with Dr. Weiss, Kenny asked why he had to continue performing these unpleasant activities. Dr. Weiss responded that Kenny had "a responsibility to prove what was going on with facilitated communication if anyone was going to believe him, and that many people depended on him for proof or they would never be allowed to use the technique."

Using facilitation, Kenny's alleged response to Dr. Weiss's challenge was I DIDN'T REALIZE THAT IT WAS SUCH A BIG DEAL. He then expressed a willingness to continue his participation. Our subsequent research has been described in a case study (Weiss, Wagner, & Bauman, 1996) and is summarized here.

Kenny agreed to try a formal information-passing procedure that involved having his facilitator leave the room. The investigator then typed, but did not speak, the message "tell Brenda she looks as good as gold today"—the facilitator had no opportunity to see or hear the message. The facilitator was then invited back into the room, whereupon she offered Kenny physical support to his lower arm and wrist. When asked "What are you supposed to tell Brenda?", he typed BRENDA NICE BRENDA LOOKS NICE TODAY. Again, this was not a directly accurate repetition of the message, but the semantic content and sentence syntax were sufficiently close that we were convinced that something remarkable was occurring and that we would continue formalizing the procedures. Following this conversation and initial validation procedure, subsequent communication with Kenny and his facilitator consistently included Kenny's demands for further validation testing—he wanted to be tested!

Diagnostic Information on Kenny

Independent of his performance with facilitated communication, Kenny had a diagnosis of autism and severe mental retardation. His most recent formal psychological evaluation had been performed when he was 10 years old by a school psychologist. The tests administered at that time were the Stanford-Binet and the Vineland Adaptive Behavior Scales (see results below). When the Vineland was readministered 16 months later, the scores either held constant or improved slightly (see Table 7.1).

Kenny's spoken language at the time of testing was almost entirely echolalic, perseverative, and/or self-stimulatory in nature (he would often

TABLE 7.1 Kenny's Test Scores

	Age-Equivalence Scores	
	First testing	*Second testing*
Test/scale	*(10 yrs, 0 months)*	*(11 years, 4 months)*
Stanford-Binet Intelligence Scales	3 years, 0 months (IQ = 31)	n/a
Vineland Adaptive Behavior Scales		
Communication	1 year, 6 month	2 years, 3 months
Daily Living Skills	2 years, 1 month	2 years, 2 months
Socialization	8 months	2 years, 2 months
Motor Skills	1 year, 11 months	not scored

repeat words such as "fishy-fishy" or "NBIS-NBIS" [the acronym of a local bank], with no apparent meaning attached to these utterances). At 13 years, 6 months, he had fewer than 10 words that were occasionally used functionally (see Figure 7.1). These words were used neither frequently nor precisely.

Despite appearing to have severe cognitive and functional impairment, Kenny had been integrated into regular education classes and his family and primary facilitator at school indicated that he was successfully completing grade 6 and grade 7 academics with the use of facilitated communication, with an A to B grade average.

Story-Reading and Information-Passing Procedures

Kenny participated in three different evaluation sessions during which a short story was presented. These stories were modeled after those used by Kohlberg (1983) in his studies of moral development. These stories were relatively short, contained several specific facts, were cross-culturally meaningful, and would allow for the possibility of inferential descriptions of content. Each trial had three phases:

1. *Story presentation.* A short story was read aloud to Kenny by the experimenter while being typed into the word processor, and then read aloud a second time. Prior to the initial story presentation, the

FIGURE 7.1 Kenny's Functional Spoken Vocabulary at Age 13 Years, 6 Months

Word(s)	Perceived Meaning
"help me"	used for assistance in dressing and use of toilet and occasionally for other self-help needs
"coke"	used when requesting a drink
"coat on"	used when requesting an automobile ride
"truck"	also used when requesting an automobile ride
"bus"	used at school, seems to be a question, like 'is it time to go home?'
"no"	seems to be used appropriately in a variety of situations
"headphones"	used to request music/tapes
"soup"	used to request something to eat
"daddy"	used to elicit adult attention/also seemed to be used to express 'yes'

test facilitator was escorted far out of the room to insure that she was unable to see or hear any of it.

2. *Consolidation phase.* Kenny was questioned about the story by the experimenter, who also served as a facilitator to elicit answers to the questions.

3. *Test phase.* Kenny answered questions about the story presented verbally by the experimenter, with physical support given immediately above the wrist by the uniformed facilitator.

During all test phases, there was no feedback of any kind after each response. The transcripts of all sessions are literal accounts of everything stated aloud by the experimenter and typed by Kenny with the assistance of a facilitator.

TRIAL 1

Probe Story:

There was a boy named Matt and his friend Jimmy. The boys were going to play together at Matt's house. It was raining by the time they got there, so they had to play in the house. They might break something, Matt said. But Jimmy convinced Matt to play ball for a little while, and sure enough one time Jimmy threw the ball too hard and broke a lamp. Well, Matt's dad heard the crash and came running. And he was mad!!!! "Who broke the lamp?" But before Jimmy had a chance to answer, Matt said, "Sorry, Dad, it was my fault." Matt's dad told Jimmy to go home, so the boys couldn't play together that day. But Matt knew his dad would have never let Jimmy come over again if he knew that Jimmy broke the lamp.

Consolidation Questions and Responses Facilitated by Experimenter:

Who were the two boys in the story?
MAQTT
Who else?
JIMMYY
What game did they play?
FBASEFBAKIOOLLT
What happened while they were playing baseball?
THEY BBRUOKDEE THE , LLAMP
What happened after the lamp broke?
MNASATTTTTTS DEEEDAED
GGORFTGB MADC
And then what?

```
HE SXEDCN TGB U JNJJIKMMYHB
HHOOM 3EDC
```

Test Questions and Responses Facilitated by Naive Facilitator:

Who was in the story?
DADDY
Who else?
MA%TT
JIMMY
What game did they play in the story?
GBASEBALL
Where did they play baseball?
UINTHE HOUSE
What happened while they were playing the game that they were
   playing?
THEY BROKE A LAMP
What happened at the end of the story . . . what was the last thing that
   happened?
DADDY FORGAVE THEM IT STOPPED RAAIINING

TRIAL 2

Probe Story:

Judy was a 12-year-old girl. Her mother promised her that she could
go to a special rock concert coming to their town if she saved up
from babysitting and lunch money to buy a ticket to the concert. She
managed to save up the fifteen dollars the ticket cost, plus another
five dollars. But then her mother changed her mind and told Judy
she had to spend the money on new clothes for school. Judy was
disappointed and decided to go to the concert anyway. She bought a
ticket and told her mother she had only been able to save five
dollars. That Saturday she went to the performance and told her
mother that she was spending the day with a friend. A week passed
without her mother finding out. Judy then told her older sister
Louise that she had gone to the performance and had lied to her
mother about it. Should Louise tell her mother what Judy did?

Consolidation Questions and Responses Facilitated by Experimenter:

What was the name of the girl in the story?
JUDY
How old was she?
TWELVE

How much money did she need to earn?
```
FYIFTEEBN
```
What did she want to do with the money?
```
CUOICER6TR
```
How much money had she saved?
```
TWEHHNTY
```
Did she get to do what she wanted?
```
CHEATEDTHE LASTIME I AM YESFGO TIO TTYHE CONXZCERT NERVOIUS
```
Who else was in the story?
```
MIOM LOUISE
```
What happened at the end of the story?
```
LOUISE COULDNTTELL ABOUT THE CONCS3ERT
```

Test Questions and Responses Facilitated by Naive Facilitator:

How old was the person in the story?
```
13
```
How much money did the person in the story have?
```
5DOLLARS
```
What was the money for?
```
A PRESENT
```
Where did the person in the story want to go?
```
4DOES SHELDON REALLY VBELIEVEWHY DID HE MAKE HIS DAFUGHTER
   GOWITH YOUDOES HDE THOINK WE
```

TRIAL 3

Probe Story:

Jim and Tom are brothers. Jim wanted a B-B gun, but his parents said, "Absolutely no! B-B guns are dangerous." Jim did not listen to his parents. One day after school Jim traded his baseball card collection for his best friend's B-B gun. Jim snuck the gun home and showed it to his brother. While the two brothers were playing with the gun, Tom accidentally pulled the trigger and broke the window. The boys' mother heard the noise and went into the boys' room. Should Tom tell on his brother for buying the gun?

Consolidation Questions and Responses Facilitated by Experimenter:

Who was in the story?
```
TKM
```
And who else?
```
JIJJMOLTGH3ER
```
What did Jim want to buy?

```
JIM WANTEDBBBGUN
```
How did he get the B-B gun . . . how did he get what he wanted to get?
```
TEADED6HEBSEBAL SCARDS
```
What happened after he traded the baseball cards . . . where did they
go with it?
```
SHCOTASS HONNJSHOMMSE
```
What happened when they went home . . . when Jim brought the B-B
gun home, who did he show it to?
```
BRO6TTHE4R TOM
```
What happened when he showed his brother Tom the B-B gun?
```
POUKLEEDDTHNER6TGBTRIER
```
What happened when he pulled the trigger?
```
VEEOL,KETHEWIINDCOLW
```

Test Questions and Responses Facilitated by Naive Facilitator:

Who was in the story?
```
MO^THER
```
Who else?
```
T^@WO BROITHERS
```
What are their names?
```
BOB JIM
```
Somebody wanted something real bad in the story. What did they want?
```
A BEBE GGUN
```
How did they get the thing they wanted in the story?
```
TRADED BAASEBALL CARDS
```
Let's for a moment assume that the kid wanted a B-B gun and traded
baseball cards for it. What did they do with the B-B gun?
```
SHOT IT IN TH#E HOUSE
```
What happened when they shot the B-B gun in the house, then what
happened?
```
BROKE A WINDOOW MOTHER WAS MAD
```

Reporting Back

Kenny was highly accurate in his responses to questions during the first
and third trials with the physical support of a naive facilitator. He named
precisely the three characters in trial 1 (DADDDY, MA%TT, JIMMY), the game
played (GBASEBALL), the location of the game (UINTHE HOUSE), and events
that took place during the game (THEY BROKE A LAMP).

Results from trial 3 showed similarly high levels of precision. Kenny
named the characters in the story (MO¢THER . . . T¢@WO BROITHERS) with
one incorrect name (BOB JIM were named, the correct responses were "*Tom*

and Jim"). All other responses were precisely accurate, including the object of desire in the story (A BEBE GGUN), how the object was procured (TRADED BAASEBALL CARDS), and the subsequent events (SHOT IT IN TH#E HOUSE, BROKE A WINDOOW).

Conversely, responses during trial 2 were inaccurate, unclear, or incorrect to the questions posed. Kenny indicated the character's age as 13—the actual age in the story was 12. Similarly, he reported that the character in the story had 5DOLLARS—the explicitly correct answer to the question was "20 dollars." However, the probe story stated that "She managed to save up the fifteen dollars the ticket cost, plus another five dollars. . . . She bought a ticket and told her mother she had only been able to save five dollars." Hence, this response was in part correct. The response to the question "What was the money for?" was incorrect—Kenny typed A PRESENT; the correct response would have been "to buy a concert ticket." The session was terminated after the following questions and statements were made through facilitated communication: DOES SHELDON [co-investigator observing session] REALLY BELIEVE . . . WHY DID HE MAKE HIS DAUGHTER GO WITH YOU . . . DOES HE THINK WE CHEATED THE LAST TIME . . . I AM NERVOUS. Clearly, it is possible that these words came from the uninformed facilitator, not Kenny. However, in light of the previous validation experience with Kenny, the fact that the facilitator had no more ability than in the prior session to know whether these answers were correct and concerns for the possibility of Kenny's discomfort, the session was terminated.

Several aspects of Kenny's performance were of great interest. First, the precise answers revealed that it was Kenny, not the uninformed facilitator, who was answering the questions. There could have been literally hundreds of possible responses to the types of questions posed to Kenny, with a corresponding probability of "1/hundreds" that the facilitator was "guessing" the correct responses. If we hypothetically assume that there could be 100 plausible answers to these questions—in actuality, there could have been far more than 100 possible responses to most questions—the a priori probability of "guessing" three correct answers is equal to $1/100 \times 1/100 \times 1/100 = p < .000001$. Kenny answered 13 questions correctly, 2 questions incorrectly, and one question in part correctly across all three of the sessions. The accuracy and consistency of these responses indicate that it is highly likely that Kenny, not the uninformed facilitator, was the source of answers about the stories.

It is also noteworthy that across the three trials there were 14 incorrect key strokes out of a total of 149 (including the absence or presence of appropriate spaces between words), or a precision rate of 90.6%. Moreover, *all* errors resulted either from striking a key immediately adjacent to the correct key (accounting for 8 errors); depressing the correct key too long, resulting in an additional letter (accounting for 5 errors); or the omitting a space between two words (accounting for 1 error). Hence Kenny and his facilitator were precise not only in the answers that they offered but also in the accuracy of the spelling and typing of these answers.

The recorded responses also appear to support the notion that Kenny was employing at least rudimentary inferential logic in answering some of the questions. The questions posed to him were *not* directly taken from the transcripts of the stories. For example, nowhere in the story presentations were there such questions as "Who was in the story?" or "How did they get the thing they wanted in the story?" In order for Kenny to answer these questions, he had to make simple inferences about the questions. Thus a "who" question involved inferring the name of a character and a "how" question involved inferring the description of an action. Kenny's ability to infer answers to questions presented in a novel manner indicated that his responses were not rote due to repetition or some form of echolalic responding, akin to a savant hyperlexia (cf. Goldberg, 1987)—this refers to a theory that some children with autism and other developmental disabilities might be able to decode words (i.e., pronounce them) without understanding them, and to do so precociously—nor a motor response in which he repeated back a learned sequence of key strokes. Kenny was primed during the "consolidation phase" of the story presentation with questions similar, but not identical, to those heard during the test phase.

Three observations are worth noting. First, few of the questions were exactly the same during consolidation and test phases. Second, Kenny's responses varied; comparison of questions and answers during the two phases of each trial do not read as repetitive production. Indeed, responses during the consolidation phase were primarily characterized by seemingly random or missed key strokes that could have been related, at least in part, to the limited competence of the experimenter/facilitator during this presentation. Third, Kenny's responses during the test phase could not be explained as a repetition of a previously learned motor program. The literal stroke-by-stroke transcripts during the two phases bear little or no resemblance to one another, indicating that Kenny did not simply "play back" a previously memorized message. Indeed, the best explanation of these data is that Kenny's correct responses to questions exemplified at least rudimentary *linguistic inferences*.

This type of simple inference is not the only evidence of his abstract information-processing abilities. There were also varying levels of higher-order transformations, inferences, and extrapolations revealed during the test sessions. For example, during trial 3, Kenny demonstrated a *phonemic transformation*. He had previously been presented with the spelling "B-B" [gun] by the experimenter, but later spelled the word as BEBE during the test phase. Though this was an isolated example, it implied that Kenny had the ability to produce a phonemic transformation analogous to "sounding out" the word and indicated that at some level he might be using a phonological system to spell.

Kenny's responses during the test phases, including DADDY FORGAVE THEM (trial 1) and MOTHER WAS MAD (trial 3), implied that Kenny may have logically inferred information from the events of the stories. In trial 1, the character "Matt" took the blame for the broken lamp because he feared that his friend "Jimmy" would not otherwise be allowed to return to their house. One plausible inference from this information (presented to Kenny, but not to the uninformed facilitator) was that Matt's father might be more "forgiving" if Matt assumed responsibility. During earlier questioning in the test phase of trial 3, there was no indication that the brothers' parents had refused to allow the boys to have the B-B gun, which supported the inference that MOTHER WAS MAD (as opposed to the mother being "forgiving"). While it is possible that the uninformed facilitator could have inferred these responses, this seems unlikely since the needed information was not available to the facilitator.

The indication that Kenny was using higher-order processing of the stories and that he was the author of the facilitated statements gains further support from his demonstration of a *conjectured extrapolation* of the story during trial 1. The story presented to Kenny included the statement, "It was raining by time they got there, so they had to play indoors." The last question presented to Kenny during the test phase was "What happened at the end of the story . . . what was the last thing that happened?" His response was DADDY FORGAVE THEM IT STOPPED RAAIINING. Review of the questions and answers during this test phase shows that there had been no prior mention of "rain" with the uninformed facilitator. Discussion of RAAIINING indicated both that this statement was authored by Kenny, not the facilitator, and that he was extrapolating on the facts of the story (i.e., that it was raining in the story)—a fundamentally abstract processing of information.

Kenny also showed memory retrieval consistent with the well-studied information-processing phenomena of primacy–recency effects first described by Ebbinghaus in 1885 (cited in Rose, 1992). When Kenny was asked "Who was in the story . . . Who else?", he responded with the last characters mentioned in the story as his first response. He did *not* follow an order consistent with a rote or programmed response. Rather, he abstracted the order of the characters in the story in a manner consistent with a *recency effect*.

A DEMONSTRATION OF INDEPENDENT TYPING:
THE CASE OF JOEY

Joey was introduced to facilitated communication in March 1992 when he was 6 years, 2 months of age. As in Kenny's case and others', we actively argued with and discouraged Joey's family and teacher from moving ahead with this technique, but to no avail. However, Joey's family and teacher were also amenable to some methods of trying to validate the authenticity of communication.

Joey's developmental status was characterized by a diagnosis of PDD and/or autism, and severe mental retardation. Some amount of expressive language was emerging by 6 years of age. However, the great majority of verbal behavior was echolalic or perseverative speech, with a small number of single-word labels and occasionally functional two- to three-word phrases. Additionally, on a number of occasions Joey would stop using expressive language for periods of days or even weeks. Joey was last formally tested at 4 years, 7 months of age, at which time he showed an IQ of 44 (31 month age-equivalence) on the Stanford-Binet. Results on the Vineland Adaptive Behavior Scales ranged from 19 to 20 month age-equivalence on the communication, daily living skills, and socialization subscales.

Excerpts of Joey's individual education plans (IEP) from the year prior to the initiation of facilitated communication follow.

Excerpts from "Student Profile" and "Current Performance Levels" (Age: 5 years, 10 months)

Joey is skilled at puzzles, pegging, sorting, and block building. . . . He is inconsistent in naming his colors and shapes . . . identifies [by pointing in a field of 2 cards] letters of the alphabet with 90 percent accuracy . . . also identifies numbers 1 to 10, but does not show 1-to-1 correspondence. . . . Joey has poor eye contact, social interaction and attending abilities which interfere with his effective communication. Joey's primary means of communicating is non-verbal. . . . He does use gestures, facial expressions and often will take an adult's hand to direct them to a wanted item. Joey engages in echolalic speech and uses a number of single words and 2- to 3-word phrases. . . . Joey's receptive language skills are poor. He is inconsistent in responding to direct requests. . . . Joey has good fine motor, self-care and gross motor skills. He can independently eat his lunch once the food or eating utensil is placed in his hand. He is toilet trained.

Examples of IEP Objectives

Joey will follow simple directions, when repeated, with 80 to 100 percent accuracy.

Joey will receptively identify common objects found in his environment
with 80 to 100 percent accuracy.

Joey will take the correct object to demonstrate comprehension of ad-
jectives when told, "you can take the (big) one," with 80 percent
accuracy.

Joey will find a desired object when told it is (on) an object with minimal context cues, to show comprehension of three prepositions at
the 80 percent accuracy level.

Joey will receptively and expressively name [primary] colors . . . shapes
. . . with 80 percent accuracy.

Joey will count objects up to 10 and match the quantity with its symbol
with 80 percent accuracy.

Joey will match the letter sound to the letter with 80 percent accuracy.

Joey will trace along vertical and horizontal lines with 80 percent
accuracy.

During this two-year period we were attempting to develop Joey's recognition of letters, numbers, and sight words. However, at his previous
school some prominent personnel who had extensive experience with PDD,
autism, and mental retardation resisted attempting these procedures; they
argued that there had been no demonstrable evidence that he could recognize or attach meaning to these types of stimuli. We had lengthy disagree-
ments over the merits of including more abstract curricula, such as reading and math readiness activities, in his IEP. Consequently, Joey's parents
moved him to a new school program that included the "experimental"
curricula, seen in his IEP above (e.g., letter and number recognition, sight
word reading).

It was at this new school that one of Joey's teachers first introduced the
idea of using facilitated communication. His teacher reported regularly
attempting to use facilitation with Joey over a two-month period before
any alleged responses were elicited (a chronicle of significant facilitated
communication–related events reported by his family and teachers is
shown in Figure 7.2).

Increasingly, the facilitators became convinced that they could feel
Joey's hand moving across the keyboard with intent, and his attention to
task and general conduct showed remarkable improvements, particularly
when he sat in front of the keyboard. This gave a subjective impression that
Joey was actively engaged in the facilitated communication activities. His
family and teacher were convinced he was the author of typed communications. However, there was no clear preliminary evidence similar to what
we had observed with Kenny or the few other individuals with whom we
were involved. Hence, consultations were regularly made to the family and

FIGURE 7.2 Chronology of Joey's Significant Facilitiated Communication Events

3/10/92:	FC first attempted.
5/8/92:	First alleged success at producing coherent responses to questions with FC physical support offered had-over-hand.
5/92 to 2/93:	Continued use of FC on a routine basis, but *no* reports of accurate and precise information being typed that was unknown to the facilitator (i.e., absence of anecdotal evidence).
2/21/93:	First demonstration of independently typed words, typically involving typing the letters from a flashcard showing both a picture and word (i.e., copying from sample).
2/23/93:	First demonstration of typing words from *only* a verbal prompt (no picture, simply told to type "green" and "elephant"), and began typing with index fingers on *both* hands in alternation (previously only using index finger on right hand).
2/25/93:	First accurately answered fill-in-the-blank questions about "personal information."
3/1/93:	First accurately answered fill-in-the-blank questions about book read on previous day.
3/7/93:	First spontaneous elaboration of picture stimuli with simple descriptor words.
3/30/93:	First description of a picture using a complete sentence.

school personnel, but specific plans to validate Joey's facilitated communication were not pursued, awaiting some informal evidence.

During the subsequent year, Joey's teacher and parents regularly incorporated facilitated communication into his daily routine for spontaneous communication as well as for language, spelling, and reading related drills aimed at developing these curricula. Joey was also maintained in his use of augmentative communication systems such as the Mayer-Johnson Picture Symbol Communication system, in developing phonic representations of letters (i.e., matching printed letter and sound), in sight word recognition, and in functional use of verbal behavior. Joey's progress with these systems continued to be slow, but steady, and no overt efforts were made to validate his use of facilitated communication. However, almost one year after Joey began using facilitation a remarkable event occurred: Joey began to type without physical support.

The first demonstration of independently typed words occurred on February 21, 1993, during a work session at home. His father was presenting Joey with flashcards showing a brightly colored picture with its accompanying word printed below. Joey would be asked to both name and then give some descriptive detail about each picture presented. His alleged responses were then typed using facilitation, with physical support offered at the hand or wrist. After Joey and his father had worked for a brief period, Joey's father left him sitting in front of the computer while he went into an adjacent room. Upon his return, Joey's father found the word BABY typed repeatedly across the computer screen. Indeed, the next picture sitting on the stack of flashcards was that of a "baby." Joey's father called to Joey's mother, inquiring if she wanted to continue working with him, as she had seemingly started to do. Joey's mother indicated that she had *not* been working with Joey and that she was busy in the other room; at which point they realized that *Joey* had typed the word BABY several times *independently*. They then presented Joey with approximately 25 additional words, which he typed largely without physical support. On some trials Joey would not respond to the keyboard until his mother or father lifted or gently pushed his hand, arm, or elbow toward the keys, or gave verbal prompts such as directing Joey to the first letter of the word. But the prompt to strike the first key was typically all that was necessary to elicit the entire word.

A conservative interpretation of this startling development was that he had learned to copy a sample. That is, he was simply hitting the corresponding keys to the printed word that he saw on the card. This seemed plausible given the confluence of skills and activities that Joey had been working on during the previous year: (1) He had spent regular time sitting in front of a keyboard during the year—retrospectively, he clearly had learned how to quickly locate appropriate keys; (2) he had recently shown accuracy in letter identification in school by independently pointing to letter flashcards (see the "Student Profile" excerpts above); and (3) the picture–word flashcards were always present during these sessions, including when he first independently typed. Hence Joey may have just developed the ability to find the corresponding computer key for each letter in a given word and copied it. If this were all that Joey had achieved, it would have been a remarkable development, for Joey had never before done anything remotely this sophisticated. However, the events that took place over the following days and weeks revealed a level of competence and a rate of growth that could not be easily explained in terms of conventional educational or cognitive development theory and were more than mere copying.

Two days after Joey first showed the ability to independently type words from a flashcard, he then showed he could type words with *only* a verbal prompt. For example, his parents would simply say, "how do you spell 'green'" or "Joey, type 'elephant.'" The family only attempted to use words that Joey had had some level of prior experience with, but the list of words that he spelled correctly was exhaustively long. Clearly, Joey was not simply copying; at a minimum, he had memorized a lengthy list of words that he could decode from a spoken presentation to correctly spell.

This demonstration alone did not reveal whether Joey understood what he was spelling—just that he could decode. However, he soon was accurately answering fill-in-the-blank questions about "personal information." This was done by presenting Joey with a typed question that he would then answer by independently typing the response (all names were followed by the family's last name, left out here for confidentiality):

1.	My name is:	JOEY
2.	I am ____ years old:	required prompts and assistance
3.	My address is:	13 COTE STREET
4.	My telephone number is:	required prompts and assistance
5.	My mother's name is:	CARMELINA
6.	My father's name is:	DAVID
7.	My sister's name is:	JENNIFER
8.	My brother's name is:	DAVID
9.	My dog's name is:	required prompts and assistance
10.	The color of my house is:	YELLOW
11.	My favorite color is:	GREEN

By March 1—8 days after first typing independently—Joey was answering questions about a book he and his mother had read the previous day, using a similar fill-in-the-blank procedure. And by March 7 he could elaborate on his descriptions of pictures that he previously would only name—this was done by presenting Joey with a flashcard that showed a picture, with the printed words covered, and by asking "What is this?" Joey would type the name of the object in the picture. His father would then ask "What else can you tell me about the picture?" Joey's elaborations typically included appropriately naming the dominant color(s) in the picture, and, in a number of trials, he would then identify other aspects of the picture. For example, after correctly identifying the picture CAT, Joey then appropriately elaborated with YFLLOW EYES. For the picture of a goat, he typed GOAT and then added the word BELL, presumably to note the bell around the neck of the goat in the picture. By March 30, with encouragement from his teacher and parents, Joey began describing the contents of pictures in complete sentences. He typed, for example, THE MOTHER IS HOLDING THE BABY and THE EGG IS THE COLOR WHITE.

Based on these observations, we can make several interpretations. First, Joey can correctly spell extremely large numbers (i.e., hundreds) of words from pictorial or verbal presentations of words. Second, Joey understood many questions and could formulate appropriate responses. Third, it is likely that Joey had some level of these skills prior to showing them through independent typing. The fact that he traversed from simple copying of words to correctly answering and spelling answers within a matter of about one week—he was working on these skills for about one hour daily—implied that he may have had rudiments of these skills for some time. This indirectly supports the hypothesis that some undefined amount of facilitated communication may have been authored by Joey prior to independent typing. Fourth, failure to show either observational or experimental evidence of valid communication with facilitation did *not* necessarily imply that either comprehension or competence were lacking. We found neither incidental evidence nor any formal demonstration that Joey was capable of valid communication with facilitation prior to his independent typing. His independently typed communication dramatically exceeded the expectations of a multitude of professionals experienced in PDD, autism, speech and language development, and special education. It is quite likely that Joey had competencies that we simply did not know how to tap. Fifth, Joey was far more capable of answering questions correctly by spelling out his responses on a keyboard than he was of producing spoken responses. For the great majority of questions that Joey answered appropriately with a typed word or phrase, he was unable to answer with a spoken response.

Clearly, there are many more questions than answers regarding the breadth and extent of Joey's competencies (literacy, comprehension, expressive abilities, and motor skills) and the nature of his disability. Our assessment of him has been completely observational and awaits empirically controlled study. However, the progression of Joey's expressive skills were important contributors to our growing recognition that the phenomenon of facilitated communication indeed existed and required considerably closer study.

WHAT WERE WE TO CONCLUDE?

We entered this area of inquiry as hostile skeptics, looking to protect our clients from what we perceived as extremely dangerous misinformation. However, our findings of observational and experimentally controlled validity, the emergence of independent typing, and data implying validity of this technique (Calculator & Singer, 1992; Cardinal, Hanson, & Wakeham, 1996; Crossley, 1992; Heckler, 1994; Intellectual Disability Review Panel [IDRP], 1989; Karp, 1993; Karp, Biklen, & Chadwick, 1993; Steering Committee, 1993; Rimland & Green, 1993; Sheehan, 1993; Sheehan & Matuozzi, 1994; Vazquez, 1994) have given us some guidelines with which to proceed.

Facilitated Communication Exists. "Facilitated communication" as described by Crossley, Biklen, and their associates (Biklen, 1990, 1993; Biklen

& Schubert, 1991; Crossley, 1992; Crossley & Remington-Gurney, 1992) exists in some form, for at least some persons with significant disabilities. Despite the wide range of unanswered questions surrounding this phenomenon, the fact that at least a small number of individuals have demonstrated remarkable and unexpected literacy with facilitated communication may call a great many of our current theories of human development into question. Bear in mind that several advances in the assessment of central nervous system (CNS) processes were linked to a small number of unique individuals who were studied on a case-by-case basis. Classic examples of this date back to the work of Broca and Wernicke, whose early observations created the basis upon which a great deal of CNS function and verbal behavior are now understood (cf., Kandel, 1991).

Facilitated Communication Is Evanescent and Fragile. Since our first clear evidence of valid facilitated communication was revealed, we have initiated a small number of additional case studies that are currently progressing. Although these studies are not yet complete enough to report, they have contributed to our subjective impressions that this phenomenon is fragile vis-à-vis its reliability; some days we get it (i.e., valid communication) and some days we do not. For example, we are currently investigating facilitated communication with a young man who, with his partner-facilitator, has succeeded at passing information accurately about 10 to 15% of the time. Similarly Kenny, described above in our case study (Weiss et al., 1996), did not show valid communication in the second of our three trials. Therefore, had Trial 2 been the only trial administered, we would have concluded that facilitation was not a valid form of communication. There are at least two hypotheses regarding the reliability of facilitated communication that we must evaluate further. It may be that facilitated communication *can* exist (i.e., it is valid) but is not always operative (i.e., lower reliability). Alternatively, the actual validity and reliability of facilitated communication may be quite high, at least for some, but many of the experimental designs employed thus far have been unreliable in capturing the phenomenon.

It is clearly premature to speculate on the reliability of this phenomenon. However, recognizing the morass of complications associated with the fragility of facilitated communication may help us to interpret some findings and navigate our future research efforts. First, generalizing conclusions from a single evaluation is, at best, misleading. It seems essential to evaluate the phenomenon repeatedly and from a variety of experimental and experiential perspectives, to do it often and in varied ways. The majority of individuals who have been assessed in validation studies have revealed high levels of facilitator influence (cf., Green & Shane, 1994). This may be because there *is* a high level of facilitator influence, or it may be due to the type of research designs used; it may be due to practice or stimulus effects, or to other experimental considerations. It is evident from our limited studies that we, too, would have shown predominantly facilitator influence if we had stopped with only isolated assessments of our clients.

Second, in research studies of the method, deviation from the reported phenomenon *for an individual* should occur only gradually. Start by assessing the phenomenon as it is reported by those who know the facilitated communication user well, and initially stay with what works for that person. Only start to deviate from a routine after logging several repetitions over a lengthy time period.

The Incidence of Facilitated Communication Competence Is Not Yet Known. Related to the seemingly fragile nature of the method, conclusions concerning the incidence of who can or cannot use facilitated communication are quite premature. It is too early to generalize from reported statistics (e.g., Rimland & Green, 1993) what the actual incidence of this phenomenon may be. The most that we may conclude at this time is that some people can succeed in expressing themselves through facilitated communication. Questions of who and how many await further investigations.

Look Long and Close at Those Who Have Validated. We likely have a great deal to learn from those who have validated in their use of facilitated communication. Rimland and Green (1993) reported 17 individuals who had shown varying forms of validation. Subsequently, others have reported new cases of validation (Cardinal et al., 1996; Weiss et al., 1996). The crucial questions to be addressed revolve around who these individuals are and what the range and variety of their competencies are. Moreover, who are the individuals who served in the roles of facilitators for those individuals who have validated? To gain a more complete understanding of the many questions remaining about facilitation and associated factors, including sensory, motor, cognitive, and neurologic development, we must explore what these individuals can tell us, both overtly as well as through experimental investigations (cf., Marcus & Shevin, Chapter 6, this volume). Unfortunately, it seems that it will take a long time to unravel the many intricacies that we may learn from these individuals.

As we stated at the outset, it may seem odd that experimental psychologists, particularly those who are skeptical by nature and training, are embarking on studies of facilitated communication. However, it now strikes us as odd that most serious students of human development are not stopping to take a close look at this very interesting and important phenomenon. Much will be learned, and we intend to be present as these new findings are revealed.

CHAPTER 8

The Multiple Meanings of Independence: Perspectives from Facilitated Communication

Douglas Biklen

How do people who communicate via facilitation think about independence (i.e., typing without any physical support). What does independence mean to them? How do they define independence? This study, comprised of interviews with and observations of eight public school students who use facilitated communication, was conducted in the symbolic interactionist tradition (Blumer, 1969; Glaser & Strauss, 1967), focusing on the meanings these students make of their worlds and, more specifically, the issue of independence.

Often a topic such as this is conceptualized simply as a technical question, as a treatment, decontextualized. Thus researchers may ask how many persons "are independent," implying that independence is something a person *has* or *has not*, something the person has learned or not learned, something that can be understood primarily as a skill (Halle, Chadsey-Rusch, & Reichle, 1994, p. 149). From the symbolic interactionist perspective, events, objects, and knowledge are all presumed to be contextually located. Concepts such as independence, ability, and disability are treated as social constructs, not innate, natural facts or truths. Where the positivist may consider it possible to create communication experiments by which to establish facts and even the truth about communicative ability or style, the interactionist hopes to capture viewpoints, understandings, hypotheses, and theories by observing and interacting with people in their natural contexts. The interactionist observer hopes not just for an inventory of events observed or viewpoints given but for evoked understanding. In other words, truth does not exist, it is enacted (see Addelson, 1990) and therefore changing. We can expect to derive understandings of how individuals think about such things as typing with physical assistance and typing without it, but not about what independence is or is not.

THE DISCOURSE ON INDEPENDENCE

Research and commentary on independent typing by people who had been introduced to facilitation says little about it, except that those who came to type without support did so after several years of typing only with support and did so only when their facilitators sat next to them or diagonally behind them. In the book *Silent Words*, Eastham (1992) describes her son's typing without physical support as something he learned with techniques his teachers borrowed from the field of visual impairments:

> A pencil was used to touch David's shoulder instead of the teacher's hand, it was pointed out that we could gradually fade the object more easily than a person's touch. The professors were used to working with blind persons and knew what a strong motivation touch was. (p. 80)

David Eastham's teacher sat a little more than a foot from him (p. 84). As with Kochmeister (1994) (see also Watts & Wurzburg, 1994), Eastham typed in this manner with one of several facilitators sitting next to him, but not without the familiar facilitator seated nearby.

Oppenheim (1974) is less precise about her students' communication, although she explains that the teachers were able to fade their hand-over-hand support of her students' writing. Nevertheless she found they sometimes needed a light touch on another bodily surface—for example, the head or back—to continue. Crossley reported that within several years of beginning with facilitation, more than 30 of her clients typed independently (Crossley, 1992), although, like Oppenheim, she found they sometimes seemed to require a touch on the head or back.

PARTICIPANTS AND THEIR WORDS

This study focused on *all* of the students who used facilitated communication in four different sites, a first-grade class in a rural elementary school and a middle school (grades 4–6), junior high school (grades 7–8), and high school in a suburban district; by the end of the study, the students who had been at the middle school had transitioned to the junior high school but were still in the study. These sites were chosen because the teachers were working at having their students type and write without support.

At the time this study was completed, the participants in the study ranged in age from 7 to 19 (see Table 8.1). The 7-year-old attended first grade, three of the others attended junior high school, and four were in high school. The study occurred over the last seven months of one school year and the first seven months of another. Each of the students had used facilitated communication at sentence level for conversation and academic work for more than two years and with multiple facilitators.

Four of the students were classified as autistic, three as mentally retarded, and one as mentally handicapped with a developmental disability. Their presumed reading levels prior to being introduced to facilitated communication were characterized variously as "nonreader," "preprimer," and "first grade," with the exception of one student (who was in the sixth grade at the time) whose speech teacher said he had been judged to have the ability to "decode words at the fourth-grade level." The first grade student was able to read at or above grade level. The sixth-grade student could speak in functional sentences but was unable to elaborate on topics. The other students had extremely limited communicative ability. In addition

TABLE 8.1 Student Demographics and Communication Information

Name	School Level	Age	Disability	Prior Communication	Prior reading level	Regular Classes	Support for sentence-level typing
Cathy	El. 1	7	Autism	Words, phrases	Grade level	Full-time	None
Lindsay	Jr. H.S.	15	M.R.	Words, phrases	Non-reader	1	Mid-forearm & Elbow
Patrick	Jr. H.S.	14	Autism	Words, phrases	Preprimer	1	Elbow & Shoulder
Joseph	Jr. H.S.	16	M.H./D.D	Sentences, echoed speech	Decoding, 4th grade level	0	None
Courtney	H.S.	18	M.R./N.I.	Words, phrases	First Grade	1	Mid-forearm
Stephen	H.S.	17	M.R.	Sentences, often unintelligible	First Grade	1	Mid-forearm
Maggie	H.S.	18	Autism	Yes, No, echoed speech, greetings	Preprimer-First Grade	Full-time	Shoulder*
Evan	H.S.	19	Autism	No speech, functional word book (unreliable)	Non-reader	Full-time	Elbow

* Maggie typed some school work without physical support; see the example provided above of science definitions.

to the sixth-grade student, one other student could say short sentences, but could not initiate or converse in complex sentences, one student did not speak and was unable to use a book of keywords reliably, and the others could say individual words and sometimes phrases but could not converse at sentence level.

Three of the students in this study now type some or all of their communication without physical support. The other five students participated in another study in which their teachers confirmed their authorship (Biklen, Saha, & Kliewer, 1995; Chapter 3, this volume).

METHOD

During the study, all but one of the students attended some academic classes that included peers without disabilities. Joseph, the one exception, spent one period in a resource room with learning-disabled students but for the rest of his school day attended a separate special class. Three of the students attended regular classes (i.e., including students with and without disabilities) for the entire school day except for a daily meeting with a speech teacher (i.e., speech pathologist). In the tradition of participant observation (Bogdan & Biklen, 1991; P. M. Ferguson, Ferguson & Taylor, 1992; Taylor & Bogdan, 1984), I conducted observations in settings that the students frequented, including regular classes, special classes, and speech class. It was in the latter that I interviewed each of the secondary-age participants about the meaning of independent typing for them. These observations also included conversations with the teachers and teaching assistants who acted as facilitators. I made a minimum of five observations of each student, focusing mainly on the high school–age students at the outset and then on the junior high students and the elementary student during the last half of the study. The elementary-age student attended a typical class full-time, so all my observations of her were in this setting. Due to her age, I felt observations would yield more useful data than interviews.

Because the students typed on electronic typewriters and computers, transcripts of their typing were available to me. The 7-year-old child used both typing and handwriting. For spoken language, I took notes and, in the cases of five students for whom I had permission, I videotaped my conversations with them on at least two occasions each. The videotapes enabled me to accurately record speech and also level of support in facilitation (e.g., no physical support, facilitator's hand on shoulder, hand at elbow, hand on forearm, hand at wrist, hand under hand). Although I did not videotape the elementary-age student in her first-grade class, I was able to secure three videotapes of her at the age of 4 in preschool class, typing with facilitation. This was at a preschool where all students—those with and without disabilities—are introduced to letters, words, and typed or written communication at age 3. I was also able to observe videotapes of all but one of the other students when they were first introduced to facilitation. For all of the students, I was able to secure examples of their typing from the early months in which they had been introduced to facilitation.

THE MEANINGS OF INDEPENDENCE

The students' conceptions of independence were in a constant state of formulation and reformulation, filled with contradictions, never simple. They did not think of it as a "thing" or "state" as much as a way of being or becoming. The following subsections are the themes that the students used to characterize independence.

Nothing Terrifies as Much

For several students, typing without support was cause for anxiety, even fear. Maggie, who did most of her typing with a facilitator's hand on her shoulder—I observed her typing this way with a teacher, a teaching assistant, and her mother—said she regarded her steps to independent typing as INTELLECTUALLY RIGHT [but] EMOTIONALLY EXCUCIATINGLY DIFFICULT. I HAD TO FREE MY SELF EVERY STEP OF THE WAY (Watts & Wurzburg, 1994). By the time the study ended, she was typing in upper- and lowercase letters and typed some sentences related to her academic work without physical support (described below). Yet she was fearful of losing facilitation and especially of losing a favored facilitator: I AM AFRAID I WILL NOT ALWAYS HAVE MRS. F. TO HELP ME. I WILL HAVE TO HAVE A REPLACEMENT OF HER TO SURVIVE.

Courtney received forearm support for most of her typing. Although she did not type sentences without physical support, she did type individual words (e.g., SNEAKERS, CHURCH, BIOGRAPHY, BICYCLE, NICE) when asked to do so by her teacher, without any touch. She, too, expressed fright at others' potential expectation of independence: FEEL SCARED BASED VAST EXPECTATIONS FOR ASKING FACSILETATE AAS INDEPENDENT AS WANTED ADDS SRTRESS. She had no confidence in her eventual success: THING FOR ME THE HARD PART IS TRASTING (?) THAT I CAN DO IT ALONE.

Patrick said GET VERY NERVOUS, AND I GEWT LOST SO EASY MAKING ME MAKLE A LOT MISTZKES. He typed with forearm or elbow support, except for his name and the date, which he could type with no support.

Stephen's concern was similar: He regarded independence as important but wanted assurances that his teachers and I understood that he might be slow to achieve it: ONLY YOU THE UNDER YOU UNANDERSTASND THAT I AM SLOW THAT I AM SLOW THE TO TYPE THE TIME WHEN I TOKE INDEPENDENTLY.

Typically, Evan received facilitator support of a hand above or just below his forearm. His typing was filled with typographical errors. He jabbed at the keyboard as he selected letters and, on two occasions, he attempted to throw the typewriter. Each time that he became visibly upset, his typing paralleled his behavior—he jabbed more forcefully and produced more typographical errors. If fear of breakdowns was a gap for Maggie, Courtney, Patrick, and Stephen to bridge, for Evan it was a chasm:

> WHY DFRUIOVE [drive] RTHHE [the] INDEPISSUE [independence issue] TYOPTHE [to the] FRONT NOTHING TERRIFIESZ ME AS TRULY AS EZXEXP E4CTATION [expectation] OF INDE [independence] I GET 1 INSWIDER [inside] TRE TENSES SA LIJJKE [like] IMAVGSEES [images] O F ATEST6 [of a test] IA D CARE T G TOOO MUCNH AB [I care too much about] PODEEOPLEAXS [peoples] REACTIONS TOWAERD [toward] THE DIFDICULTYUS [difficulty] WE THINK THEY WREGARD [regard] US ADS [as] SAERETARDED [retarded] AFTEDFR THE FAILURSR5 [failure] ABNDS [and] IOT [it] SD SCAREES [scares] DUNDERSTYANDING [understanding] AWAY [When Evan typed, he often hit two or three keys simultaneously, thus for the word "drive" he hit an "f" next to the "r", a "u" instead of an "i", and then an "i" and the "o" next to it. My translation of his typing is based nearly entirely on removal of extra letters. Occasionally, Evan typed the beginning letters of a word, enough for readers to guess it (e.g., INDEP for "independence" and BEC for "because"), and then proceeded to a next word.]

The risk for Evan of typing without physical support was not merely that he might look bad but that he might be regarded as incompetent, a reputation that facilitation had allowed him to escape.

Like the Olympics

As students discussed their typing without physical support, they seemed to be describing a performance skill not unlike learning to ski down an expert slope, perform a triple toe loop in skating, or walk a tightrope. Some wondered whether they could ever master it. Patrick, for example, lamented what he felt was slow progress, even though he thought he knew why:

I FEEL THAT MY GOOD PROGRESS HAS BEEN SLOW NOT
BSADMOSDTOLY [bad mostly] SLOW AMDF SOMERTHING DELAHYED
VBY MY TROUBLE IN KEERPING MY ATTRENTIONM [attention] TAKES
SOME TERRIFIV CINC CINCSDRB CONCEMTYRDATION.

Lindsay regularly practiced trying to type without physical assistance. She could type her name, the date, and some individual words without support and had learned to do a multiple-choice test without support, albeit with her facilitator sitting next to her. It appears that Lindsay had difficulty at first getting words out in the right order, but then got her point across, crediting her improvements to determination and visualizing:

ARE THEY THE BEST ALL THE THAT THEY DO/TO USE VISTALING
TO SEE IT BEST
ALL THE ATHLETES IN THE OLLMOPICS SEE FAR INTO THE MIND
BEFORE THE RSACE SND WAT CH IN THEIREM [watch in their
mind] TO SEE IT DONE GOOD FOTR PRACTICXE BEGDORE

Deciding to Try

Both Evan and Patrick regarded independence as their teachers' agenda more than their own. Patrick revealed a humorous side when he typed, MRS M TREWLLSA [tells] ME I WANT TO,. Then he added, I KNOW IT IS RIGHT. Similarly, Evan remarked that the goal of independence was not his agenda:

ITS NOT MJTY6 [my] GOOAL ITS YTHE TEWARTTEAMS [teams]
YESA I8 DECIDED WJH ATR [what] I WANT6 IUS MORE CIOE
MFORT [comfort] ANDLOE4SS [less] RTLO [to] EHIN ERRRORED BY
TTESTYTTING

This was far from a declaration to achieve independence at any cost. And it was produced with much emotion. He pounded out the message, jabbing at the keys, then pulled the paper from the typewriter several times, walked around the room, tossed books on the floor, and pushed the typewriter against the wall, before sitting back down to complete his typing. Several months later he typed to me, TYOU NMUST SEE ME AS A FAILURE IN INDEPENDENCER ASS CALOWAYS [as always] THE TENSION IS HIGH AND THATS BEC ASE4 [because] I9 [I] WANT RTO PLEASE YO. Then he typed that he was ready to work with his teacher to SORT5 PRACTGT5ICAL RTHI9NGS OUT ABOUT INDEP. After months of worrying about independence, he was ready to proceed, explaining that his life was QUIETER NOW

THAN IN THE BEGINNINVG and he was ABL;E AWWUME OWN POWER TO CREATE.

For the others, all of whom were typing with the same or less physical support than Patrick or Evan, becoming able to type without physical support was a kind of symbol of normality and competence, a way of being seen by more other people as thinking individuals. Lindsay typed that it was GOOD TO TRY BERING INDRPENDEDENT FEE. LS [feels] BETTER EVEN IN CASE PEOPLW THS THINK I ANM NOT WIRED RIGHT.

Joseph, a junior high–age student, could type without any physical support, although success with staying on topic seemed to require his teachers or me to converse with him by typing our side of the conversation; if we did not do that, he tended to produce one-word and three- or four-word sentences and to leave out details. Once he had typed sentence-level communication without physical support, Joseph said that he was impressed with his own abilities. Several years earlier, when he began to communicate through typing, his teacher supported him at the forearm for conversational communication, pulling back on his arm—in effect restraining him—a strategy she found necessary to keep him from producing echoed responses (see Chapter 3).

For Maggie, independence was related to the larger goal of finding acceptance:

> I . . . HAD AN AGENDA OF HOW I WOULD BE COMFORTABLE IN THE WORK LD OF NORMAL PEOPLE AND HOW TO GO TO IT. I WANTED INITIALLY TO STAY IN MY LIFE OF MY WORLD AND NOT BE A PART OF THE OTHER WORLD THAT YOU LIVE IN. BUT I SLOWLY BEGAN TO DO SOME INTERESTING THINGS THAT MADE ME NEED BECOME MORE AND MORE A MEMBER OF THE REAL WORLD.

She was sometimes exuberantly optimistic about achieving her goal: I WILL EVENTUALLY BECOME INDEPENDENT IN MOST IF NOT ALL COMMUNICATION THAT ALSO HAS MANY STAGED BUT I WILL SING AND DANCE ON THE M ALL. And sometimes she was more measured: I HOPE I CAN WORK HARD AND BE NORMAL SOMEDAY. NOT AS AUTISTIC. I WANT TO COMUNICATE MORE EASILY.

At other times she seemed impatient about typing without physical support. She was more interested in a concept of independence that was larger than and different from physical independence, namely, freedom to make decisions about her life:

> I AM ALWAYS TRYING TO BE INDEPENDENT AND ALWAYS FAILING. I AM TOO RESTRICTED. I AM SO TREATED LIKE A FOOL. I AM

NOT ALOWED TO MAKE A DECISION AT ALL. I AM AT MY WITS
END OVER MY SCHEDULE FOR NEXT YEAR AND NO ONE IS LISTEN-
ING TO ME AT ALL. I WANT TO MAKE AN INDEPENDENT DECISION
BUT I HAVE BEEN OVER RULED AND I AM ANGRY ABOUT IT
STILL. I WANT TO BE GIVEN CONTROL. I AM SO WEARY OF
BEING TOLD WHAT TO DO AND I AM SO ALWAYS AIMED AT INDE-
PENDENTS. I WANT A LOCAL DIPLOMA AND THEY ARE MAKING ME
TAKE REGENTS WHEN I DO NOT WANT TO [She wanted to complete
a non–college preparatory curriculum].

Despite these protestations, Maggie and her first facilitator had planned together and she took at least co-ownership for the plan and outcome:

IT [the agenda to achieve independence] HAD WELL STRUCTURED
PLANS THAT WE [she and her facilitator] DE VIED AND STUCK
WITH. She explained, WE PLANNED THE STEPS TO
INDEPENEDENCE TOGETHER AND SHE WAS THE STRENGTH I
NEEDED TO MAKE EACH JUMP. ALTHOUGH THE MANY JUMPS
WERE NOT GR GREAT TO OTHER PEOPLE THE LEAPS WERE
LIKE JUMPING OVER SKYSTAPERS TO M ME.

When Maggie began to type without any physical support, the content was school work—her facilitator sat next to her as she typed. She typed definitions for science terms after first reading the relevant passages in her text. She typed responses that synthesized—not merely copied—what she had read:

PHYSICAL PROPERTIES-FEATURES THAT DESCRIBE A PIECE OF
MATTER; PHYICAL CHANGE—ANY CHANGE IN THE PHYICAL PROPER-
TIES OF A SUBSTANCE THAT DOES NOT CHANGE THE ARRANGEMENT
OF ATOMS; CHEMICAL REACTION—CHEMICAL CHANGE REARRANGING
OF THE ATOMS OR MOLECULES TO FORM A NEW SUBSTANCE;
CHEMICAL PROPERTY—DESCRIBE HOW A SUBSTANCE REACTS WITH
OTHER SUBSTANCES; BALANCED EQUATION—THE NUMBER OF ATOMS
OF EACH ELEMENT IS THE SAME ON BOTH SIDES.

Practice, Practice, and More Practice

I often observed teachers creating opportunities for students to type without physical support or with reduced support. Teachers asked their students to type their names and the date without support on the top of each sheet of paper or before any extended conversation; the first-grade student typically wrote her name. The teachers of the older students asked them to practice typing individual words (i.e., not multiple words together and not sentences) without support. Several students attempted making multiple-choice selections on computer games without physical support; they also used worksheets with fill-in-the-blank and matching activities. With Maggie, Joseph, and Cathy, their teachers simply gave them opportunities to try typing something without support; when they did, the teachers encouraged more.

The teachers' independence strategies included having students take over some of the tasks of facilitation. For example, the teachers encouraged the students to pull back their pointing hand after typing a letter—Patrick's teacher asked him to touch his chest with his pointing finger between selections. On other occasions, teachers asked the students to type words from lists or from dictation. The teachers asked students to look at the letter they wanted to type before doing so and to slow down or even pause between selections if they were moving at a rapid pace and if they were inaccurate. I observed two facilitators (middle school and high school) let go of a student's hand or lift off a student's shoulder as she typed a familiar part of a word (e.g., "-ing" ending of a word) or a familiar word (e.g., "yes," "no," or "the"). One teacher asked her students where they wanted to be supported on a given day. When this was asked of Lindsay, she had her teacher move the support from her forearm to her ELBOE.

The practice required effort. REAL HATRD WORK, Patrick declared, I ASM SEWWEAS SWEATIMG [I am sweating]. Maggie called it a STRUGGLE . . . MANY THOUSANDS OF HOURS OF PAINSTAKING THAT HAVE GONE IN TO GETTING HERE.

Giving Up Speed and Meaning

It seemed that for all of the students, except Cathy and Joseph, typing without any physical support compromised fluency, speed, and complexity of content. This had previously been a problem for Joseph; during his first two years of using facilitation he had been seemingly unable to type sentences, or anything that could be interpreted as meaningful, except when given strong backward resistance by the facilitator. Without support, the other students typed what their teachers regarded as echoed (previously heard) phrases and nonsense letters or typed single words and not sentences and did so extremely slowly, with numerous typographical errors. Unless she had a specific task, such as the science assignment described above, Maggie, too, produced highly echoed typing when trying to type without support. The following was typed by Maggie without facilitation and without the structure of a course assignment, as she was waiting for a facilitator to sit down next to her:

```
HI MAGGIEE HOW ARE YOU TODAY FINE GOOD TEST SO DO I WOW
GREAT HAPPY YES RIGHT OK YES FRIDAY MAIN OFFICE DAY DAY
MONDAY 5 PM MONDAY LLY M BAKER LUNCH WEEK WEEK DURING
LUNCHES WEEK LUNCH GOOD WEEK LAB GAD LAB DAY DOUBLE DAY
HAPPENS ME MRS. D. LEAVE THAT NO IDEA DOESNT CUT
WHITE . . .
```

When asked how she felt about the goal of typing without physical support, Maggie described a dilemma:

```
I CANNOT DO WITHOUT MRS. F. AND MRS. D. THEY ARE TOO
IMPORTANT TO ME STILL. I AM TOO NERVOUS ABOUT SCHOOL AND
TOO UNFOCUSED TO BE ALONE OR EVERLESS HELPED. I NEED THE
DIRECITON. I GO OFF TRACK AND THEY REDIRECT ME. I NEED
THAT TOO MUCH STILL BECASEU MY THOUGHTS ARE HARD TO KEEP
TOGETHER. I AM WILLING TO TRY WRITING A LITTLE WITHOUT
AS MUCH AS I GET NOW BUT I MAKE A LOT OF MISTAKES AND I
HAVE TO DO GOOD WITH MY SCHOOL WORK AND SO IT LEAVE
LITTLE TIME TO PRACTICE.
```

Maggie typed this message about desperately needing support to complete her work expeditiously, and yet the amount of support she received seemed minimal—a facilitator's hand on her left shoulder for conversation and the facilitator sitting next to her when she typed some coursework content. In conversational communication, even as she typed with her left hand she would reach in with her right hand and delete incorrect letters. It seemed that she *believed* she could not type conversational communication without support, and so she could not.

It Depends on the Situation

The content and complexity of what students typed without physical support seemed to depend on the communication context. In this sense, there was no such thing as independent communication; it was always contextually situated. For no student was this more apparent than for Cathy, the 7-year-old in first grade. She had begun to communicate using facilitation when she was 3, first typing her name and words, receiving support at her hand and on her forearm, just behind her wrist. Before she left preschool, she could type a few favorite words without a facilitator's touch, one of which was "barney," and with facilitation she produced simple sentences (e.g., I THINK I NNEED SOLME HUGS; START; IT I WAS GREKAT; and I LIKEIR [like it]). She could read individual letters and was observed reading typed words. She did not speak in sentences, except for short ones (e.g., "No," "Not now," "Not me," "Don't do it"). During this study, she was a full-time member of a first-grade class along with 23 other students.

In a class lesson we see the kinds of speech she produced, which then can be compared to her typing and writing:

> Mrs. Castle [Cathy's teacher] wrote the word "Robot" on the chalkboard, with a long vowel sound over the first "o" and a short one over the second one. She asked the students if they knew what the word spelled. Seven students raised their hands. She called on one boy, who said "rowboat." She pointed out that this was close but that the sound of the second "o" was different and that it sounded like "ah." Another student identified the word as "robot." Mrs. Castle then asked, "What's a robot?" Students volunteered various answers, including: "It's an enemy; you fight it" and "It's metal and they don't think." Mrs. Castle asked, "Cath, what do you think this is?" Cathy spoke, "Mr. Robot." Mrs. Castle then asked, "Right, and what do you think a robot is?" She responded, "Lunch." The teacher smiled at her answer and remarked, "You've been reading ahead. That will become clear to everyone in a few minutes!"

After the class discussion, the students got out their books and read a story entitled "Mr. Robot," about an animal that had purchased a robot that could serve lunch. As the class read the story aloud, Cathy followed along, placing her finger on the words as they were said. An instructional specialist asked her to read aloud, and she began to do so, but she read very softly and only when it was demanded of her.

Although Cathy could speak, her teachers generally had to structure their questions to get expected and brief responses. For example, when Mrs. Castle showed the class a picture of Martin Luther King and Coretta Scott dressed in wedding clothes and asked Cathy what they were doing, Cathy said, "Making." The teacher said, "What are they doing, Cathy?" Another student said, "Getting married." Cathy said, "Married." Later, Mrs. Castle asked Cathy how she thinks Martin Luther King must have felt when other kids his age would not play football with him because he was black and they were white. Cathy had been fidgeting, with legs stretched out around a desk leg, near the rug, with her face on the leg, trying to bite the bolt on the leg. She did not make any expression and did not say anything. Mrs. Castle said, "Cathy, how would you feel if your good friend Stephanie said she would not play with you?" Cathy made a sad face and said, "Sad." During that same lesson, Mrs. Castle showed a picture of a casket and asked Cathy what had happened. Cathy said, "He died."

Despite the fact that she did not converse with others in spoken sentences, other than brief commands, Cathy wrote and typed with no physical support. At the end of October, for example, she wrote the following lines: ME AND THE COLOR BEARS. MY FOWAT COLOR IS PURPLE. MY FOWAT KED IS JACK. MY FOWAT NABYR IS EIGHT. MY FOWAT MOFEY IS WAIBOKS. She had typed FOWAT for "favorite," KED for "kid," NABYR for "number," and MOFEY for "movie." She typically needed verbal encouragement to initiate or continue her work (e.g., "write out what you think about that," and "keep going, finish your sentence"), stopping after each word and not continuing until her teacher encouraged her: "Finish your sentence."

Cathy's production of full sentences seemed to have little to do with physical support and much to do with the teaching/learning and communication context of how material was presented to her and what was expected of her. The support she needed appeared to be more in the structure of dialogue. Sadly, she did not have a way to engage in spontaneous, complex conversations or arguments with her classmates as they did regularly with each other.

Joseph, who had learned to type all of his conversational sentences without physical support, often settled for brief responses, typically one or two words, or general sentences, for example, IT WAS FUN or HE WAS HAPPY or I WENT THERE. However when pushed into extended dialogue, he showed more complex thoughts. The following is a conversation that Joseph and I typed to each other:

RESEARCHER: Tell me about your school work and life in general.
JOSEPH: SCHOOL WORK IS DOING VERY GOOD.
RESEARCHER: How about some specifics about school?
JOSEPH: CLASSES ARE DOING GOOD GYM IS DOING GOOD.
RESEARCHER: Tell me about gym.
JOSEPH: I BEEN DOING ACTIVES LIKE BASKETBALL AND SOCCOR.
RESEARCHER: I assume you probably watched some of the world cup soccer on television. What were your thoughts about it? Remember, give me specifics.
JOSEPH: I ENJOYED THE WORLD CUP SOCCOR FANIL ON T.V. THIS PAST YEAR.
RESEARCHER: What do you think of popular interest in soccer?
JOSEPH: PEOPLE COME TO MOST SOCCOR EVENTS EVERY YEAR AND SOME WATCH IT ON T.T.V. [In this case, the word MOST is probably an automatic completion for "more".]

Transcripts of Joseph's conversations revealed that he never produced compound sentences or elaborated on topics unless encouraged to do so.

Presumably, he had patterned his typing after his limited speech and needed some prodding to expand his style of expression. In one conversation, I asked him to describe a character in a play he had read. He typed, HE IS A BOY. I typed back, asking him "what else?" Joseph added, HE IS A HAPPY PRESON. "What else," I asked again. HE GETS EXCTIED, he typed. "Yes." I typed, "He uses words like 'Right!' and 'With a capital U!' "He also seems inquiring," I typed. To this, Joseph typed, I THINK HE ASKED SOME GOOD QUESTIONS. Asked to explain or give an example, he pointed to the text and typed one of his character's questions, CAN WE MAKE IT LIKE A DUMP?

Joseph appeared to have no difficulty typing without physical support; he even used both hands to type. Like his peers without disabilities, he communicated in ways that were reflective of a given context. To reveal thoughtfulness or insight, he required dialogue. The process whereby I typed to him and pursued topics with him seemed to elicit more complex commentary than he showed through his speech or than he otherwise typed.

CONCLUSION

In his autobiographical book, *I Don't Want to Be Inside Me Anymore,* Birger Sellin (1995) asks:

> which would you rather
> for me not to live(,) without help and stay handicapped
> or for me to become independent
> if so you must just demand more from me. (p. 184)

This was a prevailing theme among the eight students in this study. Being pushed to do more typing with less physical support seemed to be a *sine qua non* for doing it, yet going without physical support was an impossibility unless the student was willing and/or wanted it. And then, the student still required prodding and thoughtful interaction, as described with Joseph and Cathy.

To hear a person's ideas on this or any topic required an expectant listener. In the course of the study, I observed that the students were forthcoming, even expansive, when engaged in conversation and parsimonious with their words when asked to give routine responses, to engage in conversations absent of ideas (action for action's sake), or to express themselves in ways that ignored the conditions imposed by their mode of communication. They demanded what students everywhere have always demanded—to be taken seriously.

Their requirement for dialogue was not different from that described by Stumbo (1989) in an account of her writing project with students in Appalachia, where through a school magazine she arranged for her students to interview coal miners, ministers, housewives, and older people. Her school principal told her that she "shouldn't really expect too much of most of the students, and that for some of them, just coming to school was an accomplishment" (p. 91). Perhaps it was because she was the daughter of a coal miner herself that she never imagined her students unable to think and never took her principal's words seriously. She taught Shakespeare and Chaucer and other traditional texts, but it was the magazine that taught her about teaching:

> This is why I wanted to be a teacher. I want to know about the worlds that my students bring into the classroom with them. I have discoveries to make about them and the people that live in them. If teaching is the creative process that I believe it is, I have to listen; I have to understand that some of my students bring scars and terrible experiences into the classroom with them. But I believe with every fiber of my being that we cannot sell students short because of those experiences and scars. (p. 96)

Of course, many great teachers have talked about the same phenomenon. Freire (1970) called it dialogical teaching, or "conscientizacao." His educational approach began with thematic investigation, inquiring as to the themes of his students. The identification of themes was followed by a decoding process, wherein the teacher—Freire refers to a co-ordinator—"must not only listen to the individuals but must challenge them, posing as problems both the codified existential situation and their own answers" (p. 110), not unlike the problem-posing of qualitative research.

As students in this study revealed their multiple understandings of "independence," it became clear that characterizing independence merely as a technique would drastically oversimplify the issue. For some, the word embodied a terrifying expectation; mention of the word evoked intense anxiety. For them, indeed for all of the students, movement toward typing without physical support required what other researchers have described as essential ingredients for self-determination (see Ippoliti, Peppey, & Depoy, 1994) or generally more competent-seeming performance (Gold, 1980), namely positive regard from others, a reassuring atmosphere, supportive concern, and trust. Paradoxically, whether we speak of independence as typing without support or as self-determination, both required collaborative circumstances: people who expected words to be typed and goals or decisions to be articulated; people who would read and listen to the words; people interested in the ideas and willing to heed them; and people willing to sit by them, literally as well as figuratively.

In retrospect, representing the term "independence" as synonymous with "no physical support" may obscure the students' understanding and experience of facilitated communication. Students who were able to type certain content without physical support (e.g., name, date, yes/no responses, multiple-choice selections, school work, dictated words) wanted and seemed to require physical support for other tasks. Although some individuals were able to type conversationally without physical support, for all of the students in the study any instance of typing without touch did not mean that they had no support. In every instance, the student had a facilitator sitting nearby, no more than a foot or two away. Their experience seemed quite like those of David Eastham, who could type "alone" if his teacher sat within 34 centimeters of him (Eastham, 1992), or of Kochmeister (1994; Rivin, 1993; Watts & Wurzburg, 1994), who could type conversationally so long as her father, stepmother, or sister sat next to her.

NOTE

1. The videotape documentary, *Every Step of the Way* (Watts & Wurzburg, 1994), was made in part at Maggie's high school and included her as one of the principal interviewees. Since this occurred at the time of the study, and the video was available, the filming became part of the observations for the study. Also note that in this typed text and in all of the students' typing, all typographical errors have been retained just as they appeared in their conversations.

CHAPTER 9

Suggested Procedures for Confirming Authorship Through Research: An Initial Investigation

Donald N. Cardinal
Douglas Biklen

In this chapter we present a set of protocol conditions that we believe are essential to the valid and reliable authentication of authorship in controlled, quantitative facilitated communication studies. By examining numerous studies of facilitated communication, we identified a variety of procedural conditions that researchers concluded were important to verifying authorship. Against a list of these conditions, we compared the procedures used in certain authorship studies. We hypothesized that the degree to which a certain study includes the identified procedural conditions will significantly and strongly correlate to the study's degree of measured, authentic communication by the facilitated communication user. In other words, we believe that the conditions we identified (e.g., allowing practice of "testing" protocol) largely accounted for the outcomes of previous authorship studies. The more a study used these conditions in their protocols, the more likely the facilitated communication users would validate their communication, and the less a study's protocol contained these conditions, the less likely users would be able to validate their communication. This hypothesis was tested by comparing how closely a particular study adhered to the procedural conditions we identified to the ability of the facilitated communication users to validate their communication.

Obviously, not all procedural conditions were of equal importance. This created the need to weight the importance of each item; thus we created *impact factors* (IFs), whereby very important items could be given a weight of 1.0 and lesser items, but still important ones, could be assigned, for example, an IF of 0.25. We arrived at the weighting of procedures by examining the emphasis that researchers in the various studies placed on the procedures. For example, most studies emphasize the experience of participants with facilitation, use of familiar facilitators, and numbers of trials or sessions (i.e., practice), whereas feedback to participants on their performance during the tests, participant involvement in designing test conditions, and confidence building were given relatively less attention in the literature. The former items were assigned an IF of 1.0 while the latter items were assigned an IF of 0.25. Impact factors could range from a high of 1.0 down to a theoretic low of < 0.01.

This chapter will focus directly on quantitative procedures for confirming authorship in research studies; these may not be suited for personal confirmations of authorship. For individual confirmation of communication, we recommend a portfolio approach (see Chapter 3 for a detailed explanation of the strategy).

WHAT HAVE PAST STUDIES TAUGHT US?

Table 9.1 presents a list of procedural conditions that, when present in a quantitative experiment to measure authorship, appear to result in more authentic (user-generated) communication than studies that do not include these conditions. When studies are rated against this list of procedural conditions and the weights are applied, the mathematical product is called the *mean procedural conditions rating* (MPCR). So, the higher the MPCR of an authorship study, the more it contains the recommended conditions. Again, it is hypothesized that the greater the adherence of a study to the procedural conditions (i.e., higher MPCR), the greater the *reported authenticity* (RA). Reported authenticity is simply another measure we developed to determine the degree to which a particular study was able to measure authentic communication by the facilitated communication user. The higher the RA, the more the study was able to measure authentic communication and vice versa. A more detailed explanation of MPCRs and RAs is presented later in this chapter. A second, related hypothesis is that the higher the RA, the less the facilitator *degree of influence* (DI). The DI is simply the degree to which a particular study reported "influence" on the method's user by the facilitator—in extreme cases, concluding that the communication was coming from the facilitator, not the user. In this extreme case, a study would get a high DI rating.

We will test these hypotheses using the following six studies: Wheeler, Jacobson, Paglieri, & Schwartz (1993); M. D. Smith, Haas, & Belcher (1994);

TABLE 9.1 Recommended Procedural Conditions Rating Sheet

IF	Condition	Description
1.00	1. Extensive experience with facilitation	More than 6 months and/or conversational level communication
1.00	2. Practice using multiple trials	Practice of the exact test procedure (not test content) over 7 or more *sessions* and included as part of protocol
.25	3. Facilitated communication user consults on test and format	Participants are consulted as to what conditions may benefit or hinder their ability to communicate
1.00	4. Familiar facilitators	Study facilitators have facilitated with the participants for at least several months prior to the study using similar communication devices and tasks[a]
.75	5. Monitoring for facilitated communication user's style	Are participants being monitored for exact adherence to procedures, which should be consistent with previous facilitated communication training for that individual?
.75	6. No-risk, or low-risk, testing	Participant won't lose right to communicate or respect of others if fails test
.25	7. Build confidence: limit opportunities to fail	Uses tasks participant has demonstrated s/he can do, or intersperses easy tasks with more difficult ones.
1 00	8. Naturally controlled conditions	Procedures and location look very similar to those found in the participant's everyday environment.[b] Avoids a "clinical-like" setting that might convey the idea that the facilitated communication user was under study rather than the method.
.25	9. Ongoing feedback on performance	Participants are given feedback within the study to allow them a means to learn.
.75	10. Minimize word retrieval tasks	Tasks are created so as to minimize the participants' need to retrieve specific words (e.g., description of an object's function is permissible if the name of an object can-not be retrieved; use of multiple choice formats where the answer is available from among options; OK to use the word *auto* or *vehicle* when seeing a picture of a bus)
.50	11. Information by multiple modalities	Information is presented through as many domains (visual, auditory, tactile, etc.) as is reasonable and helpful for the participant(s)
.50	12. Age appropriate content	Materials and procedure are appropriate to the participant's chronological age level.
.75	13. Personally relevant content	Materials and procedures are interesting, important, motivating, and/or meaningful to participant, not irrelevant.
1.00	14. Extensive time to respond to questions	Time to give an answer is substantial, even 20 - 45 minutes in some instances.

IF = Impact Factor (weight of each condition). IR = Item Rating, WIR = Weighted Item Rating (IF $\times$ IR)

[a] Facilitated communication user's habits of using the method (looking at keyboard, fading, etc.) should be dealt with in similar fashion as before the experiment.

[b] This assumes that the everyday environment is one that has respect for the person's ability.

Vazquez (1994); Simon, Toll, & Whitehair (1994); Steering Committee (1993); and Cardinal, Hanson, & Wakeham (1996). As explained in greater detail later, these studies represent a range of approaches to controlled verification of authorship and also yield widely divergent results, ranging from no reported authentic communication to a majority of authenticated communication.

The following are brief summaries of the six studies:

(A) Wheeler, D. L., Jacobson, J. W., Paglieri, R. A., & Schwartz, A. A. (1993). An experimental assessment of facilitated communication. *Mental Retardation, 31,* 1, 49–60.

As we noted in Chapter 1, *none* of the individuals gave correct responses when shown items different from those shown to the facilitators, with two exceptions. (1) In two instances, individuals named categories for the items they were asked to identify, but not the precise items; these responses were VEHICLE instead of "van" and FOOD instead of "bread." (2) Three individuals gave five correct responses when neither they nor their facilitators knew they had been shown the same item cards; these same individuals did not give any of the facilitators' items when the cards they were shown were different. The latter data are not provided in Wheeler and colleagues' article in *Mental Retardation* but are reported in their report of the same study published by the New York State Office of Mental Retardation and Developmental Disabilities (Wheeler, Jacobson, Paglieri, & Schwartz, 1992). Seven of the twelve participants typed the names of pictures shown to their facilitators that were *not* shown to them.

(B) Smith, M. D., Haas, P. M., & Belcher, R. G. (1994). Facilitated communication: The effects of facilitator knowledge and level of assistance on output. *Journal of Autism and Developmental Disorders, 24*(3), 357–367.

All of the six participants in the study took part in six experimental sessions, three with one facilitator and then three with another. They were shown four items from each of three different categories: (1) pictures (two action scenes and two pictures of common objects) that were kept out of the view of the facilitator, (2) "everyday objects presented to the subject inside a paper grocery bag outside of the facilitator's field of vision," and (3) messages spoken to the participant while the facilitator was out of the room (p. 361). The facilitators asked participants to type a response pertaining to the items they had seen or to the messages heard.

Participants received "three different levels of support," ranging from (1) no physical support, (2) "hand-over-hand assistance to the subject . . . [that] did not prevent errors," and (3) "hand-over-hand assistance while the subject typed . . . [that] prevented errors by pulling the subject's hand back between key selections and from incorrect key selections" (pp. 361–362). The authors regarded only the latter level of support as comparable to the way the literature described facilitated communication. These different levels of support were designed to reveal influence. "In no instance did a subject type a correct communication when the facilitator had been exposed to a different stimulus than the subject" (p. 363).

(C) Vazquez, C. A. (1994). Brief report: A multitask controlled evaluation of facilitated communication. *Journal of Autism and Developmental Disorders, 24*(3), 369–379.

This study concluded that the two individuals with autism in this study could communicate with facilitation. "As in the Intellectual Disability Review Panel Report (1989)," the author reported, "the results are mixed" (p. 373). Vazquez used "a variety of tasks" with participants who had been perceived as being very good at using facilitation. She concluded, "This study provides evidence for genuine communication from these highly select subjects, as well as strong evidence for direct cuing between subject and facilitator. (The author did not specifically describe instances of influence or cuing.) Erratic in their performance, each subject was able to report information unknown to the facilitator in one out of four controlled sessions" (p. 373). The activities included viewing and describing videos, labeling pictures, and naming objects.

(D) Simon, E. W., Toll, D. M., & Whitehair, P. M. (1994). A naturalistic approach to the validation of facilitated communication. *Journal of Autism and Developmental Disorders, 245*, 647–657.

Four of the seven participants named activities or objects associated with activities in which they had participated that were unknown to the facilitators. For example, a student typed ATE after going to eat a sandwich. Another typed a word that included BOOK after going to the library. And a student typed SOFA AND CHAIRS after visiting a "life skills center" where there were a sofa and chairs. Student 7 reported WENT KITCHEN after an activity in which he had put dishes in the kitchen dishwasher. He also was the participant (see Chapter 1) who had indicated on another occasion that he had gone to a vending machine, put in a dollar, and bought a particular item. (Subsequently, however, Simon et al., 1995, questioned this communication.)

In the naive condition, Subject 3 got a half of ten items, Subject 5 got one of eight, and Subject 3 got three of ten. In the misguided condition, subjects 3 and 4 each got one of ten. All subjects got some incorrect misguided items! Subjects 1, 2, and 6 were influenced but did not produce any of their own communication.

(E) Steering Committee, Division of Intellectual Disability Services. (1993). *The Queensland report on facilitated communication*. Brisbane: Department of Family Services and Aboriginal and Islander Affairs.

As noted in Chapter 1, the Steering Committee report analyzed transcriptions of participants typing and found that "thirteen (65%) of adult clients were able to communicate information using visual language which was accurate and not previously known to the facilitator" (p. 10). This is what is commonly referred to as message passing. In addition, nine adults and three children (50% of all the subjects and 75% of the children) responded correctly to questions in a multiple-choice format, where the content was unknown to the facilitators (p.10). And "twenty-one (87.5%) of the client sample of 24 had their communication validated using content and structural analysis" (p. 10).

Only one of the 24 clients was able to communicate more than "basic need" information by speaking. Of the 20 adults in the study, 11 had autism, 2 had cerebral palsy, 1 had Down syndrome, and 6 had no specific diagnosis other than mental retardation. Without facilitation, all tested in the profoundly retarded range.

(F) Cardinal, D. N., Hanson, D., & Wakeham, J. (1996). An investigation of authorship in facilitated communication. *Mental Retardation, 34*(4), 231–242.

This study examined the source of authorship of facilitated communication (i.e., who originates the facilitated output, the facilitated communication user or the facilitator?). The experiment used two main protocol conditions: naturally controlled environment and practice effect. Data were gathered on 43 students who completed 3,870 attempts to transfer information to a "blind" facilitator over a six-week period. There were two main findings of this study. One, under the conditions of this study, some facilitated communication users can pass information to a facilitator when that facilitator is not privy to the information. Two, the measurement of facilitated communication under test conditions may be significantly benefited by extensive practice of the test protocol when *practice* is defined as it is in this study. This latter result could partially account for the inability of several past studies to verify output originated by facilitated communication users.

How the Impact Factors Were Assigned

As noted above, IFs represent the weight or importance of each procedure compared to the other procedural conditions. For example, an IF of 0.75 is viewed as three times more important than an IF of 0.25. As mentioned earlier, procedures were chosen because of their appearance in authorship studies. The more credit a certain procedure receives from a study's author(s) for fostering the measurement of authentic communication, the higher the IF it receives. Conversely, when authors suggest that a certain procedure can actually hinder a subject's performance, that procedure may not be included at all. Where we were unsure about whether to rate a condition relatively low (e.g., 0.25) or higher (e.g., 0.50 or 0.75), we discussed in detail our reasoning for the differences and came to a compromise. As more research is evaluated using the rating system, fine-tuning can be done on the impact factors, providing even better information to future researchers.

How the Level of Reported Authenticity Was Assigned

The following rating scale was used to categorize each of the six selected studies as to its level of RA:

1 = No authentic interaction (There were no reports of authenticity.)
2 = Mild production (There were some reports of authenticity but still a question as to who it could be attributed to, the facilitated communication user or the facilitator.)
3 = Moderate production (There was clear authentication of the interaction in about half of the subjects communicating beyond expected levels or they did so in more than half of their individual trials.)
4 = High production (Most of the people in the study communicated to unexpected levels of communication using facilitated communication or, in the cases of a very small n, did so in nearly all of their sessions.)

Note: The "expectations" of a person's ability to communicate is seen here as the formal evaluation of their unfacilitated communicative skills as evidenced by test scores or professional observations of functional usage.

Why Choose These Six Studies?

The studies were selected since they were representative of three of the four levels of RA. Studies A and B are good examples of investigations in which the researchers concluded that no authentic interaction occurred, thus warranting an RA rating of 1. Studies E and F are generally accepted as investigations that have measured moderate levels of authentic interaction, and both received an RA rating of 3. Although Study E is not a peer-reviewed study and thus may have less than full acceptability in the professional community, it is included here since its research procedures have been used and cited by many facilitated communication studies that *are* peer-reviewed.

Finally, Studies C and D were selected because of their reports of modest, but otherwise unexplained, occurrences of authentic interaction. It should be noted that Studies C and D both report that in the majority of cases, the subjects did not confirm the authenticity of their interactions, but both found that students were able to report information that was unknown to the blind facilitators (pages 373 and 655, respectively). Studies C and D both received RA ratings of 2.5 since their studies reported more than mild authentication of authorship for some participants. No studies were found that could warrant an RA rating of 4, that is, where it could be reported that most subjects' interactions were always authentic and not due to possible facilitator influence. However, for particular subjects, under certain conditions, an RA rating of 4 might be possible.

How the Degree of Influence Was Assigned

The "Results" and "Discussion" sections of each study were examined for reports of possible influence by the facilitator on the facilitated communication user. For example, in Study A, most of the subjects typed some responses to pictures seen by their facilitators but *not* by them. This was clear evidence of some type of facilitator influence and thus received a DI score of 4, on a scale of 1 to 4. In all except Study C, adequate information was provided to arrive at a judgment of the DI detected in the investigation. In Study C, the author states specifically that her study provides "strong evidence for direct cuing between subject and facilitator" (p. 373), yet we were unable to find data to support this contention. Given the author was so direct in her statement about facilitator cuing, we assume that she was aware of some data that support her statement but that were not included in the final report. Therefore, a "mild/moderate" degree of influence (DI = 2.5) was attributed to this study.

Degree of Influence Reported

The following rating scale was used to categorize each of the six selected studies for degree of influence.

1 = None or nearly none (The study revealed no facilitator control or influence that may have provided the facilitated communication user with information that would materially increase the user's accuracy in the testing situation.)

2 = Mild (The study revealed some influence but it was unclear that this influence resulted in a significant benefit to the facilitated communication user's performance.)

3 = Moderate (The study revealed facilitator influence that could have positively affected some of the facilitated communication user's test performance, but the evidence for this influence fell short of absolute facilitator control of the facilitated communication user's responses and fell short of control across all, or nearly all, of the testing conditions.)

4 = High degree (The study revealed absolute facilitator control and reported this control in all, or nearly all, of the trials and conditions of the study.)

Item Ratings

An item rating (IR) is the assignment of a numerical value to each recommended procedural condition and represents the degree to which that condition was met for a particular study. Item ratings can range from 1 to 5 and are usually assigned as whole numbers, although continuous numbering (e.g., 2.5, 3.25) is permitted when the evaluator believes that the "true" rating falls somewhere between ratings of two whole numbers. The rating scale for IRs is as follows:

1 = No or very poor adherence to the condition
2 = Some attempts to adhere to the condition, but they were mild
3 = A moderate attempt to adhere to the condition
4 = A very good attempt to adhere to the condition
5 = The procedural condition was very evident and primary to the study's protocol

N/I = No information on which to judge. An N/I score does not penalize the study's overall rating since the N/Is are not used to arrive at the MPCR.

How the Mean Procedural Conditions Ratings Were Computed

The mean procedural conditions rating is a mathematically computed score that represents the degree to which the experimental procedures of a particular study adhered to the "best practices" presented here and referred to as recommended procedural conditions. MPCR is computed by dividing the sum of the *weighted item ratings* (WIRs) by the number of items scored (not necessarily by the 14 possible conditions), allowing a fair and standardized comparison across studies. The WIR is the product of an individual condition's IF (see "How the Impact Factors Were Assigned") and the individual IR (see "Item Ratings") for a particular condition. For example, Study A scored an IR of 2.0 for Condition 12 (see Table 9.2). An IR of 2.0 indicates "some attempt to adhere to the condi-

Contested Words, Contested Science

TABLE 9.2 Procedural Conditions Rating Matrix—Individual, Weighted, and Mean Scores

Cond	IF	Study A		Study B		Study C		Study D		Study E		Study F	
		IR	WIR	IR	WIR	IR	WIR	IR	WIR	IR	WIR	IR	WIR
1	1.00	4	4.00	1	1.00	4	4.00	3	3.00	4	4.00	3	3.00
2	1.00	1	1.00	2	2.00	3	3.00	3	3.00	3	3.00	5	5.00
3	.25	1	.25	N/I	N/I	N/I	N/I	N/I	N/I	N/I	N/I	4	1.00
4	1.00	4	4.00	2	2.00	3	3.00	3	3.00	4	4.00	4	4.00
5	.75	1	.75	1	.75	3	2.25	3	2.25	3	2.25	3	2.25
6	.75	1	.75	N/I	N/I	N/I	N/I	N/I	N/I	N/I	N/I	4	3.00
7	.25	1	.25	2	.50	2	.50	4	1.00	3	.75	4	1.00
8	1.00	2	2.00	1	1.00	2	2.00	4	4.00	3	3.00	5	5.00
9	.25	1	.25	1	.25	2	.50	1	.25	3	.75	1	.25
10	.75	1	.75	2	1.50	2	1.50	5	3.75	2	1.50	3	2.25
11	.50	2	1.00	3	1.50	4	2.00	4	2.00	3	1.50	3	1.50
12	.50	2	1.00	2	1.00	3	1.50	4	2.00	4	2.00	3	1.50
13	.75	1	.75	N/I	N/I	4	3.00	3	2.25	3	2.25	1	.75
14	1.00	1	1.00	1	1.00	N/I	N/I	N/I	N/I	2	2.00	3	3.00
Mean PCR			1.27		1.14		2.11		2.41		2.25		2.40

IF=Impact Factor (weight of each condition), IR=Item Rating, WIR = Weighted Item Rating (IFxIR)

tion" was made to meet this condition. The IF for Condition 12 was 0.50, indicating that Condition 12 was twice as important to the overall ability of a study to measure authentic communication as a condition with an IF of 0.25 and half as important as a condition with an IF of 1.0. To arrive at a condition's WIR, the product of IR and IF is computed, IR [2] times IF [.50] = WIR [1.00]. Finally, to arrive at a study's MPCR—the degree of adherence of that study to the recommended procedural conditions—the WIRs for *all* conditions are averaged. Study A, for example, had a MPCR of 1.27.

EVALUATING OTHER STUDIES USING THE PROCEDURAL CONDITIONS RATING SYSTEM

Remember: The individual weight given to each procedural condition in this model is continually being reevaluated by the authors. It is not necessary for the reader to set new weights in order to evaluate additional studies (although we have found it interesting to adjust the weights and view the relative changes among studies). To compute the MPCR of a new study, follow the steps below:

1. Select a study that investigates authorship in facilitated communication. Several additional studies of this type are listed in this book's References. The more detail provided within a study, the more you can reliably evaluate all 14 procedural conditions.
2. Using the recommended procedural conditions ratings sheet (Table 9.1), evaluate the degree to which each of the 14 conditions exist in the study. Assign each condition an item rating from one to five using the IR rubric. Assign N/I (no information) to conditions you are unable to evaluate due to inadequate information.
3. Now, multiply each item rating times its corresponding impact factor and enter those numbers in the column titled WIR.
4. Total the WIRs and divide that sum by the number of items you were able to evaluate. For instance, if you were unable to assign a number to 4 of the 14 conditions, then you would divide the sum by 10—the number of conditions you were able to evaluate.
5. Next, using the RA rubric, assign a rating (1–4) to the overall degree to which the study's conclusions support authentic output by the facilitated communication user. That is, did the facilitated communication user(s) produce output that was originated by them? Take the following into consideration when doing this evaluation:
   (a) Some influence exists any time two or more people speak. Therefore interpret the notion of "influence" as meaning that the facilitated communication user was a passive participant in the interaction—looking for the degree to which output was controlled by the facilitator.
   (b) Interpret the "results" of the study, not the author(s) "discussion" of the study. Although journal editors and reviewers most likely will insist that the discussion sections follow the results, some journals enforce this more than others.
   (c) Be sure to consider the degree to which each user was able to produce original output over that which they were able to do prior to using facilitated communication. You are looking for the benefit of facilitated communication and therefore should only consider output that the facilitated communication user was unable to achieve without facilitated communication.
6. You have now completed the basic analysis and can compare the study's reported authenticity score (RA) and its mean procedural conditions rating (MPCR) to the studies reported in this chapter. You may also wish to conduct further analysis by developing the study's degree of influence. Refer to the degree of influence reported rubric in this chapter for details on how to compute this measure.

RESULTS

Testing the Hypotheses

The two hypotheses outlined earlier were (1) the greater the adherence of a study's procedures to the recommended procedural conditions (MPCR), the greater the reported authenticity (RA), and (2) the greater the reported authenticity (RA), the less the facilitator degree of influence (DI).

Hypothesis 1. To test hypothesis 1, we conducted an analysis to determine the degree of relationship between the MPCR and the RA of each study (see Table 9.3), and to determine if that relationship was statistically significant. The analysis resulted in a significant and strong degree of relationship between the two variables ($r = 0.945$, $p < .001$). This result indicates that the greater the adherence of a study's procedures to the recommended procedural conditions, the greater was the study's ability to measure authentic communication. This result suggests that the failure to measure authentic communication from facilitated communication users in some past studies may be the result of the study's experimental procedures rather than solely the facilitated communication users' inability to communicate.

Hypothesis 2. To test hypothesis 2, we conducted a second test of relationship, between the studies' reported authenticity ratings (RA) and their degree of influence (DI) (see Table 9.3). This analysis resulted in a significant and strong—but inverse—relationship between these two measures ($r = -0.82$, $p < .05$). This result indicates that the greater the authentic communication measured in the study, the less the likelihood was of reported facilitator influence. A logical explanation for this result could be simply that facilitator influence impedes and, in some forms, may even completely block authentic communication. Further, the results of this inquiry suggest that some procedural conditions increase the likelihood of influence occurring and therefore may retard authentic communication (e.g., the introduction of distractors, or lack of experience of using facilitated communication).

TABLE 9.3 Ratings Matrix Across all Six Studies

Study	RA	DI	MPCR
Wheeler et al.	1	4	1.27
Smith et al.	1	4	1.14
Vazquez	2.5	2.5	2.11
Simon et al.	2.5	3	2.41
Steering Comm.	3	1	2.25
Cardinal et al.	3	1	2.40

Validity of This Rating Method

The question is *not* whether these ratings are valid for the six cited studies. They are assumed to be, since the categories and weights were derived partially from these studies. Rather, the question is how valid this rating system is in predicting the outcomes of future studies. Only time will tell that. However, these suggestions for experimental design conditions are the result of a systematic method for the planning of future studies based on what has been learned from prior ones. Therefore we suggest that future studies be designed in accordance with these conditions and weights, taking into consideration that new conditions will be discovered, thereby modifying this system. Additionally, the designer of further studies will most likely have to make trade-off decisions when designing their studies' procedures. For example, "information by multiple modalities" (Condition 11) may conflict with "minimizing word retrieval tasks" (Condition 10) and a decision may have to be made to discount one of the recommended procedures, in which case, we recommend removing or modifying the condition with the weakest individual IF.

No single study has all of the procedural conditions listed. However, those studies that possess the greatest degree of adherence to these procedures tend to report greater communicative performance by the subjects in their studies. The procedural conditions rating system does appear to measure that which it purports to measure and thus can be viewed as having validity.

Reliability

To test the degree of reliability of the rating procedures, interrater reliability coefficients were developed for each rating process, including (1) the item ratings (IRs) of the recommended procedural conditions, (2) the degree of influence (DI) ratings, and (3) the reported authenticity (RA) interaction rating. The IR reliability results indicate a mean coefficient of $r = 0.95$, ranging from $r = 0.91$ to $r = 0.98$. The ratings of the degree to which each study adheres to the recommended procedures appear to be highly reliable. The DI and RA reliability coefficients were $r = 0.99$, $p < .001$ and $r = 0.97$, $p < .001$, respectively, indicating that each measure used in this analysis was reliable.

Further Research

This current study is viewed by us as preliminary in that, as this book goes to press, we are gathering new data for an expanded study with modifications. For example, we have discovered that in computing MPCR, using n (the number of the Item Ratings minus the number of N/Is) as the divisor is less sensitive than using the mean Impact Factor, computed by adding the IFs that were able to be rated and then dividing by their n. For example, if all 14 procedures were able to be rated for a particular study, then the total of their individual PCRs would be divided by the total possible IF, 9.75 (the *sum* of all 14 IFs), not by 14 (the total *number* of IFs).

Another change we have considered for this study is to control for the degree of expertise of the evaluator. To test whether the expertise in facilitated communication of the evaluator (the person assigning PCR, RA, and DI ratings) influences those ratings, we are gathering data from naïve evaluators (familiar with research methods, but not with facilitated communication). These new data can then be compared to data presented in this study.

CONCLUSIONS

In this chapter, we have presented evidence that controlled studies, which are designed to measure authentic communication produced by facilitated communication speakers, may be highly sensitive to their protocol conditions. Stated in a slightly different way, people who use facilitated communication may be more sensitive to test conditions than are individuals using other methods of communication. The question then becomes: What are the procedural conditions that are most optimal to the measurement of authentic interaction between the facilitator and the facilitated communication user? For now, the 14 conditions outlined in this chapter, when present in a study, appear to represent the best practices for protocol development.

Further, certain conditions may be far more important than others, even to the point of determining the presence or absence of authentic communication. It appears, for example, that extensive experience with the method, practice of the "test" conditions, and conducting the study in the participant's natural environment are especially crucial factors. At the same time, we are mindful that any single person's experience in such testing must be treated as its own case study. Particular people may be more sensitive to some conditions than to others: One person may have extreme anxiety with any testing and may benefit especially from practice; another person might be stymied by word-retrieval tasks. For this reason, any future research must always be based on the assumption that the research design, including the procedural conditions, may be as crucial to the results as are the particular skills of the individual participant.

This chapter focused directly on quantitative procedures for confirming authorship in research studies, which may not be suited for personal confirmations of authorship. For individual confirmation of communication, we recommend a portfolio approach.

CHAPTER 10

Reframing The Issue: Presuming Competence

Douglas Biklen
Donald N. Cardinal

In this chapter we examine the discourse of facilitated communication, focusing on the nature of the arguments and perspectives on the method. The discourse has been most contentious when it has concerned allegations of abuse made via facilitation and the legal wrangling over whether to pay attention to them. Because the abuse issue tends to push arguments and assumptions to extremes, it is a good lens through which to examine the contrasting understandings of facilitated communication.

POWER, AUTHORITY, VOICE

Social science arguments are generally thought of as having more or less authority depending on methodology and design, evidence, source of data, position or reputation of the authors, and whose interests they serve—those with power or those without. In such equations, people at the margins of power and authority—for example, poor people or people with disabilities—often have limited or no voice. They can be left unrepresented and unheard.

Our roles as researchers and discussants lay in the tradition of what Giroux calls "border crossers" (1992), what Delpit refers to as "participants in the culture of power" (1995, p. 4), and what hooks (1989) and others call "oppositional discourse." All arguments are located in a context of power and authority. Some represent more dominant views and others more marginalized ones. Our role is to question the politics of dominance by challenging methodological assumptions as well as assumptions about content and meaning. All researchers have agendas, and ours is to foster, in whatever ways possible, the conditions in which people with disabilities can be heard—that they might be border crossers, participants in the culture of power, a heard opposition.

As hooks reminds us, researchers are obliged to recognize their own positions of privilege, particularly when their research touches on the lives of traditionally silenced groups. Researchers who write about groups to which they do not belong are required, she explains, to consider "the ethics of our action" and "whether or not our work will be used to reinforce and perpetuate domination" (hooks, 1989, p. 43). Court cases involving facilitated communication raise this question of representation in a most direct way. Will people with disabilities be permitted to represent themselves or will they be represented as incompetent and thereby silenced in court? Is the giving of testimony a border for crossing? Is the court a forum of contesting voices?

In one of the first cases of alleged abuse involving facilitated communication, family court judge Karen Peters (Ulster County, New York) heard a case involving a nonverbal 16-year-old girl with autism. J, the girl, allegedly accused her father, Mr. S, of sexually abusing her. Reciting the poetry of Ogden Nash, Judge Peters defined the case as a contest over authorship: Could the court hear a solitary prisoner's "knocking in the skull," a "beating on a wall," a "frantic cry" (In the Matter of Department of Social Services, 1994, pp. 1–2). "The question before the court is simple," Judge Peters lamented, "have we heard the frantic cry of a child?" (p. 2). Were the plaintive words the child's words?

Although J had been removed from the parents' custody for 10 months pending the judge's decision, the case was never tried and testimony on the facts never given. Judge Peters acknowledged her role as arbiter but then refused to hear the case. She declared the method too new, too little researched, not yet something she could find valid:

> Regrettably, the proponents of this technique have failed to conduct the necessary studies to ensure the reliability and validity of this communication technique sufficiently to permit the court to accept J's alleged statement into evidence. (pp. 24–25)

Without the studies, the judge admonished, "we will never know if there is a knocking in the skull, an endless silent shout, of something beating on a wall, and crying, let me out" (p. 25). In a decision emblematic of what Lincoln (1993) has referred to as "*etic* views" of the silenced—"the views of those with the power and access to control the naming process (e.g., what is communication and what is not), even while being outsiders to marginal lives" (p. 29)—Judge Peters did not invite J to prove her own communicative competence, whether through a message-passing exercise or any other means. Goode (1992) describes this etic perspective as one of fault-finding, sanctioned by official authority, as contrasted with the empathic emic perspective which would attempt to understand how the person with a disability experiences the world from her vantage point.

RULES FOR BEING HEARD

There are rules about how a voice is heard and by whom, whether in court or in research. The question in courts is: On what basis should the words typed be seen as legitimate communication of people with disabilities? Related to this, can research fairly evaluate facilitation? And can research examine and represent marginal voices in a way potential readers can hear them? Giroux (1992) reminds us that in such matters, power and knowledge are intertwined, "as both the practice of representation and the representation of practice to secure particular forms of authority" (p. 29).

In the case of Luz P, we see an important shift in how a person using facilitation could be represented. Here, the victim is transformed from a silent object to a subject who would have some, albeit limited, voice in shaping her own representation as well as facilitated communication's representation. Like J, Luz P (In the Matter of Luz P, 1993), age 11, classified as autistic and mentally retarded, could not speak. Typing with her teacher at a special school in Orange County, New York, Luz alleged her parents had sexually abused her.

Initially, an Orange County family court judge dismissed the case, finding facilitated communication inadmissible. However, the appellate division of the State Supreme Court of New York subsequently ruled that the question before the court was not whether facilitated communication was favored by particular experts or whether it had been accepted within the scientific community:

> The test for the court in cases such as these is a pragmatic one. Can the interpreter, or in this case the facilitator, effectively communicate with the witness and reliably convey the witness' answers to the court? A determination of these questions does not require expert testimony. To the contrary, the proffered facilitated communication lends itself to empirical rather than scientific proof. Thus, the test proposed by the County Attorney, whereby the court could question Luz outside the presence of the facilitator and then hear her responses through facilitated communication, should adequately establish whether this

is a reliable and accurate means of communication by Luz. Fact specific questions can be devised which should demonstrate whether the answers are subject to the influence, however subtle, of the facilitator. If the court is satisfied
from this demonstration that the facilitator is "qualified" to transmit communications from Luz to the court, then the facilitator may be appointed as an
interpreter. (p. 5)

When the judge remanded the case to family court, the testing began.
Luz P now had to prove her communicative ability. If she passed, the case
could proceed. If she failed or refused the test, the judge would dismiss
the case. The parents' attorney demanded and won from the judge a pic-
ture-labeling test similar to that used in the study by Wheeler, Jacobson,
Paglieri, and Schwartz (1993). Lew Borofsky, the prosecutor in the Luz P
case, had no idea how she would perform. After several weeks of practic-
ing the type of test proposed by the court, Borofsky, Luz, and her teacher/
facilitator discovered something that the research community prior to that
point had largely missed—but which *is* represented in the studies in this
book—namely, that *practice* improves performance. After numerous sessions, Luz began to succeed under the controlled conditions. The next step
was to demonstrate this ability to the court[1]:

> Of the 10 pictures that were different from those of the teacher, the child
> [Luz] identified five correctly and failed to identify five.
> When the teacher and the child were shown the same picture, the child
> identified six correctly and failed to identify four.
> In no case did she give the picture that the teacher saw when it was differ-
> ent from hers. (E. Martin, 1993, p. 2)

Luz had passed the double-blind test that *all* participants had failed in the
studies by Wheeler and colleagues (1993), Moore, Donovan, Hudson,
Dykstra, and Lawrence (1994), and Klewe (1993) (see Chapter 1).
    Luz's success raised several issues for the research community. Was Luz
different from other people using facilitation? Was the test Luz took in some
subtle way different from other authorship tests? Or did her ability with
such a test suggest that others could also pass similar tests so long as they
could practice beforehand?
    The court now agreed to take testimony from Luz, with her facilitator
masked by headphones and white noise from the questions asked. However, the father's attorney interrupted her testimony and demanded that
Luz's facilitator not look in the direction of the person asking the questions—the attorney worried that the person could read the lips of the person asking questions—and not look at the keyboard. These requirements
proved too much. Luz was unable to communicate under the changed

condition. This time, she was not given the months of practice time that the county attorney believed she would need to meet the new rules, particularly the second of the two. The case was dismissed.

The attorney for Luz's father argued that her performance demonstrated that she was incapable of communicating. But another, equally plausible interpretation of her test performance could be that the new test procedure rules were too difficult, a relatively common experience for all those hooks calls outsiders. It is easy to converse within one's own group, where ways of sharing ideas are implicit, but far more difficult when crossing boundaries. Delpit (1995) has described the problem that emerges when people speak a different implicit language. Every culture transmits information implicitly to its members about how to be and what to do. However, outsiders often miss the implicit codes of another culture. In fact, the outsiders *and* the insiders wonder about the other: "Each cultural group is left saying, 'Why don't those people say what they mean?' as well as, 'What's wrong with them, why don't they understand?'" (Delpit, 1995, p. 25). D. Williams (1994a) warns nondisabled observers that they cannot presume to know the thinking or experience of people with autism (and presumably others with developmental disabilities) who do not speak.

Some critics seem to set testing criteria based on their assumptions about how they themselves would perform if presented similar tasks. Levine and Wharton (1995) have argued that, "any child with the ability to spell and write sentences, and the motor ability to guide an adult's hand to specific letters, has the potential to develop independent communication skills through augmentative communication" (p. 52). This statement is problematic on at least two grounds: Most facilitated communication users have not described their typing as involving guiding "an adult's hand to specific letters"; and, as we have seen in Chapter 8, some users of facilitation do *not* think they can so easily, if at all, learn to type without support—at least it is not something they would glibly assert as possible. It seems that Levine and Wharton forget their own position of power, in effect treating the person who uses facilitation as like themselves, nondisabled. We are reminded of Delpit's (1995) admonition that such impositions of definition are common: "Those with power are frequently least aware of—or least willing to acknowledge—its existence. Those with less power are often most aware of its existence" (p. 26).

GOOD FACTS

Getting a new argument heard often requires "good facts" or a "good case." In the landmark *Brown v. Board of Education* case on segregated schooling, plaintiffs' lawyers documented that conditions of schools attended by black and white students were certainly not equal, but they also demonstrated that segregation created demonstrable feelings of inferiority in the excluded group. In the *Pennsylvania Association for Retarded Citizens v. Commonwealth of Pennsylvania* case, which established the right to education, children with disabilities were shown to have been forcibly segregated from their nondisabled peers, to have been denied even basic access to education, and to have regressed after years of neglect; most important, experts made the single, observable point that all children could benefit from an education.

The first case on facilitation that reached trial involved an alleged victim, JK, 12 years old at the time of trial, who was classified as autistic and severely retarded. Before learning to communicate with facilitation, he was able to identify only five letters, had no spoken language, and could sign a few words, including "yes" and "no." After using facilitated communication for three months, JK began to type sentences. One day, when queried about whether he liked various individuals with whom he came into contact, he indicated he liked them all except one. When asked what he didn't like about the one, JK typed DONTASK. Through a series of questions over several days, JK indicated that a care worker, Marc Warden, hurt him by putting his penis in MY BYYT (the "y" is next to the "u" on the typewriter keyboard). Earlier he had typed, ASK ABOUT FUK and then, when asked what that meant, he typed MUKBUTTHURT.

Prior to the start of the court case, JK succeeded in a message-passing test arranged by the school psychologist, where he selected a word, typed it with one facilitator, and then typed it with a facilitator who was unaware of what word he had chosen—a procedure similar to the research design described by Cardinal, Hanson, and Wakeham in Chapter 2. There was no formal testing of his facilitation as part of the legal proceedings.

In the court case, JK was asked if Warden hurt him. He typed ASS. When he typed the letters FUK, he was asked if that meant "fuck." JK pointed to "yes" twice. Then JK pointed to "no" in response to questions of whether Warden fucked him with his nose, mouth, or a suppository. JK was asked if he knew what a penis was, and he pointed to "yes." Asked if Warden used his penis to fuck JK's butt, JK pointed to "yes."

The Kansas court created what Giroux (1992, p. 27) calls "enabling conditions," in a sense putting aside its own privileged position of people who communicate easily and fluently and considering an alternative mode, with attention to the conditions for expression that this mode demanded. The court searched for strategies to ensure that the person be heard. This expression-sensitive approach is not unlike the kind of awareness Delpit (1995) and others associate with multicultural openness, where the "dominant group" attempts to listen to and hear the other side and, "after hearing, to speak in a modified voice that does not exclude the concerns of their minority colleagues" (Delpit, 1995, p. 20). The court reasoned why the jury could regard JK's facilitated statements as his own.[2]

> Conrad [the facilitator] testified she had no knowledge of the abuse before JK began typing about it; JK exhibited other unusual behavior before describing the abuse (he threw a tantrum when his caregiver had his pants off); the spelling, grammar, and word choice in JK's statements were inconsistent with Conrad's; Conrad had no vested interest in the statements; Conrad facilitated with a student who gave a statement to Conrad that Warden had never abused him; and JK's statements were validated by Warden's confession. (*State v. Warden*, 1995, p. 1090)

Warden's two confessions, first to the police and then to a coworker, most likely determined the conviction. Warden at first denied he had done anything inappropriate but then told a police investigator that "he had rubbed his penis on JK's anus." He made a similar confession to another care worker who testified in the case. Warden later testified "he confessed to something he did not do because he was scared and 'wanted to get out of there'" (p. 7) and that "his admission to Holly Miller (the care worker) was merely to repeat what he had told Detective Beeson" (p. 7).

From the perspective of the prosecution winning its case against Warden, these were the "good facts." As hooks (1989) has explained in discussing another area of social activism, "extreme cases . . . make people confront the issue, and acknowledge it to be serious and relevant" (p. 87).

THE EXCEPTIONAL PERSON

In addition to good facts, attempts to silence are most often defeated by extraordinary performances. Thus segregation barriers were broken by heroic, exceptionally determined individuals, such as Rosa Parks, Medger Evers, Martin Luther King, and Ed Roberts. It seems even that the catalyst for change is often exceptionally skilled, especially strong, a "superrepresentative" of the group that has been silenced.

This requirement presumably emanates from the fact that ordinary competence becomes lost in the predisposition not to hear the other. hooks (1989) describes this phenomenon as it affects African American scholars: "Given the politics of domination—race, sex, and class exploitation—the [society's] tendency . . . is to place more value on what white people are writing about black people, or non-white people, rather than what we are writing about ourselves" (pp. 43–44).

In the debates over facilitated communication, Sharisa Kochmeister's experience is, as LeCompte (1993) would put it in her "framework for hearing silence," a story that "begs to be told" (p. 10). The first time that Sharisa Kochmeister, previously believed severely retarded, ever typed *without* a facilitator touching her and *without* a facilitator shadowing her arm as she moved (i.e., facilitator's hand located a foot or so above her arm) was in a court case. She has described the circumstances for her breakthrough:

> I've just been through the most incredible 10 weeks of my life. I became quite ill in March when a family court judge said I had to either type independently or be tested, or I wouldn't be allowed to testify against my abuser. After 3 weeks of vomiting, excessive sleep, and almost complete shutdown, I made the agonizing decision to type independently with my dad next to me but his hands in front of him or in his lap. On 4/11, I met the judge in chambers and convinced him I could type, and am, indeed, the one who is communicating. He ruled I'd be allowed to testify during the first week in June with only he and my attorney allowed to ask questions personally.
>
> On 5/12, there was a family court hearing and my abuser consented to a finding of sexual abuse in the case against her. She had to agree to go to the mental health center for evaluation and treatment. She had to give up visitation and agree to stay away from me. She may only contact me via letter-writing and I certainly don't have to answer. At least that part of my long struggle is over. It's my impression that the mere threat of my testimony was enough to convince her and her attorney to just give up and not risk a trial. Amazing, huh? (Kochmeister, 1994, p. 7)

PAYING ATTENTION TO DETAIL/
OFFERING OPPOSITIONAL ARGUMENTS

Excluded groups always endure multiple exclusionary practices, cultural as well as political and economic. In *Race Matters*, Cornell West (1993) describes the results of exclusionary ideology on black America as a "nihilistic threat to its very existence" (p. 12). It is, he says, "the profound sense of psychological depression, personal worthlessness, and social despair so widespread in black America." When he speaks of cultural forces he refers to "families, schools, churches, synagogues, mosques, and communication industries (television, radio, video, music)" (p. 12). He describes nihilism as "the lived experience of coping with a life of horrifying meaninglessness, hopelessness, and (most important) lovelessness" (p. 14).

For the person with a disability, nihilism occurs in many forms and forums, from being too invisible on television and in advertising, to being portrayed as objects of pity, to being denied access to opportunities in schooling, higher education, employment, and political life (see Fine & Asch, 1988; Shapiro, 1993). One of the ways inclusion or its opposite, exclusion, occurs is through how issues are framed.

In the discourse concerning allegations of sexual abuse conveyed via facilitation, as with any issue, the way arguments are framed plays a large role in determining "findings." A predominant frame has been one that considers the potential for *false* allegations and dismisses the possibility that real abuses could be reported via facilitation. Making no reference to the possibility that those making the purported allegations could have been harmed, Jacobson and colleagues (1994) decry what they say are "many instances" in which family and staff have been accused of abuse by people using facilitated communication—often with "no physical evidence"—and "characteristically, the individuals . . . are removed from their lifelong family homes, or their caregivers are arrested and jailed, at least temporarily" (pp. 75–76). The potential for such events poses, for Jacobson and colleagues, a "great danger to caregivers" (p. 76).

Jacobson and colleagues provide no accounting of particular cases in which corroborating evidence was absent. Further, they offer no comparison of how allegations of abuse by speaking individuals are handled and how these compare to cases that do not involve facilitation. Similarly, Green and Shane (1994) call for "rigorous safeguards" in sorting out abuse allegations in order to guard against "invalid conclusions with terrible, perhaps irreversible, consequences," while they express no similar concern for or even mention of the possible harm that could come to a person whose cry for help might be ignored or otherwise not heard (p. 160). Wharton, Levine, Shane, and Emans (1995) present the most extreme version of this frame: "Facilitated communication, a technique with no scientific validation . . . has no legitimacy for the disclosure of sexual abuse" (pp. 1288–1289).

Presumably, no reasonable person would favor forcible removal of children from their home or even the bringing of charges against an individual based on information that could not be corroborated or where the statement itself could not be confirmed for authorship. Yet concern for safeguards is different from Wharton and colleagues' position, which would leave no room for an individual to prove his or her communicative competence.

An alternative frame examines such allegations in the context of abuse allegations in general. A medical team responsible for evaluating individuals who allege abuse conducted a three-year review of all such cases that had come through their regional medical center. The study (Botash et al., 1994) found that for the period "between January 1, 1990, and March 10, 1993, 1096 children were evaluated for suspected sexual abuse at the CARE program. Thirteen (1.2%) of these children disclosed abuse via FC" (p. 1283). Botash and colleagues continue:

Thirty-one percent (4/13) of the children who disclosed sexual abuse via FC had corroborating evidence. An additional five had supportive evidence. Two children had physical examination findings considered suspicious for sexual abuse. Seven children had nonspecific physical examination findings. (p. 1283)

Of the four cases where there was "evidence of sexual abuse: two had physical findings consistent with sexual abuse, one also disclosed the allegation verbally, and one perpetrator confessed" (p. 1282). The study authors concluded that in abuse cases which were alleged through facilitated communication "the indication rate for abuse and neglect is consistent with the upstate New York rate [where the study took place] of approximately 47 percent," which "demonstrates that allegations of abuse that are initiated owing to an FC disclosure should be taken seriously" (p. 1287).

PRESUMPTIONS OF COMPETENCE AND INCOMPETENCE

Said (1994) has described intellectual work as the role of questioning that which is taken for granted by exercising "a perpetual willingness not to let half-truths or received ideas steer one along" (p. 23). The judges in In the Matter of Luz P (1993) and State v. Warden (1995) adopted this role. They did *not* presume intellectual incompetence in the accusers, a stance that would have silenced them by discrediting them; rather the test of authorship, as outlined in these cases, is just that—a circumscribed examination to admit the witness's testimony and allegation into evidence, not a judgement of overall competence. In effect, the court rejected the concept of "presuming *in*competence" and at the same time still required validation of particular words in a legal context, in much the same way that the legal system often calls into question the words of acknowledged, competent people (i.e., people with speech). Maurer (1995) summarizes this argument in an extensive law review article on the place of facilitation in the courts: "The individual should be presumed competent, with the burden to show incompetence resting with the party opposed to the testimony" (p. 271).

Often, prevailing thoughts and interpretations are treated as truths handed down by impartial oracles. The most common assumption, or "truth," in disability research has to do with the idea of competence and incompetence. The prevailing cultural and professional theory about people with developmental disabilities is that they have a deficit and that the role of science is to measure and understand the deficit, and even to certify who is and is not competent, who is and is not mentally retarded. Presumptions of incompetence in people labeled developmentally disabled, autistic, mentally retarded, and so on are so often repeated by researchers, diagnosticians, and practitioners in texts and classification manuals that their mere restatement becomes a kind of evidence of their truth. Yet we must question these as any claims of truth, preferring instead a condition of uncertainty, fueled by competing discourses, competing truths. In Giroux's (1992) terms, we align ourselves with "refusals of all 'natural laws' and transcendental claims that by definition attempt to 'escape' from any type of historical and normative grounding" (p. 44); Fine (1992) refers to this as "denaturalizing" the "natural". And so, too, did the courts in the cases of Luz P, Kochmeister, and JK, for they were forced by circumstance to consider whether particular people, irrespective of label, were communicating their ideas in particular situations with a particular method.

Taking the critical point of view seriously, the persons with disabilities must have a central position in the discourse about facilitation, not as objects of research but as participants in research and as researchers themselves, as people who are presumed competent. That is essentially what several judges have done (again, the cases of Luz P, JK, and Kochmeister) by involving people with disabilities in making their own representations of their communication competence, and it is a theme encountered in the emerging autobiographical literature (Sellin, 1995).

While the courts have certainly not done all that might have been possible to hear the voices of people who use facilitation, the constitutional provisions within which they operate *have* provided a locus and rules of contestation by which some facilitated words have been heard by some judges. This experience deserves careful consideration for the lessons it may afford the research community as well as the broader community. Increasingly, the courts have leaned toward finding ways of hearing the words of people with disabilities, even when that requires finding ways of determining whether the words of the person are his or her own (see especially *State v. Warden*, 1995, and *Callahan v. Lancaster-Lebanon Intermediate Unit*, 1995). While there is as yet no definitive court standard as to the methodologies for determining authorship, recent decisions (In the Matter of Luz P, 1993; *State v. Warden*, 1995) suggest that the measures used must be appropriate to the means of communication and to the person being tested; a single test may not be appropriate for all individuals. Maurer (1995) cites numerous precedents for the multiple approaches (see also Dwyer, 1996; Phipps & Ells, 1995).

NOTES

1. A table was set up with a cardboard barrier running down the center. The idea was to show the child and teacher a different picture. Neither could see the other's picture. The pictures could be identified by a typical child of about 5.

The teacher ignored her own pictures most of the time and looked at the child. She facilitated with a light touch on top of the child's wrist.

2. The Kansas Supreme Court seems to have recognized that for JK to be heard required intensive efforts by the court to hear him, including asking him clarifying questions, asking questions in different ways, seeking correction of typographical errors, comparing his communication with his facilitator's and with that of others who worked with the same facilitator, considering that he had successfully performed a message-passing test, and comparing his words to other evidence, especially the two confessions. These strategies resemble those described in Chapter 3.

CHAPTER 11

Summing Up: What Should Not and What Can Be Said About Facilitated Communication

Donald N. Cardinal
Douglas Biklen

In critical theory, social scientists are interested in exploring "who speaks, under what conditions, for whom, and how knowledge is constructed within asymmetrical relations of power" (Giroux, 1992, p. 26). In this book, we have endeavored to conduct and report research in a way that is conscious of power relations in the fields of disability (e.g., psychology, special education). For example, people with disabilities typically have had no voice in research studies having to do with them; by contrast, we have attempted in several chapters to include the responses of research participants to the studies in which they were involved and, in one instance, a person with a disability is his own researcher. Many researchers present their controlled experiments more or less uncritically as valid contexts for examining the meaning and effects of disability; by contrast, this book includes studies in which the researchers have looked at how test conditions may explain performance. Similarly, many researchers have presented uncritical and decontextualized characterizations of people with disabilities, for example, as "profoundly retarded," "severely retarded," and "autistic"; by contrast, we highlight the importance of context, noting people's uneven performances, and acknowledging that failed or erratic performance is *not* defining of a person's ability.

From the standpoint of methodology, our approach has been to widen and deepen the available discourses of facilitated communication, not to restrict ourselves to a single discourse (e.g., controlled studies). While limiting consideration to a certain type of study such as the controlled experiment may be persuasive in some circles, it could also be unnecessarily exclusionary. Delpit (1995) cites the work of James Paul Gee when explaining that status or authority of voice is often maintained by one group over another by demanding adherence to particular discourses. In the debate over facilitation, the discourse has been about what constitutes science and data. In Delpit's (1995) example the topic was dialect, where dominant groups "apply frequent 'tests' of fluency in the dominant discourses, often focused on its most superficial aspects—grammar, style, mechanics—so as to exclude from full participation those who are not born to positions of power" (p. 153).

As we have seen in the court cases and in the research literature on facilitated communication, requirement that a person pass the wrong test (e.g., a test that requires word-retrieval skills, a test that includes activities in which the person has no prior experience [i.e., practice]) under the wrong conditions (e.g., that the person complete a response in limited time) can easily produce poor, even nihilistic, results. Our point is not to disagree with the idea of the controlled experiment—or even with particular results. The controlled experiment has a place among various research approaches; it can yield informative data, particularly if thoughtfully and sensitively constructed. However, controlled studies should not be equated with the whole of science or defined as the single way of knowing. No single protocol should be regarded as *the* protocol; protocols can and are often misleading, ill conceived, even wrong. At the same time, there is much to learn by expanding our notion of research to include qualitative and autobiographical accounts (Crossley & McDonald, 1984; Sellin, 1995; D. Williams, 1994a, 1994b); these can be especially useful as we attempt to interpret the results of other studies. Eugene Marcus has created a hybrid of autobiography and controlled experiment by conducting a self-study under the conditions first used by Wheeler, Jacobson, Paglieri, and Schwartz (1992), adapting the study conditions to aid his performance and, perhaps most important, providing narrative description of his subjective experiences. In several other chapters we used traditional qualitative research methods, including the researchers' subjective understandings of their work and reporting the perspectives of teachers/facilitators as well as of facilitated communication users. We are mindful that in the focus on authorship, facilitated communication as a concept can easily be reduced to being perceived as hand-holding rather than as the complex array of elements originally used to describe it (see Biklen, 1990). Autobiographies and qualitative research can be antidotes for such reductionism, as can careful attention to the language and arguments used in discussions of controlled experiments.

Our approach has been to challenge the peculiarly modernist notion of inviolable objectivism (i.e., presuming social science facts are not socially created) in deference to the proposition that all ideas are imbued with values, all ideas are contextualized. We embrace careful observation, systematic investigation, and other qualities of being objective, but always within a recognition that ideas carry with them assumptions and interests. Our ideas, as anyone's, can be located within a paradigm that "might be viewed as in opposition or in support of the dominant ideology, but it cannot be judged independently of it" (Giroux, 1981, p. 49).

Expanding the pool of data elaborates the varieties of voices heard and creates the opportunity for ever more rigorous, searching analysis. There may be a tendency to see the words of people with disabilities as less theoretical, less derived from systematic examination, and less authoritative, but this need not be the case; they, too, may be systematically gathered and organized. Lincoln (1993) has described the necessity of formulating accounts that include affected people (e.g., outsiders, marginalized people) in such a way that they accommodate the rules of the people themselves *and* of traditional social science. They must, she argues, "speak to disciplinary and policy communities, . . . [and] serve the interests and aspirations of the silenced themselves" (p. 36). This is an emerging trend in social science research, one that endeavors to hear the voices of affected people and to do so within a framework that will be heard by traditional social science and policy groups. Although speaking about the struggles of people of color, West's analysis of the social scientist's role could equally apply to the topic of facilitation. West (1993) has described an eclectic, adaptive stance as "the most desirable option" for those who would create a "new cultural politics of difference" (p. 33). It involves, West explains, staying "attuned to the best of what the mainstream has to offer—its paradigms, viewpoints and methods—yet maintains a grounding in affirming and enabling subcultures of criticism" (p. 33). He calls for "intellectual freedom fighters" who "position themselves" within or alongside the mainstream but also "aligned with groups who vow to keep alive potent traditions of critique and resistance" (p. 33). hooks (1994b) espouses a similar pragmatism, drawing ideas from diverse corners, including the dominant side: "I cross boundaries to take another look, to contest, to interrogate, and in some cases to recover and redeem" (p. 5). Activist (i.e., critical) researchers must, as Fine (1992) puts it, position themselves "explicitly, but with questions . . . not answers; as mobile and multiple, not static and singular; within spaces of rich surprise, not predetermined 'forced choices'; surrounded by critical conversation, never alone" (p. 230).

In this chapter we attempt to summarize our findings, linking them to specific studies in this book as well as to other available literature. We draw some conclusions but more often we raise additional questions, pointing out the complexities of facilitated communication and of social science research on disability and ability. Naturally, we make no claim of producing value-free interpretations; we consider that impossible. Rather, we construct this discussion within a disability-rights framework.

SUMMING UP WHAT WE KNOW

It is becoming clear that the inability of some experiments to measure authentic facilitated communication has been at least as much a result of the testing/experimental procedures used as it has been the failure of the method or the person(s) using the method. As discussed in Chapters 4 and 9, certain procedures in a controlled experiment seem to improve the likelihood of facilitated communication users producing authentic communication.

Experiments are frequently viewed as valid only as they are able to control for threats to internal and external validity. In the physical and biological sciences, the pure experimental research method is clearly believed to be the best approach for determining the causal effect of an isolated, single variable on its dependent variable, because of the potential for a high degree of control of extraneous conditions (Babbie, 1995). Even in the social sciences the traditional experiment (aka: pure or true experiment), and to a lesser degree its sibling designs of preexperiments and quasi-experiments, can be superior methods to test hypotheses (Campbell & Stanley, 1963; Cook & Campbell, 1979). Unfortunately, for studying human behavior in educational settings (as in facilitated communication authorship studies), the pure experimental method can, at times, disrupt the intended target phenomenon, since control is most easily achieved with research on humans in restrictive and artificial settings (Babbie, 1995; Cook & Campbell, 1979). The problem is that humans react to these controlled conditions differently from the way they react to naturally occurring conditions; thus the degree to which results can be generalized to the greater world is severely limited (Cook & Campbell, 1979).

An "experiment" is much better designed to be explanatory rather than descriptive (Babbie, 1995). This may be why early experiments in facilitated communication attempted to "explain" whether facilitated communication worked or not, not to empirically "describe" why people were unable to validate their communication.

The systematic observation of people using facilitated communication in their natural environment, as well as discussions with users of the facilitated communication method and their facilitators, can assist in the scientific endeavor to measure the authenticity of facilitated communication by systematically "describing" the phenomenon. Using natural, but empirical, observations to develop experiments, as witnessed by several of the studies presented in this book and elsewhere, has provided research designs that can boast of scientific validity as well as generalizability. Dialogue between these two research methods has yielded experimental designs that have, at least in part, begun to overcome the experimental pitfall of artificial conditions and therefore a lack of generalizability, while maintaining the optimal experimental controls necessary for valid findings (i.e., they meet prevailing standards of validity).

So, what do we really know about authorship and facilitated communication? The following is what we understand about facilitated communication when considering the entire body of research on it and related topics. We have stated our understanding in terms of what we think *should not* be said or claimed about facilitated communication and what *can* be said about it:

What Should Not Be Said About Facilitated Communication:

- Facilitated communication has been proven to be a hoax or a fraud.
  Contraindication: No scientific evidence or factual reports exist to indicate an orchestrated intent to deceive or to fraudulently obtain personal gain from facilitation. Litigation charging that it is a hoax has been consistently dismissed by state and federal courts (*State v. Warden*, 1995; Dwyer, 1996; *Storch et al. v. Syracuse University et al.*, 1995).
- Facilitated communication has been proven to be not real.
  Contraindication: Although the literature presents mixed results regarding the ability to measure authentic communication from facilitation, it has been authenticated under both natural and controlled conditions and these reports have appeared in highly respected peer-reviewed journals.
- Facilitated communication originates with the facilitator rather than the facilitated communication user.
  Contraindication: Some controlled studies have reported that facilitated communication *can* be influenced by the facilitator or that the facilitated communication user may recognize cues from the facilitator (see Simon, Toll, & Whitehair, 1994; Wheeler et al., 1993). Other controlled studies have reported authentic, user-originated communication (e.g., Cardinal, Hanson, & Wakeham, 1996; Sheehan & Matuozzi, in press; Vazquez, 1993; Weiss et al., 1996). Therefore the general statement above would be inaccurate and misleading. Further, as noted in Chapter 9, certain conditions and/or procedures foster influence or cue seeking while others minimize it.

- Facilitated communication is magic or a trick.
  Contraindication: No reputable studies have concluded that facilitated communication is a trick or illusion. The few instances when "trickery" has been alleged demonstrate how one *could* manipulate a person to press letters on a keyboard, assuming one was unethical. No evidence exists to suggest that unethical behavior exists in facilitated communication to a degree greater than with any other communication training method.
- Facilitated communication works for everyone.
  Contraindication: Some studies report that even under conditions where some people can demonstrate their authorship using facilitated communication, others were unable to do so (e.g., Cardinal et al., 1996; Simon et al., 1994). Evidence about the range of people with whom the method might be useful and the particular conditions under which it proves useful will undoubtedly evolve as use of the method and refinements in research techniques also evolve.
- No one has ever "validated" their communication through facilitation.
  Contraindication: Many people using facilitation have "validated" their authorship (see Cardinal et al., 1996; Intellectual Disability Review Panel [IDRP], 1989; Sheehan & Matuozzi, 1994; Simon et al., 1994; Steering Committee, 1993; Vazquez, 1994; Weiss et al., 1996). Several courts have accepted facilitated communication for crucial testimony (Kochmeister, 1994; *State v. Warden*, 1995), and some judges have required validation tests in court or as part of legal proceedings. Additionally, naturalistic studies have reported authentic communication through facilitation (e.g., Biklen, Saha, & Kliewer, 1995; Olney, 1995). The presence of even a single instance of validation, for example, in a message-passing experiment, negates the claim that "no one has ever validated authorship."
- Everyone using facilitated communication will:
      demonstrate excellent literacy skills
      write poetry
      have perfect spelling
      perform at super accelerated levels
  Contraindication: Peer-reviewed studies have reported that some facilitated communication users do communicate with typical literacy skills and others do not (Biklen, 1993a; see also, Koppenhaver, Pierce, & Yoder, 1995, for a discussion of the relationship of literacy to facilitated communication); some write poetically and most do not (Biklen et al., 1995; Biklen, Morten, Gold, Berrigan, & Swaminathan, 1992); some users are reported to have mostly perfect spelling while others do not; no controlled studies have reported accelerated levels of communication—in fairness, these studies have not typically been designed to investigate

that question—but some naturalistic studies and books have (Biklen, 1993; Sellin, 1995).
- Everyone using facilitation will:
    facilitate best (or, conversely, not at all) with their mothers and fathers
    facilitate best (or, conversely, not at all) with only one person
    learn to use facilitated communication immediately
Contraindication: Some studies have reported that a parent was the best facilitator for a particular subject but have also reported instances in which particular individuals do not communicate when their parents are facilitating; or some individuals communicate with one parent but not the other, or with certain teachers but not others. Studies indicate a wide variation in the time it takes to learn how to use facilitation. Qualitative studies and other narrative accounts suggest that ability to communicate with facilitation, generalization to multiple or new facilitators, and typing with less or even no physical support improve with effort/practice over time (Biklen, 1993; Biklen et al., 1995; Crossley, 1994; Eastham, 1992; R. Martin, 1994); this parallels the finding that authentication of facilitated communication has occurred at the highest levels (i.e., above 70%) in those studies that involved familiar facilitators in assessment activities over extended periods of time in multiple sessions (e.g., Cardinal et al., 1996; Steering Committee, 1993).

Things One Can Say About Facilitated Communication:

- Facilitated communication appears to work for some people.
    Indication: Peer-reviewed controlled studies report that some people can use facilitated communication to communicate to a degree that is significantly greater than they can without facilitation. The degree to which it works or does not work may change over time and may depend on a complex array of qualities, including the skills of the facilitator, the particular communication context, motivation, personal qualities of the person with the communication impairment, opportunities for practice, and so forth.
- Authorship studies in facilitated communication achieve mixed results, but when studies possess certain procedures, some level of facilitated communication can be measured.
    Indication: This is demonstrated thoroughly in Chapter 9. Among the features that appear particularly important are making sure that participants have had extensive experience with the method and numerous practice sessions with the research protocol; involvement of participants' "best" or familiar facilitators; naturally controlled conditions;

extensive time in which to respond to questions or tasks; monitoring of the participants' style of communicating (e.g., looking at the target, waiting for questions to be asked before trying to respond, opportunities to clarify answers); minimizing word-retrieval tasks; and using content in test tasks that is personally relevant.

- Authorship studies have reported that the facilitator can influence the user's communicative output or that participants may seek/derive cues from the facilitator.
  Indication: Some controlled studies have indicated that the facilitator can unknowingly "control" the facilitated communication output, while other studies have demonstrated that the facilitator can "influence" the facilitated output. Still other studies claim that the influence is not control but rather is much like the influence verbal speakers experience, involving giving and receiving cues, consciously and unconsciously, not only in a unidirectional way from facilitator to the facilitated communication user, but also in reverse.

- Testing for authorship of facilitated communication is still very complex and there are many unanswered questions, but our understanding of it is greater now than even a few years ago.
  Indication: All of the studies in this book as well as other studies, including those in which people have failed to "validate" authorship, have yielded insights about how better to assess authorship. Chapter 9 of this book addresses this issue thoroughly.

- Not all people with autism, Down syndrome, pervasive developmental disorder, or other developmental disabilities benefit from facilitation.
  Indication: Most studies, even the most recent ones that include many of the conditions typically associated with successful measurement of authorship, have not demonstrated authorship for all participants. The presence of a particular disability has not been shown to guarantee success with method. At the same time, several studies have identified particular disabling conditions (e.g., impaired hand function, dyspraxia) that have been hypothesized to be involved with communication impairment and therefore suggest the potential usefulness of facilitated communication. It is also noteworthy that many individuals with the above-mentioned disabilities have effective speech and writing skills and may, for this reason, have no need for any alternative means of communication.

- Not all professionals make good facilitators, regardless of experience in the field.
  Indication: Data on this point are limited; however, it seems to be confirmed by several sources. First, studies in which individuals worked with "familiar" or "best" facilitators tended to have greater success in

measuring authorship than those that used unfamiliar or new facilitators; further, the studies that have successfully measured authorship typically have implied that individuals are more fluent with certain facilitators and unable to communicate, or communicate only at a rudimentary level, with others (e.g., single words rather than sentences). The same phenomenon is richly described in qualitative research accounts and has been corroborated by individuals who have achieved independent typing.

- Many facilitated communication users have difficulty passing validation tests under controlled conditions.
  Indication: Chapters 1, 5, and 9 of this book cover this point in great detail. However, many studies, for example, Chapters 2, 5, and 6, and the Postscript, demonstrate that facilitated communication users can improve upon their ability to pass validation tests under controlled conditions. Critical factors that may foster increased success are discussed in Chapter 9. It would be wrong to consider success or failure to pass tests as dependent only on personal qualities of the participant. And it would be wrong to design authorship tests in a way that did not include those factors that have been shown to maximize success.

- Some facilitated communication users show remarkable increases in communicative performance, others show less than remarkable performance, and still others show no increase at all.
  Indication: Peer-reviewed studies, as well as additional studies in this book, have demonstrated that some people who were presumed to be severely and moderately retarded were—with facilitation under facilitator-blind conditions—able to engage in tasks, such as computer games or discussions, in which knowledge of vocabulary and mathematical reasoning was clearly in a range typical for a person without an intellectual disability (see Olney, 1995; Weiss et al., 1996). Similarly, some individuals who have learned to communicate with facilitation and who subsequently typed without physical support have demonstrated the ability to convey complex thoughts (Kochmeister, 1994; Rivin, 1993; Watts & Wurzburg, 1994). Other individuals, in these same and other peer-reviewed studies, have not demonstrated improved, dramatic changes in communicative ability, or any changes at all.

- Findings from qualitative and quantitative studies have produced convergent findings about facilitation.
  Indication: Controlled studies in which individuals have demonstrated authorship incorporate factors that have been discussed in qualitative studies, including the benefits of practice, the importance of facilitated communication technique/monitoring, and the usefulness of multiple modalities for testing. Similarly, controlled and qualitative studies have

reported similar findings: uneven performance, difficulties with generalizing to multiple facilitators, possibility of cuing or influence, and unexpected (i.e., previously not observed) literacy abilities.
• Facilitated communication is important.
Indication: Communication is fundamental to participation in community; indeed, it is central to all relationships. To the extent that facilitated communication can provide a voice to some people with disabilities, it is crucially important. For this reason, and inasmuch as speech is a basic right, the right to select a means of communication, to learn how to communicate, and to communicate one's own thoughts and feelings must also be considered a right.

CONCLUDING NOTE

In making the words "presuming competence" central to this book, we intended to challenge a central, dominant representation of people with developmental disabilities. But at the same time, we do not imagine the challenge to be a naive or antiscientific one. We do not expect readers to believe as a matter of faith that certain people can do things they have not demonstrated themselves capable of doing. But we do mean to imply that whatever a person comes to do is inextricably woven together with the person's past experiences and with the current context. Thus, in terms of facilitation, if a person is to prove his or her communication in accordance with particular standards, the person's performance will be affected by the kinds of tasks required, the conditions under which the tasks are demanded, the affect/posture of the people watching or interacting with the person, and so forth. Further, we assume that ways of measuring performance may affect the performance itself; hence the importance of considering multiple ways of observing, recording, and understanding. Adopting the concept of "presuming competence" places an onus of responsibility on educators and researchers to figure out how the person using facilitation, or any educational undertaking, can better demonstrate ability.

Taking the Test: A Facilitator's View

Rosemary Crossley

In this commentary I give a personal account of my testing experiences from 1977, when I was involved in testing Anne McDonald, to 1994, when I was facilitator F1 in the research described by Baldac and Parsons in this book (Chapter 4).

My first experience of facilitating a communication aid user who was undertaking validation testing occurred in Melbourne, Australia, in 1977. In April of that year, I started to teach Anne McDonald to read and spell. In August 1977, the state Mental Health Authority (MHA) asked two senior psychologists to test Anne to see if she really could read and spell. Leo Murphy, dean of special education at Burwood State College, and Jean Vant, former senior psychologist for the MHA, wrote a short story that they gave to Anne to read while I was out of the room. The following passage, written later, is Anne's account of what transpired that day, when Anne was 16 and grossly malnourished after 13 years in institutions:

> The text in front of me was a passage about a relative of Jean Vant's whose name was also Annie and who was a lush. For some reason, another relative had to give her a bottle of gin once a year. After I'd read it Mrs. Vant gave me three comprehension questions to answer: "What was my aunt given?", "What was her name?" and "Where did the present come from?".
>
> I started spelling the answer to the first question, and I'd got as far as g i when Mrs. Vant said "Oh, I know what you're going to say." At that stage I hated being second-guessed. It was foolish, but not being sleek and fat I had only my pride to live for. I was determined to pass the test, but to do so on my own terms. I changed the

answer from 'gin' to 'gift'. To get the 'gin' in I spelled "Jean's aunt
is called Ginnie" and to show off my vocabulary I spelled "She got the
gin from annuity." (Anne McDonald, personal communication, 1994)

Jean Vant reported that Anne "was given a passage to read whose contents were known only to Dr. Murphy and myself [Vant], then three typed
questions relating to it" to answer with my [Crossley's] support and that
Vant had supported Anne's arm while she spelled answers to other questions. She concluded, "I have observed her [Anne] working with the mag-
netic letter board both as the person supporting her and the person who
was asking the questions. I am satisfied in both instances that she did
indeed answer the questions and in each case had read the material and
the questions." Her final report, endorsed by Dr. Murphy, was provided
to the MHA in September 1977 (Crossley & McDonald, 1984).

The MHA initially accepted the Vant/Murphy report with enthusiasm.
However, when the MHA had realized the implications of finding sophisticated communication skills in a child who had been diagnosed as profoundly intellectually impaired and shut away without therapy or education for 13 years, it first ignored the report and later, in testimony to the
Supreme Court of Victoria in May 1979, denied that it existed (Crossley &
McDonald, 1980).

There are similarities and differences between this first test of facilitated
communication and the others in which I have been involved since. The
most important difference was the nature of the Vant/Murphy test, which
evaluated a skill—literacy—rather than the existence of communication
per se. If Anne's answers matched the questions, this indicated that she
had read and understood the questions regardless of whether her responses
were strictly correct. This is an important point. Most of the validation
studies producing negative results have not allowed for students getting
answers wrong—any incorrect responses have been arbitrarily ascribed to
the facilitator.

In the Baldac and Parson's study, participant 4 (P4) was shown a photograph screened from me that had been selected by his father from a random set of pictures I had never seen. When I asked what he could see, he
typed TRAM, TRAIN, TRUCK, and TRAIN again. The picture featured a
tractor. The chance of my coincidentally manufacturing a string of vehicle
names starting with the same initial letters as "tractor" is minuscule.
Equally, given that the important question is not "Can P4 correctly name
different vehicles?" but "Can P4 show that he can produce meaningful
communication when facilitated?" his responses must be viewed positively.
Because the Vant/Murphy story gave Anne the information she needed
to answer the questions, word finding was not an issue for her.

Despite allowing each participant up to eight hours for testing, Baldac and Parsons found the time too short to allow administration of all items to the slower typers; the stimulus remained in view of the participant throughout, however, and memory for the stimulus was not the issue that it is in most message-passing tests.

An implicit assumption in academic testing is that the students being tested understand and accept the value of testing and are motivated to succeed. If the participants' life experiences are significantly different from average (Anne had been institutionalized for 12 of her 16 years and had never before undertaken any tests), and/or if they have disabilities known to affect socialization and motivation, this may not be a reasonable assumption. Anne changed one answer when she was second-guessed. After the testers left, she fooled around and produced nonsensical answers along with rude comments about my tone of voice (a tone which reflected the tension I was under) before answering the questions she'd been shown. Two years later, in the Supreme Court of Victoria, Anne spelled I DON'T LIKE ANY SUGGESTIONS THAT MY COMMUNICATIONS AREN'T MINE when given a message-passing test and only performed the test on the third time of asking (Crossley & McDonald, 1984).

The most notable example of noncompliance in the Baldac and Parsons research was P3, who, when asked to describe photographs produced, instead typed totally unrelated sentences. His skills, and those of his primary facilitator, F2, would certainly have been questioned if he had not previously successfully undertaken validation tasks with the same facilitator (Intellectual Disability Review Panel [IDRP], 1989). P3 had been invited to take part in this research as a previously validated communicator in order to explore the effect of the different tasks set on his performance. In P3's case, motivation seemed as significant as any variation in task. During the research he complained that the tasks set were "babyish." After the research was complete P3, who was in eleventh grade, was due to take school exams. To ensure that his performance was not open to question, his school arranged for an external facilitator from an elementary school, who had no knowledge of the courses P3 was studying, to partner him. Once he got over the shock of his regular facilitator being replaced at the door of the examination room, P3 worked hard and achieved passing or better grades, indicating that his former test failure was unlikely to have been caused by incapacity.

After Anne McDonald won her Supreme Court action and left the institution, a committee nominated by the MHA was set up to investigate my work with 11 other residents (see Chapter 1 of this volume). The committee's report—it declared all 11 residents severely or profoundly retarded—is in direct conflict with the minutes of their investigations (made available under the Freedom of Information Act in late 1984), which record examples of successful message passing and of spelling without arm support. In answer, for example, to a question about Isaac Newton (asked in my absence), child L. is recorded in the minutes as having "spelt out NEWDON (*sic*). No arm support needed, no doubt about letters hit" (6/7/79). The Committee's papers also contain such comments as "P. is competent with fractions" and "N. can handle sums and doesn't need her arm supported all the time" (13/7/79).

My next experience of formal validation testing took place in 1988. I facilitated two of the three clients who undertook the message-passing test in the IDRP study (mentioned in Chapter 1) that was initiated by the Victorian government. One of these was "Toto," who was 15 years old, diagnosed as autistic, and had just moved from a special school for children labeled mildly retarded to a regular high school after typing with facilitation for some 18 months. Toto could type some single words or short phrases (concerned with food and money) independently, but he did so obsessively and, typically, out of context. His independent typing was not functional. Without the inhibition provided by facilitation, he could not type a sentence, or even a single word, relating to other topics, as he would become stuck on his obsessions.

Toto happily accompanied two IDRP investigators to the shopping center across the road from the DEAL Communication Centre, where they all had coffee, and Toto was given a black T-shirt and bought a chocolate easter egg with their money. He also got 20 cents worth of Smarties from a candy machine because, as the psychologists later tactfully noted in their report, he "persisted in his request until he succeeded."

On their return to DEAL the psychologists said they'd given Toto something. "So what did they give you?" I asked. "Coffee," he said. "Tell Rosie on the Communicator what else you got." Toto then used the Communicator independently to type 20C SMARTIES and CHOCOLATE. After CHOCO-LATE he typed FREDDO FROG, one of his stereotyped phrases, very quickly, instead of "easter egg."

"Okay, but we gave you something else as well," one of the psychologists said. "Tell Rosie about it." At this point Toto reached for my hand and held it while he typed SCARF.

"Did they give you a scarf, Toto?"

NO.

"Then what did they give you?"

SOX, he typed.

"Did they give you a pair of socks, Toto?"

NO.

"Then what did they give you?"

And so on through a list of different items of clothing until he finally got T-SHIRT. This performance is typical of people with word-finding problems, who get into the correct category and then have difficulty in retrieving the exact name, but recognize that their incorrect attempts are wrong.

"What color was it?" he was asked.

BLUE, he typed.

"Was it blue?"

"No."

"What color was it?"

BL [long pause] UE.

"Was it blue, Toto?"

"No."

"What color was it?"

RED.

"Was it red?"

"No."

"What color was it?"

MAUVE.

"Was it mauve?"

"No."

"What color was it?"

BLACK.

"Was it black?"

"Yes."

The correct answer was "black." "Blue" was one of Toto's stereotyped words, but as its initial letters are the same as "black," it might still have come out anyway. Typing BLUE a second time despite knowing it was incorrect indicated how hard it was for Toto to break out of his automatic completions. The psychologists reported that "he typed B and L and hesitated for some time before completing the word 'blue'."

Told that the test was over, Toto relaxed and conversed with the psychologists, who asked him why he took my hand.

I GET NERVOUS . . . CONFIDENCE. . . .

"Why are you nervous?"

WE ALL GET UPSET IF WORK IS HARD. . . .

"What was hard about today?"

GETTING MY THOUGHTS OUT.

As the session was winding up, Toto took my hand again and typed his thanks to the psychologists for the T-shirt and, as they put it, "apologized for his insistent behaviour in trying to obtain the Smarties" (IDRP, 1989, p. 37). The psychologists had not told anyone about Toto's tantrum in front of the Smartie machine, and his detailed apology for the incident was accepted as validation of his ability to type his own thoughts with facilitation. Other examiners may have relied solely on the set test (i.e., identification of the present) and ignored all associated communication, in which case Toto would presumably have been scored as a fail.

As noted in Chapter 1, the IDRP reported that the validity of the communication was demonstrated by four of the six clients in the study. Following the lead of the MHA, critics of facilitated communication have repeatedly reported the IDRP as testing three individuals, all of whom failed (see, for example, Green, 1992; Rimland, 1993), or have claimed (incorrectly) that the individuals who passed could all communicate successfully without facilitation (Palfreman, 1994). None of the people tested could type sentences without facilitation, and only one, Toto, had been able to type any recognizable words prior to using facilitation.

Toto was the first person without cerebral palsy whom I had facilitated during validation tests, and his performance raised new and important issues. The people with cerebral palsy with whom I had facilitated may have had problems due to lack of motivation, or lack of knowledge, or lack of literacy skills, but if they knew something they appeared to have no more difficulty than other students in getting it out (ignoring, that is, their obvious physical difficulties). They did not show anything like the language problems that we were finding at DEAL in people with diagnoses other than cerebral palsy. Toto clearly knew that the item he had been given was clothing and wasn't a scarf or sox, but he had a great deal of difficulty telling me what it was. Once he was conversing, and producing sentences, his spontaneous apology showed that he remembered clearly what had happened at the shops. More importantly, it showed that he had sophisticated language and literacy skills that he had been unable to show on the confrontational naming task.

This pattern, whereby clients have been more successful in more conversational tasks, has continued in all validation tests in which I have been involved since. In the Baldac and Parsons research, only 30% of responses were correct in condition A of the labeling task (no distractor), despite the options being limited to one of four line drawings visible to the facilitator. In comparison, 50% of responses were correct in the apparently more difficult message-passing task, when facilitators had no idea of what the participant was seeing but in which the participant could use sentences and choose which aspects of a complex picture to describe.

My only other experience of formal validation testing between the IDRP testing and the Baldac and Parsons research came in early 1992. Gina was a woman in her 20s diagnosed as intellectually impaired who had been involved in a facilitated communication training program for several years. She was to be assessed for guardianship proceedings by two psychologists, one who had criticized facilitated communication in media interviews and one with no background in nonspeech communication. Initially they proposed testing Gina's facilitated communication using a facilitator she had never met who had never had any formal training. The psychologists wanted Gina, who was known to have severe word-finding problems, to type the names of pictures hidden from her facilitator, who was to wear headphones and hear white noise. DEAL offered to provide a facilitator (myself) on condition that the testing conditions were modified by the inclusion of some less clinical message-passing tasks.

On the day of the testing, the psychologists, Gina, and I met in the mid-afternoon. The first thing Gina typed to me was that she and one of the psychologists had been to a local coffee lounge. This was confirmed. Gina then did as badly at the naming task as I had expected—an observer who could see the pictures said she typed the names of some correctly, said the names of others, but got most wrong. He commented particularly on one interesting and memorable error. Asked what one picture was, Gina typed RAPE. As facilitator I was quite embarrassed and assured Gina that whatever she had been shown I was sure it was not a picture of a rape. The observer told me afterwards that the picture showed a man and woman embracing. When I spoke about this to the director of Gina's day program, I was told that this was a consistent error, one that Gina made regularly in human relations classes. This raised the question of whether some of Gina's less striking errors were also consistent with her everyday language use. Psychologists, and the community at large, are used to tests of knowledge in which only factually correct answers are acceptable. The possibility that a factually incorrect answer may still validate a person's ability to communicate through facilitation has not been addressed other than in qualitative studies, which have cited consistent misspellings as evidence for communication ownership (Biklen, 1993).

Towards 5:30 P.M., after about two hours of tests, Gina spontaneously typed BLAST ROSIE and then some words about coming again and wanting ANOTHER PRESENT. I asked her if she'd been given a present. She said "Yes." One of the psychologists asked her who had given it to her, and she pointed at him. I asked her what it was. She typed C C PIR. At this point she was asked "What do you do with it?" She pursed her lips and I asked her if it was a balloon. She said "No" and typed FIRE. Again I asked "What do you do with it?" and she typed CAN. "Yes, can, go on—what can you do with it?" and Gina typed CAN DL. I said "Candle—did they give you a candle?" Gina said "Yes." The psychologists confirmed that her answer was correct.

Despite the fact that by this stage Gina and I had been together for two and a half hours, and despite the fact that the only information about her visit to the coffee shop and her receipt of a present of a candle had come through facilitated typing, the psychologists nonetheless concluded that: "At no stage did facilitated communication lead to a cue-free communication output which was more advanced than her [Gina's] speech and gestures" (Geschke, 1994, p. 53).

In addition to the six people with autism or autistic behaviors who are discussed by Baldac and Parsons, four other DEAL clients were tested using the same methodology. While the results have not yet been analyzed in detail, two of these clients—girls with Down syndrome known as P7 and P8—validated their ability to communicate with facilitation on a number of tasks, including message passing. Both of the other participants dropped out of the study after completing fewer than a quarter of the responses required. P9, an adult with cerebral palsy labeled as intellectually impaired, completed the matching task successfully. P10, a child with severe developmental delay and autistic behaviors, did not complete any tasks successfully (Baldac, personal communication, 1995). I was the sole facilitator for P7, P8, and P10. P9 was facilitated by his mother.

As P7 and P8 completed more tasks than any of the others, their performance is especially interesting. Both girls were successful with the matching and message-passing tasks, and both found the labeling difficult. Both girls were in general quite happy and cooperative, but this changed when labeling tasks were introduced. P7, who was 10 years old at the time of testing, was reduced to tears, and P8, who was 14 years old, became morose. At each testing session a range of tasks were presented, both to avoid boredom and to ascertain whether performance on the different tasks improved over time. While all participants became more relaxed in the testing situation over time, the reaction of P7 and P8 to labeling tasks remained constant.

I was concerned that the depressive effect of the labeling task might affect the overall performance of P7 and P8, and I suggested that to boost their confidence each be given an extra task that capitalized on their individual strengths. P7, who enjoyed reading, was given a word-association task in which she was shown one written word (e.g., "bracelet") and with facilitation selected the associated word (e.g., "jewelry") from a set of four written words (P7's prior familiarity with the words used was unknown). She got 7 out of 10 associations correct. P8, who enjoyed math, was shown a sum (e.g., 8 + 4) and with facilitation pointed to numbers and operators on a math board to duplicate (and answer) the sum. She relayed a total of 10 sums out of 10 correctly. When P7 and P8 started their new tasks, there was an immediate positive change in their presentation, and they were both happy with the outcome. The inclusion of tasks that the girls enjoyed and that they found relatively easy appeared to contribute markedly to their self-esteem and to their willingness to continue with testing. For this to happen, the researchers had to be flexible and willing to accept input from facilitators or others who knew the participants well.

P7 and P8 each gave detailed descriptions of at least one photograph screened from me and were able to identify others, but both showed word-finding difficulties. For one picture, for example, P8 started by typing BED. I asked her "Is it a bed?" She said "No." She then typed BET and BEG and BEAST but answered negatively to each of them when I said it aloud. She typed A GREAT BIG AUSTRALIAN BE but couldn't finish the word. Finally one of the researchers pointed to something in the picture (still concealed from me by a screen) and asked P8 to tell me what the item was. She typed SAND (correctly), and I was able to guess that she was looking at a picture of a beach. Once we'd broken through that impasse, she was able to describe the details of the picture with no difficulty. Of course, if she had only been allowed to give one answer, she would have scored a fail.

The Baldac and Parsons research raised several issues for me as facilitator. First, ironically, it was easy for me to misdirect the communication aid users because I didn't have any idea of what they were trying to spell. In ordinary conversation, if P8 is stuck on a word I cue her by pronouncing what she's typed. Without a context, when P8 typed BE and paused, I didn't know how to pronounce it and said "be" as in "bell." In attempting to ask clarifying questions, I could derail the communication. While describing a photograph, P4 typed PEOPLE. The obvious questions to encourage him to elaborate were "how many?" "what sex?" and "how old?" If P4 had been a fluent typist, he could have easily explained why these were inappropriate questions, which he couldn't answer. As it was, without a more suitable question, P4's communication would either have stopped there or have been thrown right off track. (He went on to type PEOPLE ARE SAILING. The photograph was a bird's-eye view of a marina with boats going out, and the people were black dots on the decks.) Without a context it was also easy to misinterpret what was typed. P8, for example, was shown a picture of seals. She typed SEA. I assumed that was a whole word and asked her if she had a picture of the sea. She said "No" (correctly) and I typed a string of spaces to separate her answers before asking her to try again. Not surprisingly, P8 was confused, and she typed a number of related but incorrect words before again attempting and completing SEALS. These errors on my part had nothing to do with the techniques of facilitation. Rather, they exemplify the general difficulty of communicating with disfluent communicators when you have no idea of what the topic is. Such misunderstandings occur frequently in nonspeech communication and also occur in communication with people with severe articulation difficulties. They point up the fact that communication is a cooperative enterprise in which both parties have a role and which requires more than the bare bones of language to succeed.

The second issue was the varying levels of stress produced by the different tasks, not just in the communication aid users, but in me as facilitator. Overall, the aid users appeared to find all conditions of the labeling task equally stressful. As facilitator, the conditions of both the matching and the labeling tasks that explicitly checked for facilitator influence were more stressful than those that just examined communication success. Every time aid users started to give an answer that matched the card in front of me, I became concerned that I might be influencing their communication. Consequently condition C, in which the card in front of me was never the correct answer, was the most relaxed. Interestingly, in both tasks the highest scores were obtained in condition C, though as only a minority of participants undertook this condition, no firm conclusions can be drawn.

Certainly, my long-term involvement in validation testing has made me conscious of the effect of stress, both on me and on the aid user(s) being tested. In part, stress is related to the circumstances of testing, and in that respect the testing of Anne McDonald in the Supreme Court was undoubtedly the most stressful. Other issues that affect stress are the nature of the tasks, the testing setup, and the friendliness (or otherwise) of the testers. The most relaxed testing in which I have facilitated was that conducted by the IDRP—it took place at DEAL, no special equipment or cameras were used, the task was conversational in nature, and the presents given to the aid users established a friendly relationship between them and the testers. The most stressful was the testing of Gina, in an unfamiliar location with inappropriately sized furniture, video equipment, cassette recorders, a screen, and earphones. One candle couldn't do much to improve the situation. When the psychologists decided a second testing session was required, they did not give Gina another present; instead they had her collected from her home at noon on a Sunday, with no warning and no lunch, but with a streaming cold, and sat her down to label pictures. Unsurprisingly, her performance deteriorated significantly.

The Baldac and Parsons study was conducted at DEAL, and the researchers made every effort to establish friendly relationships with the participants and allowed the participants practice time before testing started. Nonetheless it was hard for participants to remain relaxed while undertaking confrontational naming tasks at a table divided by a high screen in front of two video cameras and their operators. While I did not find the setup particularly stressful, this may be a reflection of my substantial test experience. Certainly the other facilitators expressed some anxiety.

It is generally accepted that the performance of people with autism and people undertaking word-finding tasks deteriorates under stress. The effect of stress on communication partners has not been formally investigated. The most common effects I have noticed when facilitators are conscious that their performance is being observed are a loss of concentration or an increase in muscle tension in the supporting hand and arm, which may lead the facilitator to be less sensitive or responsive to the aid user's movements. Normally competent facilitators who lose concentration are likely either to forget to monitor the aid user's eye contact or forget to slow the aid user's pointing down. As the test situation provides many visual distractions and the effect of tension on aid users often speeds up their pointing, any loss of concentration by the facilitator may have significant effects on the aids user's output. Future research could usefully examine how individual facilitators perform under different conditions.

Variations in performance apparently resulting from different tasks, different language/memory abilities, and different degrees of motivation are common features in validation testing. Another common thread running through all the testing in which I have been involved is the way in which positive results have been handled by those to whom they are an embarrassment. The Baldac and Parsons results are too recent to have attracted comment, but the wheel came full circle in 1994 when a commentator purporting to summarize Anne McDonald's story as told in *Annie's Coming Out* (Crossley & McDonald, 1984) concluded, "There is still no convincing, objective evidence that she . . . even knows the letters of the alphabet" (Palfreman, 1994, p. 55). The commentator omitted all reference to either the Vant/Murphy tests (Crossley & McDonald, 1984) or the MHA's unsuccessful attempt to conceal their report from the Supreme Court (Crossley & McDonald, 1984).

References

Addelson, K. P. (1990). Why philosophers should become sociologists during their observations (and vice versa). In H. S. Becker & M. M. McCall (Eds.), *Symbolic interaction and cultural studies* (pp. 119–143). Chicago: University of Chicago Press.

American Psychological Association. (1994). *Resolution on facilitated communication*. Washington, DC: Author.

American Speech-Language Hearing Association. (1994). *Position statement on facilitated communication*. Silver Springs, MD: Author.

Ashton-Warner, S. (1986). *Teacher*. New York: Simon & Schuster. (Original work published 1963)

Babbie, E. R. (1995). *The practice of social research* (7th ed.). Belmont, CA: Wadsworth.

Barron, J., & Barron, S. (1992). *There's a boy in here*. New York: Simon & Schuster.

Berger, H. J. C., van Spaendonck, K. P. M., Horstink, M. W. I. M., Buytenhuijs, E. L., Lammers, P. W. J. M., & Cools, A. R. (1993). Cognitive shifting as a predictor of progress in social understanding in high-functioning adolescents with autism: A prospective study. *Journal of Autism and Developmental Disorders, 23*(2), 341–359.

Biklen, D. (1990). Communication unbound: Autism and praxis. *Harvard Educational Review, 60,* 291–314.

Biklen, D. (1993). *Communication unbound*. New York: Teachers College Press.

Biklen, D., & Duchan, J. (1994). "I am intelligent": The social construction of mental retardation. *Journal of the Association for Persons with Severe Handicaps, 19*(3), 173–184.

Biklen, D., Morton, M. W., Gold, D., Berrigan, C., & Swaminathan, S. (1992). Facilitated communication: Implications for individuals with autism. *Topics in Language Disorders, 12*(4), 1–28.

Biklen, D., Saha, N., & Kliewer, C. (1995). How teachers confirm authorship of facilitated communication. *Journal of the Association for Persons with Severe Handicaps, 20,* 45–56.

Biklen, D., & Schubert, A. (1991). New words: The communication of students with autism. *12*(6), 46–57.

Biklen, S., & Moseley, C. (1988). "Are you retarded?" "No, I'm Catholic": Qualitative methods in the study of people with severe handicaps. *Journal of the Association for Persons with Severe Handicaps, 13,* 155–162.

Bligh, S., & Kupperman, P. (1993). Brief report: Facilitated communication evaluation procedure accepted in a court case. *Journal of Autism and Developmental Disabilities, 23*(3), 553–557.

Blumer, H. (1969). *Symbolic interactionism*. Englewood Cliffs, NJ: Prentice-Hall.

Bogdan, R., & Biklen, S. (1991). *Qualitative research for education: An introduction to theory and methods*. Boston: Allyn & Bacon.

Botash, A., Babuts, D., Mitchell, N., O'Hara, M., Manuel, J., Lynch, L. (1994). Evaluations of children who have disclosed sexual abuse via facilitated communication. *Archives of Pediatric Medicine, 148*, 1282–1287.

Brealey, G. (1984). *A test of love* [Film]. Sydney: Film Australia.

Bruner, J. (1984). Interaction, communication and self. *Journal of the American Academy of Child Psychiatry, 23*(1), 1–7.

Calculator, S. N., & Singer, K. M. (1992). Letter to the editor: Preliminary validation of facilitated communication. *Topics in Language Disorders, 12*(4), ix–xvi.

Callahan v. Lancaster-Lebanon Intermediate Unit 13 (1995). 22 Individuals with Disabilities Education Law Report 104.

Campbell, D., & Stanley, J. (1963). *Experimental and quasi-experimental designs for research*. Chicago: Rand McNally.

Candland, D. K. (1993). *Feral children and clever animals: Reflections on human nature*. New York: Oxford University Press.

Cardinal, D. N., & Hanson, D. (1994a, March). *An analysis of findings regarding the validity of facilitated communication*. Paper presented at the 4th Annual Integration Institute, Costa Mesa, CA.

Cardinal, D., & Hanson, D. (1994b). Research brief: Preliminary results of a validation study regarding facilitated communication. *Facilitated Communication Digest, 2*(4), 3–4.

Cardinal, D. N., Hanson, D., & Wakeham, J. (1996). Investigation of authorship in facilitated communication. *Mental Retardation, 34*(4), 231–242.

Committee of Inquiry to Investigate Claims about Children at St. Nicholas Hospital. (1980). *Report* (Victorian Legislative Assembly Paper No. 83). Melbourne, Australia: Government Printer.

Cook, T. D., & Campbell, D. T. (1979). *Quasi-experimentation: Design and analysis issues for field settings*. Chicago: Rand McNally.

Crossley, R. (October, 1988). *Unexpected communication attainments by persons diagnosed as autistic and intellectually impaired*. Unpublished paper presented at International Society for Augmentative and Alternative Communication, Los Angeles, CA.

Crossley, R. (1992). Getting the words out: II. Case studies in facilitated communication training. *Topics in Language Disorders, 12*(4), 46–59.

Crossley, R. (1994). *Facilitated communication training*. New York: Teachers College Press.

Crossley, R. (In press). *Speechless*. New York: Signet/Dutton.

Crossley, R., & McDonald, A. (1984). *Annie's coming out*. New York: Viking Penguin.

Crossley, R., & Remington-Gurney, J. (1992). Getting the words out: Facilitated communication training. *Topics in Language Disorders, 12*(4), 29–45.

Cummins, R. A., & Bancroft, H. H. (1981). *Supplementary report to the report of the Committee of Inquiry to Investigate Claims about Children at St. Nicholas Hospital*. Melbourne Australia: Authors.

Cummins, R., & Prior, M. (1992). Autism and assisted communication: A reply to Biklen. *Harvard Educational Review*, 62(2), 228–241.

Damasio, A. R., & Maurer, R. G. (1985). A neurological model for childhood autism. In A. M. Donnellan (Ed.), *Classical readings in autism* (pp. 383–405). New York: Teachers College Press. (Original work published 1978)

Darley, F. L., Armson, A. E., & Brown, J. R. (1975). *Motor speech disorders*. Philadelphia: W. B. Saunders.

Davidson & Co. (1988). *Word attack plus* [Computer program]. Torrence, CA: Author.

Davidson & Co. (1989). *Math blaster mystery* [Computer program]. Torrence, CA: Author.

Davidson & Co. (1989). *Spell it plus* [Computer program]. Torrence, CA: Author.

Davidson & Co. (1994). *Spell it 3* [Computer program]. Torrence, CA: Author.

DEAL Communication Centre (1992). *Facilitated communication training*. Melbourne, Australia: Author.

Delpit, L. (1995). *Other people's children: Cultural conflict in the classroom*. New York: The New Press.

DeMyer, M. K., Alpern, G. D., Barton, S., DeMyer, W., Churchill, D. W., Hingtgen, J. N., Bryson, C. Q., Pontius, W., & Kimberlin, C. (1972). Imitation in autistic, early schizophrenic, and non-psychotic subnormal children. *Journal of Autism and Childhood Schizophrenia*, 2, 264–287.

DeMyer, M. K., Hingtgen, J. N., & Jackson, R. K. (1981). Infantile autism reviewed: A decade of research. *Schizophrenia Bulletin*, 7(3), 388–451.

Devenny, D. A., Wilverman, W., Balgdy, H., Wall, M. J., & Sidtis J. J. (1990). Specific motor abilities associated with speech fluency in Down's syndrome. *Journal of Mental Deficiency Research*, 34, 437–443.

Donnellan, A. M. (1984). The criterion of the least dangerous assumption. *Behavioral Disorders*, 9, 141–150.

Drake, S. (1993). Interactions of task demands, performance, and neurology. *Facilitated Communication Digest*, 1(4), 3–5.

Duchan, J. (1987). Perspectives for understanding children with communicative disorders. In P. Knoblock (Ed.), *Understanding exceptional children and youth* (pp. 163–199). Boston, MA: Little Brown & Co.

Duchan, J. (1993). Issues raised by facilitated communication for theorizing and research on autism. *Journal of Speech and Hearing Research, 36,* 1108–1119.

Duchan, J., & Lund, N. (1983). *Assessing children's language in naturalistic contexts*. Englewood Cliffs, NJ: Prentice-Hall.

Dunn, L. M., & Dunn, L. M. (1981). *Peabody Picture Vocabulary Test-Revised*. Circle Pines, MN: American Guidance Service.

Dwyer, J. (1996). Access to justice for people with severe communication impairment. *Administrative Law Review*, 3(2), 73–120.

Eastham, M. (1992). *Silent words*. Ottawa: Oliver Pate.

Eberlin, M., McConnachie, G., Ibel, S., & Volpe, L. (1993). Facilitated communication: A failure to replicate the phenomenon. *Journal of Autism and Developmental Disorders*, 23(3), 507–530.

Elliott, D., Weeks, D. J., & Gray, S. (1990). Manual and oral praxis in adults with Down's syndrome. *Neuropsychologia*, 28(12), 1307–1315.

Ferguson, D. L., & Horner, R. H. (1994). Negotiating the facilitated communication maze. *Mental Retardation, 32*(4), 305–307.

Ferguson, P. M., Ferguson, D. L., & Taylor, S. J. (Eds.). (1992). *Interpreting disability: A qualitative reader.* New York: Teachers College Press.

Fine, M. (1992). *Disruptive voices: The possibilities of feminist research.* Ann Arbor: University of Michigan Press.

Fine, M., & Asch, A. (1988). *Women with disabilities: Essays in psychology, culture and politics.* Philadelphia: Temple University Press.

Freire, P. (1970). *Pedagogy of the oppressed.* New York: Seabury.

Fulkerson, S. C., & Freeman, W. M. (1980). Perceptual-motor deficiency in autistic children. *Perceptual and Motor Skills, 50,* 331–336.

Galishoff, S. (1993). *Resistance to change in medicine: A historical perspective.* Unpublished manuscript, Georgia State University.

GameTek, Inc. (1989). *Jeopardy Junior* [Computer program]. Sausalito, CA: Author.

Geschke, N. (1994). *Report on the investigation of the removal and placement of a client of Intellectual Disability Services because of allegations made by facilitated communication.* Melbourne, Australia: Government Printer.

Geschwind, N. (1975). The apraxias: Neural mechanisms of disorders of learned movement. *American Scientist, 63,* 188–195.

Giroux, H. A. (1981). *Ideology, culture, and the process of schooling.* Philadelphia: Temple University Press.

Giroux, H. A. (1992). *Border crossings: Cultural workers and the politics of education.* New York: Routledge.

Glaser, B., & Strauss, A. L. (1967). *The discovery of grounded theory.* Chicago: Aldine.

Goddard, H. H. (1912). *The Kallikak family: A study in the heredity of feeble-mindedness.* New York: Macmillan.

Goffman, E. (1961). *Asylums: Essays on the social situation of mental patients and other inmates.* Chicago: Aldine.

Gold, M. (1980). *Did I say that? Articles and commentary on the Try Another Way System.* Champaign, IL: Research Press Co.

Goldberg, T. E. (1987). On hermetic reading abilities. *Journal of Autism and Developmental Disorders, 17,* 29–44.

Goode, D. (1992). Who is Bobby?: Ideology and method in the discovery of a Down syndrome person's competence. In P. M. Ferguson, D. L. Ferguson, & S. J. Taylor (Eds.), *Interpreting disability: A qualitative reader* (pp. 197–212). New York: Teachers College Press.

Goode, D. (1994). Defining facilitated communication in and out of existence: Role of science in the facilitated communication controversy. *Mental Retardation, 32*(4), 307–311.

Gould, S. J. (1981). *The mismeasure of man.* New York: Norton.

Grandin, T., & Scariano, M. N. (1986). *Emergence labeled autistic.* Novato, CA: Arena Press.

Green, G. (1992, October). *Facilitated communication: Scientific and ethical issues.* Paper presented at the E. K. Shriver Center for Mental Retardation UAP Research Colloquium. Boston.

Green, G., & Shane, H. C. (1994). Science, reason, and facilitated communication. *Journal of the Association for Persons with Severe Handicaps, 19,* 151–172.

Halle, J. (1994). A dispassionate (if that's possible) observer's perspective. *Mental Retardation, 32*(4), 311–313.

Halle, J. W., Chadsey-Rusch, J., & Reichle, J. (1994). Editorial introduction to the special topic on facilitated communication. *Journal of the Association for Persons with Severe Handicaps, 19*(3), 149–150.

Hanson, F. A. (1993). *Testing: Social consequences of the examined life.* Berkeley: University of California Press.

Heckler, S. (1994). Facilitated communication: A response by child protection. *Journal of Child Abuse and Neglect, 18,* 495–503.

Heller, K. A., Holtzman, W. H., & Messick, S. (Eds.). (1982). *Placing children in special education: A strategy for equity.* Washington, DC: National Academy Press.

Hitzing, W. (1994). Reply to Levine et al.'s "Plea to professionals." *Mental Retardation, 32*(4), 314–317.

Hobson v. Hansen, 269 F. Supp. 401 (1969).

hooks, b. (1989). *Talking back.* Boston: South End Press.

hooks, b. (1994). *Outlaw culture: Resisting representations.* New York: Routledge.

Horner, R. H. (1994). Invited commentary: Facilitated communication: Keeping it practical. *Journal of the Association for Persons with Severe Handicaps, 19,* 185–186.

Hudson, A., Melita, B., & Arnold, N. (1993). Brief report: A case study assessing the validity of facilitated communication. *Journal of Autism and Developmental Disorders, 23,* 165–173.

In the Matter of Department of Social Services, on behalf of J. S. against Mr. & Mrs. S. Decision, Docket No. N-530–91P, County of Rockland, New City, New York, May 12, 1994.

In the Matter of Luz P. (anonymous). Supreme Court of the State of New York, Appellate Division, Second Judicial Department, 92–07565, March 29, 1993.

Intellectual Disability Review Panel (IDRP). (1989). *Investigation into the reliability and validity of the assisted communication technique.* Melbourne, Australia: Department of Community Services, Victoria.

Interdisciplinary Working Party on Issues in Severe Communication Impairment. (1988). *D.E.A.L. Communication Centre operation. A statement of concern.* Melbourne, Australia: Author.

Ippoliti, C., Peppey, B., & Depoy, E. (1994). Promoting self-determination for persons with developmental disabilities. *Disability & Society, 9*(4), 453–460.

Jacobson, J. W., Eberlin, M., Mulick, J. A., Schwartz, A. A., Szempruch, J., & Wheeler, D. L. (1994). Autism, facilitated communication, and future directions. In J. L. Matson (Ed.), *Autism in children and adults: Etiology, assessment, and intervention* (pp. 59–83). Pacific Grove, CA: Brooks/Cole Publishing Company.

Kaiser, A. P. (1994). Invited commentary: The controversy surrounding facilitated communication: Some alternative meanings. *Journal of the Association for Persons with Severe Handicaps, 19*(3), 187–190.

Kandel, E. R. (1991). Brain and behavior. In E. R. Kandel, J. H. Schwartz, & T. M.

Jessell (Eds.), *Principles of Neural Science* (3rd ed.). (pp. 5–17). New York: Elsevier.

Kaplan, M. (1994, May). *The visual evaluation of the nonverbal person with autism.* Paper presented at the third annual Facilitated Communication Institute Conference, Syracuse University, Syracuse, NY.

Karp, E. (1993, May). *Strategies for increasing independent typing.* Paper presented at the second annual Facilitated Communication Conference, Syracuse University, Syracuse, NY.

Karp, E., Biklen, D., & Chadwick, M. (1993, November). *Strategies for increasing independent typing.* Paper presented at the annual meeting of the American Speech-Language-Hearing Association, Anaheim, CA.

Kerr, R., & Blais, C. (1985). Motor skill acquisition by individuals with Down syndrome. *American Journal of Mental Deficiency, 90*(3), 313–318.

Klewe, L. (1993). Brief report: An empirical evaluation of spelling boards as a means of communication for the multihandicapped. *Journal of Autism and Developmental Disorders, 23*(3), 559–566.

Kochmeister, S. J. (1994). Reflections on a year of turmoil and growth. *Facilitated Communication Digest, 2*(4), 6–8.

Kohlberg, L. (1983). The development of children's orientations toward a moral order: Sequence in the development of moral thought. In W. Damon (Ed.), *Social and personality development: Essays on the growth of the child* (pp. 388–404). New York: W. W. Norton.

Kootz, J. P., Marinelli, B., & Cohen, D. J. (1982). Modulation of response to environmental stimulation in autistic children. *Journal of Autism and Developmental Disorders, 12*(2), 185–193.

Koppenhaver, D. A., Pierce, P. L., & Yoder, D. E. (1995). AAC, FC, and the ABCs: Issues and relationships. *American Journal of Speech-Language Pathology, 4*(4), 5–14.

Leary, M. R., & Hill, D. A. (1996). Moving on: Autism and movement disturbance, *Mental Retardation, 34*(1), 39–53.

LeCompte, M. D. (1993). A framework for hearing silence: What does telling stories mean when we are supposed to be doing science? In D. McLaughlin & W. G. Tierney (Eds.), *Naming silenced lives* (pp. 9–27). New York: Routledge.

Legacy Software (1991). *Mutant math challenge* [Computer program]. Los Angeles: Author.

Levine, K., & Wharton, R. H. (1995). Facilitated communication: What parents should know. *The Exceptional Parent, 25*(1), 40–53.

Lincoln, Y. S. (1993). I and thou: Method, voice, and roles in research with the silenced. In D. McLaughlin & W. G. Tierney (Eds.), *Naming silenced lives* (pp. 29–47). New York: Routledge.

Majure, L. A. (1994). First person accounts by three persons with autism using facilitated communication. *Dissertation Abstracts International, 55.*

Martin, E. (1993, July 31). Facilitation theory tested. *Times Herald Record,* pp. 2, 18.

Martin, E. (1994, January 12). Autistic child falters in test. *Times Herald Record,* p. 4.

Martin, R. (1994). *Out of silence: A journey into language*. New York: Holt.

Maurer, N. M. (1995). Facilitated communication: Can children with autism have a voice in court? *Maryland Journal of Contemporary Legal Issues, 6*(2), 233–282.

McCall, G. J., & Simmons, J. L. (Eds.). (1969). *Issues in participant observation*. Reading, MA: Addison-Wesley.

McLoughlin, C. S., Garner, J. B., & Callahan, M. (1987). *Getting employed, staying employed*. Baltimore: Brookes.

McSheehan, M., & Sonnenmeier, R. (1993, May). *Collaboration during facilitated communication*. Paper presented at the second annual Facilitated Communication Institute Conference, Syracuse University, Syracuse, NY.

Miller, N. (1986). *Dyspraxia and its management*. Rockville, MD: Aspen.

Moon, E. (1992). Test child/real child. *The Exceptional Parent, 22*(4), 16–19.

Moore, S., Donovan, B., & Hudson, A. (1993). Brief report: Facilitator-suggested conversational evaluation of facilitated communication. *Journal of Autism and Developmental Disorders, 23*(3), 541–552.

Moore, S., Donovan, B., Hudson, A., Dykstra, J., & Lawrence, J. (1993). Brief report: Evaluation of eight case studies of facilitated communication. *Journal of Autism and Developmental Disorders, 23*(3), 531–539.

Oakes, J. (1985). *Keeping track: How schools structure inequality*. New Haven, CT: Yale University Press.

Ogletree, B., Hamtil, A., Solberg, L., & Scoby-Schmelzle, S. (1993). Facilitated communication: A naturalistic validation method. *Focus on Autistic Behavior, 8*(4), 1–10.

Olney, M. (1995). Reading between the lines: A case study of facilitated communication. *Journal of the Association for Persons with Severe Handicaps, 20*(1), 57–65.

Oppenheim, R. C. (1974). *Effective teaching methods for autistic children*. Springfield, IL: Thomas.

Palfreman, J. (1993, October). Prisoners of silence [*Frontline* documentary]. Boston: WGBH.

Palfreman, J. (1994). The Australian origins of facilitated communication. In H. Shane (Ed.), *Facilitated communication* (pp. 33–56). San Diego, CA: Singular Publishing Company.

Phipps, C. A., & Ells, M. L. (1995). Facilitated communication: Novel scientific evidence or novel communication? *Nebraska Law Review, 74*(4), 601–657.

Piaget, J. (1963). Preface. In J. H. Flavell, *The developmental psychology of Jean Piaget*. Princeton, NJ: Van Nostrand.

QuickBasic. (1985–86). *Magic spells* [computer program]. Freemont, CA: Learning Co.

Regal, R. A., Rooney, J. R., & Wandas, T. (1994). Facilitated communication: An experimental evaluation. *Journal of Autism and Developmental Disorders, 24*(3), 345–355.

Rimland, B. (1993). F/C under siege. *Autism Research Review International, 7*(1), 2, 7.

Rimland, B., & Green, G. (1993). Controlled evaluations of facilitated communication. *Autism Research Review International, 7*, 7.

Rivin, R. (1993, September 17). *How'd they do that?* [Television program]. New York: Columbia Broadcasting Corporation.

Rose, S. (1992). *The making of memory.* New York: Anchor Books.

Sabin, L. A., & Donnellan, A. M. (1993). A qualitative study of the process of facilitated communication. *The Journal of the Association for Persons with Severe Handicaps, 18,* 200–218.

Said, E. W. (1994). *Representations of the intellectual.* New York: Pantheon.

Sebeok, T. A., & Rosenthal, R. (Eds.). (1981). *The Clever Hans phenomenon: Communication with horses, whales, apes, and people.* New York: New York Academy of Sciences.

Sellin, B. (1995). *I don't want to be inside me anymore: Messages from an autistic mind.* New York: Basic Books.

Shane, H. (1993). FC: Facilitated or "factitious" communication. *Communicating Together, 11*(2), 11–13.

Shapiro, J. (1993). *No pity.* New York: Random House.

Sheehan, C. (1993, May). *Validity research: Problems, progress and alternative explorations.* Paper presented at the second annual Facilitated Communication Institute Conference, Syracuse University, Syracuse, NY.

Sheehan, C., & Matuozzi, R. (1994, May). *An investigation of the factors influencing the validity of facilitated communication.* Paper presented at the third annual Facilitated Communication Institute Conference, Syracuse University, Syracuse, NY.

Sheehan, C., & Matuozzi, R. (1996). Validation of facilitated communication. *Mental Retardation, 34*(2), 94–107.

Shevin, M. (1994). Proposal for a practical shift in our language. *Facilitated Communication Digest, 2*(4), 12–14.

Simon, E. W., Toll, D. M., & Whitehair, P. M. (1994). A naturalistic approach to the validation of facilitated communication. *Journal of Autism and Developmental Disorders, 24*(5), 647–657.

Simon, E. W., Whitehair, P. M., & Toll, D. M. (1995). Keeping facilitated communication in perspective. *Mental Retardation, 33*(5), 338–339.

Smith, J. D. (1985). *Minds made feeble: The myth and legacy of the Kallikaks.* Rockville, MD: Aspen.

Smith, M. D., & Belcher, R. G. (1993). Facilitated communication with adults with autism. *Journal of Autism and Development Disorders, 1,* 175–183.

Smith, M. D., Haas, P. M., & Belcher, R. G. (1994). Facilitated communication: The effects of facilitator knowledge and level of assistance on output. *Journal of Autism and Developmental Disorders, 24*(3), 357–367.

State v. Warden, 1995 WL 97443, 1–22 (KAN.)

Steering Committee, Division of Intellectual Disability Services. (1993). *The Queensland report on facilitated communication.* Brisbane, Australia: Department of Family Services and Aboriginal and Islander Affairs.

Storch et al. v. Syracuse University et al. (Decision and Order, April 12, 1995) State of New York Supreme Court, County of Ulster (Index No. 94–3208; RJI No. 55–95–00242).

Stumbo, C. (1989). Teachers and teaching. *Harvard Educational Review*, 59(1), 87–97.

Szempruch, J., & Jacobson, J. W. (1993). Evaluating facilitated communications of people with developmental disabilities. *Research in Developmental Disabilities*, 14, 253–264.

Taylor, S., & Bogdan, R. (1984). *Introduction to qualitative research methods: The search for meanings* (2nd ed.). New York: John Wiley.

Vazquez, C. A. (1994). Brief report: A multitask controlled evaluation of facilitated communication. *Journal of Autism and Developmental Disorders*, 24(3), 369–379.

Watts, G., & Wurzburg, G. (Producers). (1994). *Every step of the way* [Videotape]. Syracuse, NY: Syracuse University Facilitated Communication Institute.

Weiss, M. J. S., Wagner, S. H., & Bauman, M. L. (1996). A validated case study of facilitated communication. *Mental Retardation*, 34(4), 220–230.

West, C. (1993). *Race matters*. Boston: Beacon Press.

Wharton, R. H., Levine, K., Shane, H., & Emans, S. J. (1995). Letter to the editor. *Archives of Pediatric and Adolescent Medicine*, 149, 1288–1289.

Wheeler, D. L., Jacobson, J. W., Paglieri, R. A., & Schwartz, A. A. (1992). *An experimental assessment of facilitated communication* (Report #92–TA1). Schenectady, NY: O. D. Heck/Eleanor Roosevelt Developmental Disabilities Service Organization.

Wheeler, D. L., Jacobson, J. W., Paglieri, R. A., & Schwartz, A. A. (1993). An experimental assessment of facilitated communication. *Mental Retardation*, 31(1), 49–60.

Whitehurst, G. J., & Crone, D. A. (1994). Invited commentary: Social constructivism, positivism, and facilitated communication. *Journal of the Association for Persons with Severe Handicaps*, 19(3), 191–195.

Williams, D. (1994a). Invited commentary: In the real world. *Journal of the Association for Persons with Severe Handicaps*, 19(3), 196–199.

Williams, D. (1994b). *Somebody somewhere*. New York: Times Books.

Wood, D., Bruner, J. S., & Ross, G. (1976). The role of tutoring in problem-solving. *Journal of Child Psychiatry*, 17, 89–100.

Zoeller, D. (1992). *Ich gebe nicht auf* [I won't give up]. Bern: Scherz Verlag.

About the Contributors

DOUGLAS BIKLEN, Ph.D., is professor of cultural foundations/disability studies and director of the Facilitated Communication Institute in the School of Education at Syracuse University. He was executive producer of the nationally acclaimed documentary *Regular Lives*, which aired on PBS stations in 1988, and was the educational advisor to HBO's 1993 Academy Award–winning documentary *Educating Peter*. He teaches and does research on the sociology of disability, educational mainstreaming, and, most recently, communication. His initial study of facilitated communication, funded by the World Rehabilitation Fund, appeared in the *Harvard Educational Review* (August 1990). News accounts of his work have since appeared in *The New York Times Magazine*, *Newsweek*, *U.S. News & World Report*, *The Washington Post Magazine*; on the *CBS Evening News*, ABC's *Primetime Live*, and PBS's *Frontline*; on National Public Radio's *Talk of the Nation*; and on the nationally syndicated *Larry King Live Radio* and *Jim Bohannon Show*. Professor Biklen is author of numerous books, including *Schooling Without Labels* and *Communication Unbound*.

STACEY BALDAC is a researcher and graduate student at the School of Communication Disorders, La Trobe University, Bundoora, Victoria, Australia.

DONALD N. CARDINAL, Ph.D., is an associate professor in the School of Education at Chapman University in Orange, California. He has taught and coordinated programs in special education for Chapman, where he also directs the Center for Educational and Social Equity, since 1988. Professor Cardinal has embraced the notion of inclusion since 1974, when he began working for six years to move students from locked facilities into public schools and community living. For the next several years he worked in the public schools to develop school-to-work transition programs. At his current university, he has won honors for outstanding teaching and is the 1993–95 recipient of the prestigious Wang Fellowship, received for exemplary research. He has published numerous articles on evaluation and the measurement of quality in special education. His research revolves around the validation of facilitated communication, paradigm shifts in research, and the collaboration of postmodern and quantitative methods of inquiry.

ROSEMARY CROSSLEY, M.Ed., Director of DEAL Communication Center (dignity, education, advocacy, and language) in Australia, has worked with people with communication impairments since the early 1970s. In 1977 she taught a group of teenagers with cerebral palsy to communicate through spelling, using a technique now known as facilitated communication. She is the author, with Anne McDonald, of *Annie's Coming Out,* which was made into a feature film distributed in the United States under the title *A Test of Love.* Her most recent books include *Facilitated Communication Training* and *Speechless.*

DARLENE HANSON, M.S., C.C.C., is a speech–language pathologist with the Whittier Unified School District, Whittier, California. She works in inclusive school programs with students with autism and other developmental disabilities.

CHRIS KLIEWER earned his Ph.D. in special education from Syracuse University in 1996. His recent research interests include school inclusion, the social construction of Down syndrome, children's literacy, and facilitated communication. He is assistant professor of education at the University of Northern Iowa.

EUGENE MARCUS is a man with autism who believes in his own rights and those of others with and without disabilities. He is a product of Syracuse's inclusive school system, which he attended in the days before facilitated communication. He now is an associate of the Facilitated Communication Institute, where he has conducted research on his own means of communication and lectures frequently on facilitated communication and the rights of people with disabilities.

MARJORIE OLNEY earned her Ph.D. from Syracuse University in rehabilitation. She directs a program in community integration for individuals with traumatic brain injury. She is an adjunct faculty member in the department of counseling and human services at Syracuse University. Her current research interests include facilitated communication, program evaluation, and integrated employment.

CARL L. PARSONS, Ph.D., is a member of the faculty of health sciences, School of Communication Disorders, and associate dean for research, La Trobe University, Bundoora, Victoria, Australia.

SHASWATI SAHA, Ph.D., is Assistant Professor of special education at Texas Southern University. Her research focuses on school inclusion. She is research associate for a federally funded research and demonstration project at the University of Maine.

MAYER SHEVIN received his Ph.D. in psycholinguistics from the University of Rochester in 1976. He was, for two years, a psychologist at the Central Wisconsin Center. He was also on the special education faculty of Cleveland State University. From 1985 through 1991, he taught at the Grafton Developmental Center and elsewhere in North Dakota. From 1989 through 1991, he directed the Homemade Futures project in North Dakota and Minnesota. He is the editor of *Talking/Politics*, a newsletter focusing on the political implications of communication rights. Since 1991, he has been an associate of the Facilitated Communication Institute at Syracuse University.

SHELDON H. WAGNER, Ph.D., from Harvard University, studied and wrote with Jean Piaget at the University of Geneva. Dr. Wagner's graduate work at Harvard focused on normal and atypical development. He also spent time at the Massachusetts Institute of Technology (MIT) Artificial Intelligence Laboratory working with Seymour Papert and continued postdoctoral training at Harvard with Dr. Howard Gardner. Dr. Wagner was Assistant Professor of Psychology and Education at the University of Rochester before joining BP&FD, Inc., where he is co-director. He has published numerous articles, chapters, and abstracts related to infant and child development. He lectures internationally on a variety of topics related to child development and developmental disabilities.

JOHN WAKEHAM, M.A., is administrator and program specialist with the Whittier Area Cooperative Special Education Program, Whittier, California. His research interests focus on inclusion and experiences of students with Down syndrome, autism, and other developmental disabilities.

MICHAEL J. SALOMON WEISS received his Ph.D. from Tufts University in experimental and developmental psychology and is a licensed clinical psychologist. He is currently the director of Behavioral Pediatrics & Family Development, Inc., and has served as lecturer at McGill University, as a clinical fellow at Harvard University Medical School, and as a staff Psychologist at Children's Hospital, Boston. He has published numerous articles, chapters, and abstracts related to infant and child attentional development. His ongoing research activities include topics in perceptual–cognitive, motor, social, and educational development with infants and children at varying levels of risk for later development disabilities.

Index